2013

the best campsites
in the Netherlands
Belgium & Luxembourg

alan rogers ⌀ publishing
expert in camping for 45 years

Compiled by: Alan Rogers Guides Ltd

Designed by: Vine Design Ltd

Additional photography: T Lambelin, www.lambelin.com
Maps created by Customised Mapping (01769 540044)
contain background data provided by GisDATA Ltd

Maps are © Alan Rogers Guides and GisDATA Ltd 2013

© Alan Rogers Guides Ltd 2013

Published by: Alan Rogers Guides Ltd,
Spelmonden Old Oast, Goudhurst, Kent TN17 1HE
www.alanrogers.com Tel: 01580 214000

British Library Cataloguing-in-Publication Data:
A catalogue record for this book is available
from the British Library.

ISBN 978-1-909057-20-3

Printed in Great Britain by Stephens & George Print Group

Contents

Alan Rogers - in search of 'the best'

Alan Rogers Guides were first published over 40 years ago. Since Alan Rogers published the first campsite guide that bore his name, the range has expanded and now covers 27 countries in six separate guides. No fewer than 20 of the campsites selected by Alan for the first guide are still featured in our 2013 editions.

The Low Countries have seen a real rise in tourism in recent years (and it's not just those in search of tulips, cheese, lace or diamonds!). This guide contains impartially written reports on over 300 campsites, including many of the very finest, each being individually inspected and selected. We aim to provide you with a selection of the best, rather than information on all – in short, a more selective, qualitative approach. New, improved maps and indexes are also included, designed to help you find the choice of campsite that's right for you.

Finally, for 2013 we have launched the new Alan Rogers Travel Card. Free to readers, it offers exclusive online extras, money saving deals and offers on many campsites. Find out more on page 12.

We hope you enjoy some happy and safe travels – and some pleasurable 'armchair touring' in the meantime!

" ...the campsites included in this book have been chosen entirely on merit, and no payment of any sort is made by them for their inclusion."

Alan Rogers, 1968

How do we find the best?

The criteria we use when inspecting and selecting campsites are numerous, but the most important by far is the question of good quality. People want different things from their choice of site so we try to include a range of campsite 'styles' to cater for a wide variety of preferences: from those seeking a small peaceful campsite in the heart of the countryside, to visitors looking for an 'all singing, all dancing' site in a popular seaside resort. Those with more specific interests, such as sporting facilities, cultural events or historical attractions, are also catered for.

The size of the site, whether it's part of a chain or privately owned, makes no difference in terms of it being required to meet our exacting standards in respect of its quality and it being 'fit for purpose'. In other words, irrespective of the size of the site, or the number of facilities it offers, we consider and evaluate the welcome, the pitches, the sanitary facilities, the cleanliness, the general maintenance and even the location.

Expert opinions

We rely on our dedicated team of Site Assessors, all of whom are experienced campers, caravanners or motorcaravanners, to visit and recommend campsites. Each year they travel some 100,000 miles around Europe inspecting new campsites for the guide and re-inspecting the existing ones. Our thanks are due to them for their enthusiastic efforts, their diligence and integrity.

We also appreciate the feedback we receive from many of our readers and we always make a point of following up complaints, suggestions or recommendations for possible new campsites. Of course we get a few grumbles too – but it really is a few, and those we do receive usually relate to overcrowding or to poor maintenance during the peak school holiday period. Please bear in mind that, although we are interested to hear about any complaints, we have no contractual relationship with the campsites featured in our guides and are therefore not in a position to intervene in any dispute between a reader and a campsite.

Independent and honest

Whilst the content and scope of the Alan Rogers guides have expanded considerably since the early editions, our selection of campsites still employs exactly the same philosophy and criteria as defined by Alan Rogers in 1968.

'telling it how it is'

Firstly, and most importantly, our selection is based entirely on our own rigorous and independent inspection and selection process. Campsites cannot buy their way into our guides – indeed the extensive Site Report which is written by us, not by the site owner, is provided free of charge so we are free to say what we think and to provide an honest, 'warts and all' description. This is written in plain English and without the use of confusing icons or symbols.

Looking for the best

Highly respected by site owners and readers alike, there is no better guide when it comes to forming an independent view of a campsite's quality. When you need to be confident in your choice of campsite, you need the Alan Rogers Guide.

- Sites only included on merit
- Sites cannot pay to be included
- Independently inspected, rigorously assessed
- Impartial reviews
- Over 40 years of expertise

Written in plain English, our guides are exceptionally easy to use, but a few words of explanation regarding the layout and content may be helpful. This guide is divided firstly by country, subsequently (in the case of the two larger countries) by region. For a particular area the town index at the back provides more direct access.

Index town
Site name
Postal address (including region) T: telephone number. E: email address
alanrogers.com web address (including Alan Rogers reference number)

A description of the site in which we try to give an idea of its general features – its size, its situation, its strengths and its weaknesses. This section should provide a picture of the site itself with reference to the facilities that are provided and if they impact on its appearance or character. We include details on pitch numbers, electricity (with amperage), hardstandings etc. in this section as pitch design, planning and terracing affects the site's overall appearance. Similarly we include reference to pitches used for caravan holiday homes, chalets, and the like. Importantly at the end of this column we indicate if there are any restrictions, e.g. no tents, no children, naturist sites.

Facilities
Lists more specific information on the site's facilities and amenities and, where available, the dates when these facilities are open (if not for the whole season). Off site: here we give distances to various local amenities, for example, local shops, the nearest beach, plus our featured activities (bicycle hire, fishing, horse riding, boat launching). Where we have space we list suggestions for activities and local tourist attractions.

Open: Site opening dates.

Directions
Separated from the main text in order that they may be read and assimilated more easily by a navigator en-route. Bear in mind that road improvement schemes can result in road numbers being altered.

GPS: references are provided in decimal format. All latitudes are North. Longitudes are East unless preceeded by a minus sign e.g. 48.71695 is North, 0.31254 is East and -0.31254 is West.

Charges 2013 (or a general guide)

Maps, campsite listings and indexes

In our 2013 guide series we have changed the way in which we list our campsites and also the way in which we help you locate the sites within each region.

We now include a map immediately after our Introduction to each region. These maps show the towns near which one or more of our featured campsites are located.

Within each country section of the guide, we list these towns and the site(s) in that vicinity in alphabetical order.

You will certainly need more detailed maps for navigation, for example the Michelin atlas. We provide GPS coordinates for each site to assist you. Our two indexes will also help you to find a site by region and site name, or by the town where the site is situated.

Understanding the entries

Facilities

Toilet blocks

Unless we comment otherwise, toilet blocks will be equipped with WCs, washbasins with hot and cold water and hot showers with dividers or curtains, and will have all necessary shelves, hooks, plugs and mirrors. We also assume that there will be an identified chemical toilet disposal point, and that the campsite will provide water and waste water drainage points and bin areas. If not the case, we comment. We do mention certain features that some readers find important: washbasins in cubicles, facilities for babies, facilities for those with disabilities and motorcaravan service points. Readers with disabilities are advised to contact the site of their choice to ensure that facilities are appropriate to their needs.

Shop

Basic or fully supplied, and opening dates.

Bars, restaurants, takeaway facilities and entertainment

We try hard to supply opening and closing dates (if other than the campsite opening dates) and to identify if there are discos or other entertainment.

Children's play areas

Fenced and with safety surface (e.g. sand, bark or pea-gravel).

Swimming pools

If particularly special, we cover in detail in our main campsite description but reference is always included under our Facilities listings. We will also indicate the existence of water slides, sunbathing areas and other features. Opening dates, charges and levels of supervision are provided where we have been notified. There is a regulation whereby Bermuda shorts may not be worn in swimming pools (for health and hygiene reasons). It is worth ensuring that you do take 'proper' swimming trunks with you.

Leisure facilities

For example, playing fields, bicycle hire, organised activities and entertainment.

Dogs

If dogs are not accepted or restrictions apply, we state it here. Check the quick reference list at the back of the guide.

Off site

This briefly covers leisure facilities, tourist attractions, restaurants etc. nearby.

Charges

These are the latest provided to us by the sites. In those cases where 2013 prices have not been provided to us by the sites, we try to give a general guide.

Reservations

Necessary for high season (roughly mid-July to mid-August) in popular holiday areas (i.e. beach resorts). You can reserve many sites via our own Alan Rogers Travel Service or through other tour operators. Or be wholly independent and contact the campsite(s) of your choice direct, using the phone or e-mail numbers shown in the site reports, but please bear in mind that many sites are closed all winter.

Telephone Numbers

The numbers given assume you are actually IN the country concerned.

If you are phoning from the UK remember that the first '0' is usually disregarded and replaced by the appropriate country code. For the latest details you should refer to an up-to-date telephone directory.

Opening dates

These are advised to us during the early autumn of the previous year – sites can, and sometimes do, alter these dates before the start of the following season, often for good reasons. If you intend to visit shortly after a published opening date, or shortly before the closing date, it is wise to check that it will actually be open at the time required. Similarly some sites operate a restricted service during the low season, only opening some of their facilities (e.g. swimming pools) during the main season; where we know about this, and have the relevant dates, we indicate it – again if you are at all doubtful it is wise to check.

Sometimes, campsite amenities may be dependent on there being enough customers on site to justify their opening and, for this reason, actual opening dates may vary from those indicated.

Some campsite owners are very relaxed when it comes to opening and closing dates. They may not be fully ready by their stated opening dates – grass and hedges may not all be cut or perhaps only limited sanitary facilities open. At the end of the season they also tend to close down some facilities and generally wind down prior to the closing date. Bear this in mind if you are travelling early or late in the season – it is worth phoning ahead.

The Camping Cheque low season touring system goes some way to addressing this in that many participating campsites will have all key facilities open and running by the opening date and these will remain fully operational until the closing date.

Taking a tent?

In recent years, sales of tents have increased dramatically. With very few exceptions, the campsites listed in this guide have pitches suitable for tents, caravans and motorcaravans. Tents, of course, come in a dazzling range of shapes and sizes. Modern family tents with separate sleeping pods are increasingly popular and these invariably require large pitches with electrical connections. Smaller lightweight tents, ideal for cyclists and hikers, are also visible on many sites and naturally require correspondingly smaller pitches. Many (but not all) sites have special tent areas with prices adjusted accordingly. If in any doubt, we recommend contacting the site of your choice beforehand.

Our Accommodation section

Over recent years, more and more campsites have added high quality mobile home and chalet accommodation. In response to feedback from many of our readers, and to reflect this evolution in campsites, we have now decided to include a separate section on mobile homes and chalets. If a site offers this accommodation, it is indicated above the site report with a page reference where full details are given. We have listed three sites offering some of the best accommodation available and have included full details of one or two accommodation types at these sites.

Please note however that many other campsites listed in this guide may also have a selection of accommodation for rent.

You're on your way!

Whether you're an 'old hand' in terms of camping and caravanning or are contemplating your first trip, a regular reader of our Guides or a new 'convert', we wish you well in your travels and hope we have been able to help in some way.

We are, of course, also out and about ourselves, visiting sites, talking to owners and readers, and generally checking on standards and new developments.

We wish all our readers thoroughly enjoyable Camping and Caravanning in 2013 – favoured by good weather of course! The Alan Rogers Team

The Alan Rogers Awards

The Alan Rogers Campsite Awards were launched in 2004 and have proved a great success.

Our awards have a broad scope and before committing to our winners, we carefully consider more than 2,000 campsites featured in our guides, taking into account comments from our site assessors, our head office team and, of course, our readers.

Our award winners come from the four corners of Europe, from southern Portugal to Croatia, and this year we are making awards to campsites in 10 different countries.

Needless to say, it's an extremely difficult task to choose our eventual winners, but we believe that we have identified a number of campsites with truly outstanding characteristics.

In each case, we have selected an outright winner, along with two highly commended runners-up. Listed below are full details of each of our award categories and our winners for 2012.

Alan Rogers Progress Award 2012

This award reflects the hard work and commitment undertaken by particular site owners to improve and upgrade their site.

Winner	
UK0970	Cofton Country Holidays *England*

Runners-up	
FR86010	Castel Camping Le Petit Trianon *France*
CR6765	Camping Kovacine *Croatia*

Alan Rogers Welcome Award 2012

This award takes account of sites offering a particularly friendly welcome and maintaining a friendly ambience throughout readers' holidays.

Winner	
ES80330	Camping Las Palmeras *Spain*

Runners-up	
FR29180	Camping Les Embruns *France*
IT60280	Camping Vela Blu *Italy*

Our warmest congratulations to all our award winners and our commiserations to all those not having won an award on this occasion.

The Alan Rogers Team

Alan Rogers Active Holiday Award 2012

This award reflects sites in outstanding locations which are ideally suited for active holidays, notably walking or cycling, but which could extend to include such activities as winter sports or watersports.

Winner	
DE3003	Camping Wulfener Hals *Germany*

Runners-up	
IT62030	Caravan Park Sexten *Italy*
AU0065	Camping Seehof *Austria*

Alan Rogers Innovation Award 2012

Our Innovation Award acknowledges campsites with creative and original concepts, possibly with features which are unique, and cannot therefore be found elsewhere. We have identified innovation both in campsite amenities and also in rentable accommodation.

Winner	
NL6470	Camping de Papillon *Netherlands*

Runners-up	
FR85625	Camping Les Moulins *France*
ES92120	Camping Monte Holiday *Spain*

Alan Rogers Small Campsite Award 2012

This award acknowledges excellent small campsites (less than 75 pitches) which offer a friendly welcome and top quality amenities throughout the season to their guests.

Winner	
FR58040	Camping l'Etang de la Fougeraie *France*

Runners-up	
UK0115	Tehidy Holiday Park *England*
CZ4896	Camping Country *Czech Republic*

Alan Rogers Seaside Award 2012

This award is made for sites which we feel are outstandingly suitable for a really excellent seaside holiday.

Winner	
IT60450	Camping Marina di Venezia *Italy*

Runners-up	
FR64060	Camping le Pavillon Royal *France*
PO8202	Turiscampo *Portugal*

Alan Rogers Country Award 2012

This award contrasts with our former award and acknowledges sites which are attractively located in delightful, rural locations.

Winner	
FR74140	Camping Les Dômes de Miage *France*

Runners-up	
UK0710	Hidden Valley Touring Park *England*
NL5823	Camping Waalstrand *Netherlands*

Alan Rogers Family Site Award 2012

Many sites claim to be child friendly but this award acknowledges the sites we feel to be the very best in this respect.

Winner	
IT60200	Camping Union Lido Vacanze *Italy*

Runners-up	
NL6710	Recreatiepark de Achterste Hoef *Netherlands*
ES85400	Camping La Torre del Sol *Spain*

Alan Rogers Readers' Award 2012

We believe our Readers' Award to be the most important. We simply invite our readers (by means of an on-line poll at www.alanrogers.com) to nominate the site they enjoyed most.

The outright winner for 2012 is:

Winner	
FR85150	Camping La Yole *France*

Alan Rogers Special Award 2012

A Special Award is made to campsites which have suffered a very significant setback and have not only returned to their former condition, but can fairly be considered to be even better than before. In 2012 we acknowledge a Spanish campsite which suffered a devastating forest fire and we feel is a worthy recipient of this award.

ES80240	Camping Les Pedres *Spain*

FREE

The Alan Rogers
Travel Card

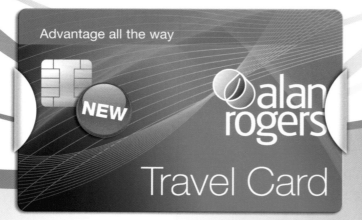

Across the Alan Rogers guides you'll find a network of thousands of quality inspected and selected campsites. We also work with numerous organisations, including ferry operators and tourist attractions, all of whom can bring you benefits and save you money.

Our brand **NEW** Travel Card binds all this together, along with exclusive extra content in our cardholders' area at **alanrogers.com/travelcard**

Advantage all the way

Carry the Alan Rogers Travel Card on your travels and save money all the way. Enjoy exclusive offers on many partner sites - as well as hotels, apartments and campsite accommodation. We've even teamed up with Camping Cheque, the low season discount scheme, so you can load your card with Cheques before you travel. So register today - hundreds of campsites already have special offers just for you.

Holiday **discounts**, **free** kids' meals, **free** cycle hire, **discounted** meals, **free** sports activities, **free** gifts on arrival, **free** wine with meals, **free** wifi, **free** tennis, **free** spa day, **free** access to local attractions.

Check out all the offers at **alanrogers.com/travelcard** and present your card on arrival.

Benefits that add up

- Offers and benefits on many Alan Rogers campsites across Europe

- Save up to 60% in low season on over 600 campsites

- Savings on rented accommodation and hotels at over 400 locations

- Free cardholders' magazine

- Exclusive cardholders' area on our website – exchange opinions with other members

- Discounted ferries

- Savings on Alan Rogers guides

- Travel insurance deals

Register today - and start saving

Step 1
Register at www.alanrogers.com/travelcard (you can now access exclusive content on the website).

Step 2
You'll receive your activated card, along with a Welcome email containing useful links and information.

Step 3
Start using your card to save money or to redeem benefits during your holiday.

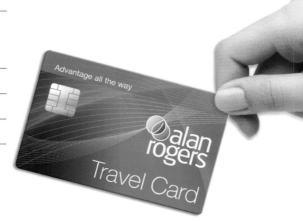

Register now at
alanrogers.com/travelcard

Getting the most from
off peak touring

£13.95/night
single tariff
2 people

There are many reasons to avoid high season, if you can. Queues are shorter, there's less traffic, a calmer atmosphere and prices are cheaper. And it's usually still nice and sunny!

And when you use Camping Cheques you'll find great quality facilities that are actually open and a welcoming conviviality.

Did you know?

Camping Cheques can be used right into mid-July and from late August on many sites. Over 90 campsites in France alone accept Camping Cheques from 20th August.

Save up to 60% with Camping Cheques

Camping Cheque is a fixed price scheme allowing you to go as you please, staying on over 600 campsites across Europe, always paying the same rate and saving you up to 60% on regular pitch fees. One Cheque gives you one night for 2 people + unit on a standard pitch, with electricity. It's as simple as that.

Special offers mean you can stay extra nights free (eg 7 nights for 6 Cheques) or even a month free for a month paid! Especially popular in Spain during the winter, these longer-term offers can effectively halve the nightly rate. See Site Directory for details.

Check out our amazing Ferry Deals!

Why should I use Camping Cheques?

- It's a proven system, recognised by all 600+ participating campsites
  - so no nasty surprises.

- It's flexible, allowing you to travel between campsites, and also countries, on a whim - so no need to pre-book. (It's low season, so campsites are rarely full, though advance bookings can be made).

- Stay as long as you like, where you like - so you travel in complete freedom.

- Camping Cheques are valid 2 years - so no pressure to use them up.
  (If you have a couple left over after your trip, simply keep them for the following year, or use them up in the UK).

Tell me more... (but keep it brief!)

Camping Cheques was started in 1999 and has since grown in popularity each year (nearly 2 million were used last year). That should speak for itself. There are 'copycat' schemes, but none has the same range of quality campsites that save you up to 60%.

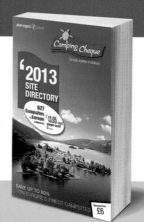

campingcheque.co.uk

A small country divided into three regions, Flanders in the north, Wallonia in the south and Brussels, the capital. Belgium is rich in scenic countryside, culture and history, notably the great forest of Ardennes, the historic cities of Bruges and Ghent and the western coastline with its sandy beaches.

CAPITAL: BRUSSELS

Tourist Office

Belgian Tourist Office Brussels & Wallonia,
217 Marsh Wall, London E14 9FJ
Tel: 020 7537 1132 Fax: 020 7531 0393
Email: info@belgiumtheplaceto.be
Internet: www.belgiumtheplaceto.be

Tourism Flanders-Brussels,
Flanders House, 1a Cavendish Square,
London W1G 0LD
Tel: 020 7307 7738
Email: info@visitflanders.co.uk

Brussels is at the very heart of Europe and doubles as the capital of the European Union. A multi-cultural and multi-lingual city full of remarkable monuments, interesting museums and highly acclaimed restaurants. In the French-speaking region of Wallonia lies the mountainous Ardennes, an area famous for its forests, lakes, streams and grottoes, making it a popular holiday destination, especially for those who like nature and walking. The safe, sandy beaches on the west coast run for more than sixty kilometres. Here lies Ostend, a popular seaside resort with an eight kilometre long beach and a promenade coupled with a bustling harbour and shops. Bruges is Europe's best preserved medieval city and is certainly one of the most attractive, whether you want to relax on a boat trip along the canals, explore the narrow streets or visit one of the many churches and art museums.

Population

10.6 million

Climate

Temperate climate similar to Britain.

Language

There are three official languages. French is spoken in the south, Flemish in the north, and German is the predominant language in the eastern provinces.

Telephone

The country code is 00 32.

Money

Currency: The Euro
Banks: Mon-Fri 09.00-15.30.
Some banks open Sat 09.00-12.00.

Shops

Mon-Sat 09.00-17.30/18.00 – later on Thurs/Fri; closed Sundays.

Public Holidays

New Year's Day; Easter Mon; Labour Day; Ascension; Whit Monday; Flemish Day 11 July; National Day 21 July; Assumption 15 Aug; French Day 27 Sept; All Saints 1, 2 Nov; Armistice Day 11 Nov; King's Birthday 15 Nov; Christmas 25, 26 Dec.

Motoring

For cars with a caravan or trailer, motorways are toll free except for the Liefenshoek Tunnel in Antwerp. Maximum permitted overall length of vehicle/trailer or caravan combination is 18 m. Blue Zone parking areas exist in Brussels, Ostend, Bruges, Liège, Antwerp and Gent. Parking discs can be obtained from police stations, garages, and some shops.

This province offers the lively city of Antwerp and the rural landscapes of the Kempen. It is a wonderful region of contrasts where people embrace the pleasures of life, whether in the bustling city streets or the idyllic countryside.

CAPITAL: ANTWERP

Antwerp has a holiday to suit every taste and budget - whether you love the bright lights of the city or the tranquillity of the forest, enjoyment is the order of the day. Why not relax on the terrace and savour a traditional Trappist beer, or treat yourself to a delicious gourmet weekend? The city of Antwerp is a fascinating mixture of the ancient and modern, famous for its welcoming atmosphere. Highlights include the 14th-century cathedral, the largest Gothic building in the Low Countries; the Central Station, said to be among the most beautiful in the world; the city zoo; and the home of Rubens, the most famous Baroque painter north of the Alps.

Venturing beyond the city, you might glimpse a deer in Kalmthout Heath – the children will love exploring the magical, fragrant pine forest. The charming cobblestone streets of Lier and Turnhout are waiting to be discovered, and Mechelen is a captivating city with a historic past. For the active holidaymaker, the Antwerp Kempen cycle network offers 2,000 kilometres of paths and roadways, and the view from St. Rumbold's Tower is well worth the climb. No trip would be complete without a visit to the Het Anker brewery, which reopened in September 2010.

Places of interest

Antwerp: a bustling city of culture and entertainment, where everyone feels at home.

Mechelen: historical city centre with late medieval St. Rumbold's tower.

Lier: charming small city known for its beers.

Turnhout: lively city near the Dutch border, within a beautiful nature reserve.

Gestel: originally the smallest community of the province, situated on the River de Grote Nete.

Attractions

Technopolis: Mechelen's science and technology centre with over 280 interactive exhibits.

Diamond district of Antwerp: look out for the 'Antwerp Cut', synonymous with quality and brilliance.

Ruben's House Museum: Rubens lived in this Antwerp house for most of his life. Now a museum, this is where most of his paintings (around 25,000) were created by him and his students.

Abbeys: in Malle, Mol, Oud-Turnhout and Westerlo, open to visitors and offering their own quality products.

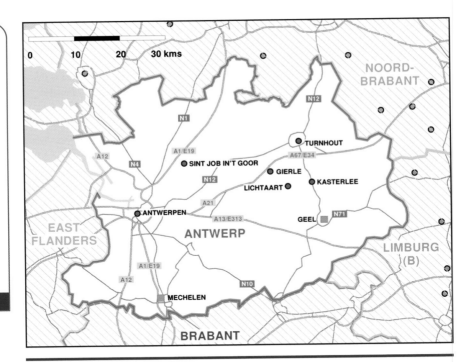

Antwerpen
Camping de Molen

Jachthavenweg, B-2050 Antwerpen (Antwerp) T: 032 198 179. E: info@camping-de-molen.be

alanrogers.com/BE0750

This is a convenient, former municipal site located on the bank of the River Schelde opposite the city centre. It is possible to walk into the heart of this ancient and interesting city, although cycling may be a better option. The site is fairly level with tarmac roads, and has 70 pitches, 65 for touring units, all with access to 10A electricity hook-ups. You will need the adapter cable (deposit payable) as the electric hook-ups are not like any you have seen before, and some long leads may be necessary.

Facilities	Directions
New toilet facilities, clean when visited, could be hard pressed at times, especially when everyone returns from a hard day of sightseeing. Basic facilities for disabled campers. WiFi over site (first 30 mins. free). Overall the facilities are quite acceptable given the very modest campsite fees. Twin-axle caravans are not admitted; American-style motorhomes may be accepted – phone first. Off site: Shops, hot food, bar, outdoor pool nearby.	From the north follow ring road around Antwerp through the Kennedy tunnel and keep right to Linkeroever. Turn right at Esso petrol station, then left at first traffic lights. Turn left at St Annastrandens tunnel on the Thonetlaan. Site is on right after 2 km. GPS: 51.22100, 4.37967

Charges guide

Per unit incl. 2 persons and electricity	€ 16.50 - € 20.50

Open: 16 March - 15 October.

Kasterlee
Camping Houtum

Houtum 51, B-2460 Kasterlee (Antwerp) T: 014 859 216. E: informatie@campinghoutum.be

alanrogers.com/BE0647

This quietly situated, family owned campsite can be found on the outskirts of Kasterlee, famous for its gastronomic restaurants. There are 175 pitches, 70 for touring, all with electric hook-ups (5A). There are plans for these pitches to be relocated to a new area of the site with upgraded facilities for the 2013 season. On-site amenities include an excellent children's play area and a popular bar and restaurant.

Facilities	Directions
New toilet block for 2013 with facilities for disabled visitors. Launderette. Motorcaravan service point. Bar. Restaurant and takeaway (open daily July/Aug, then Wed. and weekends). Playground. Boules pitch. WiFi (charged). Off site: Fishing 500 m. Bicycle hire 1.5 km. Riding 5 km.	From E34, take exit 24 towards Kasterlee. The site is signed 500 m. past the village centre, near the windmill. GPS: 51.229801, 4.979854

Charges guide

Per unit incl. 2 persons and electricity	€ 17.00
extra person	€ 3.75

Open: All year.

For latest campsite news, availability and prices visit

alanrogers.com

Gierle

Camping De Lilse Bergen

Strandweg 6, Gierle, B-2275 Lille (Antwerp) T: 014 557 901. E: info@lilsebergen.be

alanrogers.com/BE0655

This attractive, quietly located holiday site has 513 shady pitches, of which 238 (all with 10A Europlug electricity) are for touring units. Set on sandy soil among pine trees and rhododendrons and arranged around a large lake, the site has a Mediterranean feel. It is well fenced, with comprehensive, well labelled, fire-fighting equipment, and a night guard. Cars are parked away from units. The site is really child-friendly with each access road labelled with a different animal symbol to enable children to find their own unit easily. An entertainment programme is organised in high season. The lake has marked swimming and diving areas (for adults), a sandy beach, an area for watersports, plus a separate children's pool complex (depth 50 cm) with a most imaginative playground. There are lifeguards and the water meets Blue Flag standards. A building by the lake houses changing rooms, extra toilets, showers and a baby room. There are picnic areas and lakeside and woodland walks.

Facilities

One of the six heated toilet blocks has been fully refitted to a good standard. Some washbasins in cubicles and good hot showers (on payment). Well equipped baby rooms. Facilities for disabled campers. Laundry. Barrier keys can be charged up with units for operating showers, washing machine etc. First aid post. Motorcaravan service point. Restaurant (all year, weekends only in winter), takeaway and well stocked shop (Easter-15/9; weekends only). Tennis. Minigolf. Boules. Climbing wall. Playground, trampolines and skateboard ramp. Pedaloes, kayaks and bicycles for hire. Children's electric cars and pedal kart tracks (charged). Free WiFi over site. Off site: Golf 1 km.

Open: All year.

Directions

From E34 Antwerp-Eindhoven take exit 22. On the roundabout take the exit for De Lilse Bergen and follow forest road to site entrance.
GPS: 51.28908, 4.85508

Charges 2013

Per unit incl. 4 persons and electricity	€ 20.00 - € 26.50
dog	€ 4.50

Lichtaart

Camping Floréal Kempen

Herentalsesteenweg 64, B-2460 Lichtaart (Antwerp) T: 014 556 120. E: kempen@florealgroup.be

alanrogers.com/BE0665

This is an attractive woodland site and a member of the Floréal group. It is located close to the well known Purperen Heide, a superb nature reserve with 15 scenic footpaths leading through it. There are 207 pitches, of which only 26 are reserved for touring units. These are of a good size (100 sq.m. or more), all with 10A electricity and most with their own water supply. Several simple cabins are available for hikers, as well as fully equipped mobile homes. There are some good leisure facilities, including tennis and a multisports pitch, as well as a popular bar and restaurant.

Facilities

Toilet facilities are in need of some investment. When we visited cleaning and maintenance needed attention. Motorcaravan services. Shop. Bar. Restaurant. TV room. Tennis. Play area. Multisport terrain. Bicycle hire. Tourist information. Mobile homes for rent. WiFi over site. Off site: Walking and cycling tracks. Golf. Antwerp. Bobbejaanlaan amusement park

Open: All year.

Directions

Approaching from Antwerp, head east on A21 motorway as far as exit 24 (Turnhout). Leave here and head south on N19 to Kasterlee, and then west on N123 to Lichtaart. Follow signs to the site.
GPS: 51.21024, 4.90423

Charges guide

Per unit incl. 2 persons	€ 18.40 - € 25.70
extra person	€ 4.70

FREE Alan Rogers Travel Card
Extra benefits and savings - see page 12

Sint Job in't Goor
Camping Floréal-Club Het Veen
Eekhoornlaan 1, B-2960 Sint Job in't Goor (Antwerp) T: 036 361 327. E: het.veen@florealgroup.be

alanrogers.com/BE0650

Floréal Het Veen can be found 20 km. north of Antwerp in a woodland area, and with many sports facilities. There are 345 marked pitches (60 for tourists) on level grass, most with some shade and all with 10A electricity (long leads in some places) and also seven hardstandings. Amenities include an indoor sports hall (hourly charge), while tennis courts, football, basketball and softball are outside. Good cycling and walking opportunities exist in the area. English is spoken.

Facilities

Four spacious toilet blocks include a few washbasins in cubicles (only two are close to touring pitches). Facilities for disabled visitors. Laundry facilities. Motorcaravan services. Shop. Restaurant, bar, café and takeaway (daily July/Aug. weekends only at other times). Tennis. Badminton. Boules. Playgrounds and entertainment for children in season. Fishing. Canoeing. Bicycle hire. Free WiFi over site. Wooden chalets for rent. Off site: Riding 8 km.

Open: All year.

Directions

Sint Job in't Goor is northeast of Antwerp. From A1 (E19) exit 4, turn southeast towards Sint Job in't Goor, straight on at traffic lights and, immediately after canal bridge, turn left at campsite sign. Continue straight on for 1.5 km. to site. GPS: 51.30513, 4.58622

Charges guide

Per person	€ 3.80
pitch incl. electricity	€ 9.40

Turnhout
Camping Baalse Hei
Roodhuisstraat 10, B-2300 Turnhout (Antwerp) T: 014 448 470. E: info@baalsehei.be

alanrogers.com/BE0660

The Campine is an area covering three quarters of the Province of Antwerp, noted for its nature reserves, pine forests, meadows and streams and is ideal for walking and cycling, while Turnhout itself is an interesting old town. Baalse Hei, a long established, friendly site, has 459 pitches including a separate touring area of 71 large pitches (all with 16A electricity, TV connections and shared water point) on a large grass field, thoughtfully developed with trees and bushes. Cars are parked away from the pitches. Large motorcaravans can be accommodated (phone first to check availability). There is also accommodation to rent. It is 100 m. from the edge of the field to the modern, heated, sanitary building. There is a small lake for swimming with a beach, a boating lake and a large fishing lake (on payment). Entertainment and activities are organised in July and August. Walk in the woods and you will no doubt come across some of the many red squirrels, or take the lovely 1.5 km. riverside walk to the next village.

Facilities

The toilet block provides hot showers (€ 0.50), some washbasins in cabins and facilities for disabled visitors. Dishwashing (hot water € 0.20). Launderette. Motorcaravan services. Café/restaurant (daily 1/4-31/10, then w/ends only, closed 16/11-25/1). Breakfast served in high season. Shop (high season). Club/TV room. Lake swimming. Fishing. Tennis. Boules. Adventure play area. Bicycle hire. English is spoken. Overnight pitches for vehicles under 3.5t. In low season reception opens for limited hours (14.00-17.00). Charcoal barbecues only. WiFi over site (free). Off site: Riding 1.5 km. Boat launching 3 km.

Open: 16 January - 15 December.

Directions

Site is northeast of Turnhout off the N119. From Antwerp on E34/A12 take Turnhout ring road to the end (not a complete ring) and turn right. There is a small site sign to right in 1.5 km. then a country lane. GPS: 51.35467, 4.95500

Charges guide

Per unit incl. 2 persons and electricity	€ 19.00 - € 26.00
Visa cards accepted.	

For latest campsite news, availability and prices visit

alanrogers.com

The region of Brabant and Brussels is today formed by three provinces. Flemish Brabant and Wallonian Brabant were split along the language border in 1995, and Brussels became an administrative unit on its own.

CAPITALS: LEUVEN, NIJVEL AND BRUSSELS

The ancient university city of Leuven is ideal to wander through and admire the beautiful town hall, the many terraces, the Grand Convent, the Museum of M and much more. Nature is never far away – De Groene Gordel (the green belt) encircles Brussels, and in the shadow of the metropolis are dozens of beautiful parks and gardens. East of Leuven is the rural region of Het Hageland which features six charming small towns.

In French-speaking Brabant (Brabant Wallon) the best known city is Waterloo; here and in the surrounding villages are echoes of the atmosphere of the great battle of 1815. There are 500 kilometres of footpaths passing through a landscape with diverse fauna and flora. High-tech meets nature south of Brussels in the 'Ardennes brabançonnes', a region of dynamic towns (Louvain-la-Neuve, Wavre), with rich heritage and a wealth of tourist attractions, from castles and museums to rural scenery.

Brussels, the capital city of Belgium and home to the EU, offers everything you would expect from a major European city. The stunningly rich architecture of the 16th-century houses at the Great Market, in the very heart of the city, is a magnet for visitors.

Places of interest

Leuven: town hall and Great Market, new M-Museum, many cafés and restaurants.

Brussels: Great Market, Royal Museum of Fine Arts of Belgium, themed walks, cafés and restaurants.

Villers-la-Ville: impressive monastery ruins hidden in a forest.

Napoleon's last headquarters: Belgium's only Napoleon Museum with battle memorabilia and items relating to the emperor.

Attractions

The Magic Spell: themed adventure game for the whole family combining entertainment, skill and team building in a Middle Ages setting.

The Waterloo Battlefield: carefully preserved site of the famous conflict of 1815.

Horst Castle: beautiful moated castle in the green valley of the Wingebeek, among the Hageland hills.

National Botanic Garden of Belgium: one of the largest botanic gardens in the world, set in historical castle grounds.

't Wit Gebrouw: visitor centre where you can learn the secrets of, and sample, the famous Hoegaarden white beer.

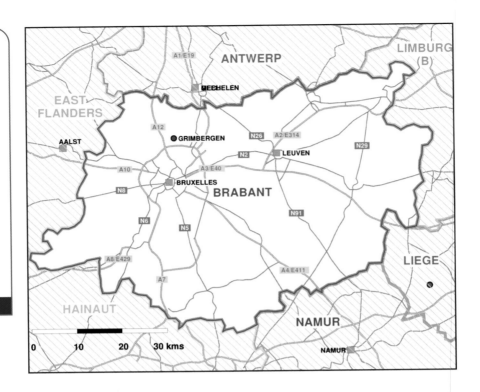

Grimbergen
Camping Grimbergen
Veldkantstraat 64, B-1850 Grimbergen (Brabant) T: 022 709 597. E: camping.grimbergen@telenet.be

alanrogers.com/BE0630

A popular little site with a friendly atmosphere, Camping Grimbergen has 90 pitches on fairly level grass, of which around 50 have 10A electricity. The site is not really suitable for large units, although some hardstandings for motorcaravans have been added. The municipal sports facilities are adjacent and the site is well placed for visiting Brussels. The bus station is by the traffic lights at the junction of N202 and N211 and buses run into the city centre every 15 minutes, as well as every hour from the campsite. In Grimbergen itself visit Norbertine Abbey, St Servaas church, and the Sunday morning market. Also worth a visit are the nearby towns of Lier and Mechelen, and the botanical gardens at Meise.

Facilities
Immaculate new sanitary facilities are heated in colder months. Separate facilities for disabled visitors. Motorcaravan services. Off site: Restaurant 100 m. Fishing 2 km. Riding 5 km.

Open: 1 April - 25 October.

Directions
From Brussels ring road take exit 7 (N202) to Grimbergen. After 2.5 km, turn right at traffic lights on N211 towards Vilvoorde (site signed), then left at second set of lights (slight oblique turn). Site entrance is on right in 500 m. (watch for blue and white Lammekenshoeve sign). GPS: 50.93486, 4.38257

Charges 2013

Per unit incl. 2 persons and electricity	€ 21.00
extra person	€ 5.50
child (under 12 yrs)	€ 1.50
dog	€ 1.00

No credit cards.

For latest campsite news, availability and prices visit
alanrogers.com

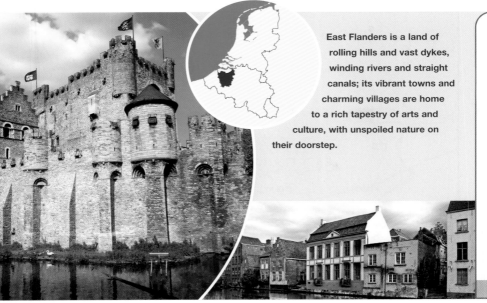

East Flanders is a land of rolling hills and vast dykes, winding rivers and straight canals; its vibrant towns and charming villages are home to a rich tapestry of arts and culture, with unspoiled nature on their doorstep.

CAPITAL: GENT

The vibrant city of Gent combines an impressive past with a lively present. Its beautiful historic centre boasts a wealth of culture, with over 900 listed buildings, several museums and a host of visitor attractions including the magnificent Citadel Park. There are also some picturesque villages waiting to be discovered just a short boat ride down the river. In the region of Scheldeland, three major watercourses converge to offer over 200 kilometres of navigable waterways with numerous landing stages and marinas – there are several boat companies and trips can be arranged. There are also many opportunities for bicycle rides and walks, both ideal for exploring the many monuments in the area, from protected chapels and Maria caves in the countryside to towering castles, strongholds and cathedrals.

The landscape is dotted with wind- and watermills; many are still working and produce their own grain, others have been converted to cosy pubs and restaurants. The beautiful rolling countryside of the Flemish-Ardennes is the home to the classic road cycling race, the Tour de Flandres, and a network of 830 kilometres of recreational cycle paths allows you to feel like a professional while taking in the captivating landscapes at your own, more leisurely pace.

Places of interest

St Bavo's Cathedral, Gent: the Van Eyck brothers' unique altarpiece, The Adoration of The Mystic Lamb, painted in 1432 and renovated in 2010.

Castle of the Counts, Gent: the 'Gravensteen', an imposing stronghold in the heart of the city .

Aalst: popular, regional museum featuring historical and contemporary exhibitions.

Ninove: Abbey church and archaeological site.

Roger Raveel Museum, Zulte: a collection of 300 paintings, 2,500 drawings and graphic works by one of the most important Belgian artists of the post-World War Two period.

Attractions

Fort Liefkenshoek: 16th-century military fort, built to protect the city and port of Antwerp against advancing Spanish troops.

The Mercator Museum, Sint-Niklaas: home to maps and globes by the famous cartographer Gerardus Mercator, alongside exhibits related to modern cartography.

Dendermonde-Puurs Steam Railway: 14 kilometres of standard gauge track, running Sundays and holidays from June to September.

Recreation Park De Ster, Sint Niklaas: 100 acres of parkland featuring minigolf, trampolines, go-karts, trains, boats, tennis, football, a running track and much more.

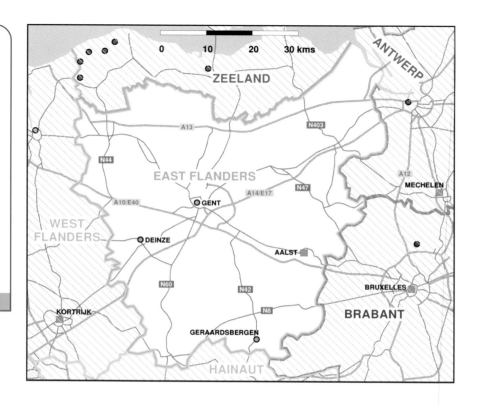

Deinze

Camping Groeneveld

Groenevelddreef 14, Bachte-Maria-Leerne, B-9800 Deinze (East Flanders) T: 093 801 014.

E: info@campinggroeneveld.be **alanrogers.com/BE0600**

Quiet and clean is how Rene Kuys describes his campsite. Groeneveld is a traditional site in a small village within easy reach of Ghent. It has a friendly atmosphere and is also open over a long season. Although this site has 98 pitches, there are a fair number of seasonal units, leaving around 50 large touring pitches with electricity (10A). Hedges and borders divide the grassy area, access roads are gravel and there is an area for tents. Family entertainment and activities organised in high season include themed, musical evenings, barbecues, pétanque matches, etc.

Facilities

Two fully updated toilet blocks provide British style WCs, washbasins and free hot showers. Motorcaravan services. Freezer (free). Bar (July/Aug. and weekends) with wide range of speciality and local beers. Small coarse fishing lake. Floodlit pétanque court. Adventure style play area. TV room. Internet access (at reception) and WiFi (free). Bicycles on loan from reception (free). Max. 1 dog. Off site: Shops and restaurants nearby. Golf 3 km. Swimming pool and kayaking 5 km.

Open: 1 April - 30 September.

Directions

From A10 (E40) exit 13, turn south on N466. After 3 km. continue straight on at roundabout and site is on left on entering village (opposite large factory). Note: yellow signs are very small.
GPS: 51.00509, 3.57229

Charges guide

Per unit incl. 2 persons and electricity	€ 20.00 - € 23.00
extra person	€ 3.00 - € 5.00
child (0-13 yrs)	€ 2.00 - € 3.00

No credit cards.

Gent

Camping Blaarmeersen

Zuiderlaan 12, B-9000 Gent (East Flanders) T: 092 668 160. E: camping.blaarmeersen@gent.be

alanrogers.com/BE0610

Blaarmeersen is a comfortable, well managed municipal site in the west of the city. It adjoins a sports complex and a fair sized lake which together provide facilities for a variety of watersports, tennis, squash, minigolf, football, athletics track, roller skating and a playground. There are 238 pitches for touring units, these are flat, grassy, individually separated by tall hedges and mostly arranged in circular groups, all with electricity. There are 40 hardstandings for motorcaravans, plus a separate area for tents with barbecue facilities. There is noise from the nearby city ring road. There is a good network of paths and cycle routes around the city.

Facilities

Five sanitary units of a decent standard vary in size. Showers and toilets for disabled visitors. Laundry. Motorcaravan services. Shop, café/bar (both daily March-Oct). Takeaway. Sports facilities. Playground. Fishing on site in winter, otherwise 500 m. Lake swimming. Communal barbecue. Off site: Bicycle hire 5 km. Riding and golf 10 km.

Open: 15 March - 1 November.

Directions

From E40 take exit 13 (Ghent-West) and follow dual carriageway for 5 km. Cross second bridge and look for Blaarmeersen sign, turning sharp right and following signs to leisure complex. In city avoid overpasses – most signs are on the lower levels. GPS: 51.04722, 3.68333

Charges guide

Per unit incl. 2 persons and electricity (plus meter)	€ 15.75 - € 19.75
extra person	€ 4.50 - € 5.50
child (5-12 yrs)	€ 1.75 - € 2.50

Geraardsbergen

Camping De Gavers

Onkerzelestraat 280, B-9500 Geraardsbergen (East Flanders) T: 054 416 324. E: gavers@oost-vlaanderen.be

alanrogers.com/BE0590

Camping De Gavers is a modern, well organised holiday site in a peaceful location adjacent to a large sports complex, about 5 km. outside Geraardsbergen. A busy site in season, there is good security and a card operated barrier. Most of the 448 grassy, level pitches are taken by seasonal units but about 80 are left for touring units. Pitches are arranged on either side of surfaced access roads with some hedges and a few trees to provide shade in parts, with electricity available to most. The site offers an extensive range of sporting activities and a full entertainment programme over a long season.

Facilities

Six modern, heated and well equipped sanitary buildings provide hot showers on payment (€ 0.50). Modern rooms for disabled visitors and babies. Launderette. No motorcaravan services. Shop (July/Aug). Restaurant and takeaway (all year). Cafeteria and bars (daily 1/4-30/9, otherwise weekends). Heated indoor pool (all year). Outdoor pool (1/5-31/8). Excellent playground. Tennis. Boules. Minigolf. Fishing. Sailing. Canoes, windsurfers, pedaloes, yachts and rowing boats for hire. Bicycle hire. Tourist train. Swimming and beach area at lake. Climbing. WiFi in bar area. Off site: Bars and restaurants within 1.5 km. Bus for Geraardsbergen leaves from outside site.

Open: All year.

Directions

From E429/A8 exit 26 towards Edingen, take N255 and N495 to Geraardsbergen. Down a steep hill, then left at site sign towards Onkerzele, through village and turn north to site. From E40/A10 take exit 17 on N42, turn left on to N495 and follow as above. GPS: 50.79098, 3.92370

Charges guide

Per unit incl. up to 6 persons and electricity	€ 13.00 - € 25.00
extra person	€ 5.00 - € 7.00
electricity per kWh	€ 0.25

FREE Alan Rogers Travel Card

Extra benefits and savings - see page 12

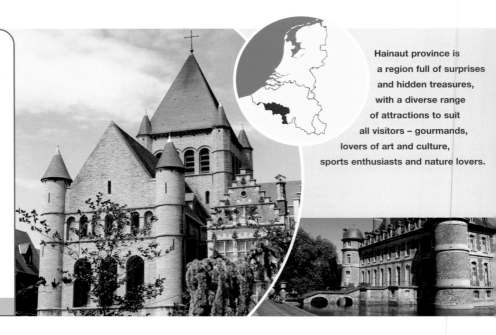

Hainaut province is a region full of surprises and hidden treasures, with a diverse range of attractions to suit all visitors – gourmands, lovers of art and culture, sports enthusiasts and nature lovers.

CAPITAL: MONS

Hainaut, formerly a thriving industrial province, is now one of the foremost agricultural regions of Wallonia. Tournaisis, Pays des Collines, Pays de Ath, Val de Sambre et Thudinie, Botte de Hainaut and the Hauts Pays typify the verdant, rural landscape while retaining their individual characters. The province is blessed with three nature parks and the lakes of the Eau d'Heure.

Apart from Charleroi, the main provincial towns have retained an atmosphere of rural charm. This is thanks to the heritage policies applied in many towns like Mons, Tournai and Enghiens, whose bustling day-to-day existence comfortably embraces the art of living. The more remarkable destinations include Tuin, located on a rock, and Chimay, which has a gem of a castle. Hainaut has 264 kilometres of navigable lakes, and is home to the Park of Canals and Castles between La Louvière, Ronquières and Seneffe.

Places of interest

Mouscron: discover the architectural heritage of Mouscron with a guided tour.

Comines: former capital of the textile industry. Go back in time in the living museum of ribbon manufacture.

Mons: prestigious art collections are housed in the city's museums, including the Museum of Fine Arts and the Museum of Decorative Arts.

Charleroi: an amazing town with a rich cultural heritage – Art Deco town hall, museums, parks, Art Nouveau façades.

Tournaisis: two natural parks, the Pays des Collines and the Plains of the Schelde, with heritage buildings and tours featuring local products.

Attractions

Mont-sur-Marchienne: admire the original pictures in the Museum of Photography.

Abbey of Aulne: impressive Cistercian ruins and the Brewery of Val de Sambre which markets the Abbaye d'Aulne branded beers.

Chimay: discover the steep streets and castle within the ramparts, seat of the Princes housing a marvellous Italianate theatre.

Le Bois du Cazier: old mine in the Marcinelle district and site of a great disaster in August 1956. Exhibits relate to the disaster and mining in the region.

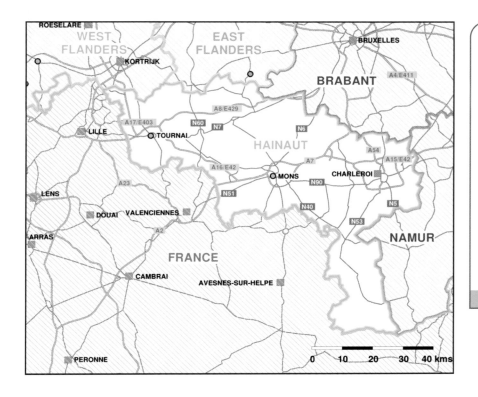

Mons

Camping du Waux-Hall

Avenue Saint Pierre 17, B-7000 Mons (Hainaut) T: 065 337 923. E: ot1@ville.mons.be

alanrogers.com/BE0530

Waux-Hall is a useful and convenient site for a longer look at historic Mons and the surrounding area. It is a well laid out municipal site, close to the town centre and E42 motorway. The 50 pitches, most with electricity (10A), are arranged on either side of an oval road, on grass and divided by beds of small shrubs; the landscape maintenance is excellent. The pitches vary in size from average to small, so manoeuvring could be difficult for larger units. A large public park is adjacent with a refreshment bar, tennis, a playground and a lake. There is direct access from the site when the gate is unlocked.

Facilities

A single, heated toilet block is of older style, basic but clean, with most washbasins in cubicles for ladies. No facilities for disabled visitors or children. Washing machine and dryer. Soft drinks machine and ice cream. Playground. Passport identity is required on arrival. Off site: Public park adjacent. Town centre shops and restaurants within easy walking distance. Fishing 300 m. Riding 2 km. Golf 4 km.

Open: All year.

Directions

From Mons inner ring road, follow signs for Charleroi, La Louviere, Binche, Beaumont. When turning off the ring road (at the Hotel St James), keep to right hand lane, turning for site is immediately first right (signed Waux-Hall and camping). Site is on the left in 200 m. GPS: 50.45138, 3.96296

Charges guide

Per unit incl. 2 persons	€ 12.00
extra person	€ 5.00
child (0-12 yrs)	€ 2.90
electricity (per kWh)	€ 0.30
No credit cards.	

For latest campsite news, availability and prices visit

alanrogers.com

Tournai
Camping de l'Orient

8 rue Jean Baptiste Moens, B-7500 Tournai (Doornik) (Hainaut) T: 069 222 635. E: tourisme@tournai.be

alanrogers.com/BE0540

L'Orient is an attractive, good quality municipal site in a quiet, green location close to the historic town of Tournai and convenient for the E42. It is immaculately kept by its manager. The 51 level, grassy, individual pitches (all for tourists) are separated by laurel hedges and have shade in some parts and electricity (16A). Adjoining the site is an attractive restaurant and bar with a superb terrace overlooking the lake where campers can fish and hire pedaloes. There is also a new, high quality pool complex with cafeteria, indoor pool with spectator seating and outdoor pool with water slides.

Facilities

Two modern sanitary units are of high quality, spotlessly clean and heated in cool weather. They include some washbasins in cubicles and roomy showers on payment. Washing machine and dryer. Facilities for disabled campers (but no ramped access). Basic provisions available from reception (bread can be ordered). Off site: Restaurant/bar adjoining site. Swimming pool (50% discount for campers) and waterslide complex. Lake with picnic and barbecue areas, lakeside walks, fishing, pedalo hire and playground.

Open: All year.

Directions

From E42 exit 32 take N7 towards Tournai centre. Turn left at first traffic lights (site signed), left at small roundabout and site entrance is immediately on the left. GPS: 50.599883, 3.413767

Charges guide

Per unit incl. 2 persons and electricity	€ 15.00

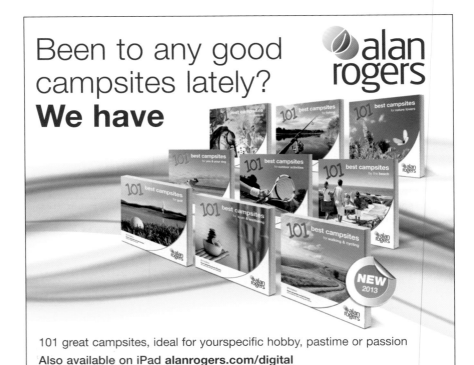

The province of Liège is characterised by green hills, the dams that create the many water reservoirs and the small villages with their distinctive Belgian houses and imposing castles.

CAPITAL: LIÈGE

The Valley of the Meuse is a vast area of natural landscape moulded by the path of the Meuse river and featuring a number of top attractions, including the mine at Blegny. The green pastures of Herve, a Walloon municipality, are criss-crossed by slowly eroding hedges, originally planted to protect the grazing animals in harsh weather. There are many orchards, so it is not surprising that alongside Herve cheese, sparkling cider and pear and apple syrups are regional specialities.

The Valley of the Vesdre was once an important source of income with its profitable wool industry located at Eupen and Verviers. Today the Vesdre is known for water, as it supplies the entire city of Liège. The East Cantons form a unique part of Belgium, being German speaking and almost entirely occupied by the nature reserve of the High Fens, a wilderness of moorland and forest. Spa is a health and wellbeing resort, home to the Belgian Grand Prix, and the perfect location to enjoy a varied holiday. Nearby there are zoos in Theux and Aywaille, castle ruins, museums in Stavelot, caves in Remouchamps and waterfalls in Coo.

Places of interest

Eupen: St Niklaas Church and some ancient houses, Chocolaterie Jacques with visitor centre, the Vesdre barrier with viewpoint and restaurant.

Verviers: Maison de l'Eau (House of Water); Maison de la Laine (House of Wool) tracing the fortunes of the local wool industry.

Stavelot Abbey: renovated and restored abbey housing three museums; the Museum of the Principality of Stavelot-Malmédy, the Spa-Francorchamps Racetrack Museum and the Guillaume Apollinaire Museum.

Liège: cathedral, interactive Archeoforum, citadel, museums, cafés and restaurants.

Attractions

Blegny-Mine: museum with exhibits and history up to its closure in 1980. The descent into the mine is a fascinating experience.

Herve: Espace des Saveurs, a multimedia show and ideal introduction to the Herve region with its groves, castles, hills and villages.

Limbourg: deservedly one of the most beautiful villages of Wallonia, located on a rock and spanning two centuries as an independent duchy.

Caves of Remouchamps: features a 600 m. long subterranean boat trip to comfortably enjoy the wonders of nature.

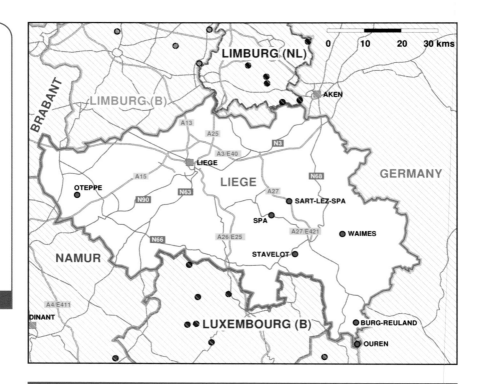

Burg-Reuland
Camping Hohenbusch

Grüfflingen 44A, B-4791 Burg-Reuland (Liège) T: 080 227 523. E: info@hohenbusch.be
alanrogers.com/BE0708

Camping Hohenbusch is located in the Our valley on the edge of the Ardennes and 30 km. from the Grand prix circuit at Spa-Francorchamps. This is a well equipped site with a swimming pool, restaurant and even a children's petting zoo. Pitches are grassy and of a good size, with a number of smaller pitches available for hikers. Hohenbusch also boasts a number of luxury pitches which are 150 sq.m. and equipped with electricity, water, drainage and satellite TV connections. A number of mobile homes are available for rent, as well as rooms in the main building. This is, of course, a great region for walking and cycling, and the long distance GR5 path passes close to the site. The Circuit de Ravel is a recently established network of routes suitable for walkers and cyclists, with one route passing through the site.

Facilities

New excellent sanitary facilities with family bathroom, launderette etc. Swimming pool (heated 26/46-1/9). Paddling pool. Play area. Petting zoo. Bar. Snack bar. Small shop. Entertainment and activities in peak season. Tourist information. Mobile homes and rooms for rent. Off site: St Vith is the closest town with shops and restaurants 5 km. Tennis. Cycle and walking trails. Fishing. Grand prix circuit 30 km.

Open: 29 March - 3 November.

Directions

From Liège, head east on the A3 and then south on the A27 to pass Spa and Malmedy. Leave this motorway at exit 15 and join the N62 following signs to Grufflingen. The site is well signed from here. GPS: 50.241249, 6.092949

Charges 2013

Per unit incl. 2 persons and electricity	€ 14.50 - € 31.50
extra person	€ 3.50 - € 5.00
child (4-11 yrs)	€ 1.50 - € 3.00
dog	€ 1.00 - € 2.50

Oteppe
Camping l'Hirondelle

Rue de la Burdinale 76a, B-4210 Oteppe (Liège) T: 085 711 131. E: info@lhirondelle.be

alanrogers.com/BE0705

This site is set in 20 hectares of woodland in the grounds of a castle that dates back to the 14th century. From the entrance one gets a glimpse of the restaurant in one part of the castle. There are 800 pitches with 300 for touring units, all with 6A electricity. The pitches are arranged around a huge playground, basketball court and a building housing a games room, a supermarket and a bar. In high season the site is bustling and lively, offering a full programme of entertainment with sports tournaments, discos and contests. This site has a lot to offer for families with children and teenagers. The large open-air pool (15x25 m) will accommodate all ages. A video circuit in all the buildings advertises and informs about the activity programmes.

Facilities

The two toilet blocks for touring units provide some washbasins in cabins, showers on payment, children's toilets and basins and a unisex baby room. Washing machine and dryer. Good provision for disabled visitors. These facilities will struggle to cope with in high season. Shop. Bar. Restaurant. Swimming pool (15x25 m). Huge adventure-style playground. Boules. Playing field. Entertainment (10/7-22/8). Games room. WiFi (free).

Open: 1 April - 31 October.

Directions

From Namen on the E42 take exit 10 towards Biewart then continue on the 80 to Burdinne. In Burdinne follow signs for Oteppe. The site is signed just before entering Oteppe. GPS: 50.56758, 5.11718

Charges guide

Per unit incl. 2 persons	
and electricity	€ 13.75 - € 21.00
extra person (over 3 yrs)	€ 2.75 - € 4.00
dog	€ 5.00

Camping L'Hirondelle

A lovely campsite set in the grounds of a majestic castle, in the heart of an area of outstanding natural beauty. This is the French speaking part of Belgium, where every village has its own castle, and close by is the mediaeval city of Huy. At the campsite you will find spacious pitches and comfortable, modern sanitary facilities. For children there's a large play area and the campsite also offers three trout lakes set beneath ancient trees. In addition there is a good swimming pool, football field, tennis courts and a multi-sport ground. You can dine inside the castle and enjoy its original 18th century wall paintings.

Rue de la Bourdinale 76a - B4210 Oteppe
Tel. +32 (0)85 711131, Fax +32 (0)85 711021
Internet: www.lhirondelle.be

Ouren

Camping International

Ouren 14, B-4790 Ouren (Liège) T: 080 329 291. E: info@camping-international.be

alanrogers.com/BE0688

This attractive, rural site is located in a wooded valley alongside the River Our in the Belgian Ardennes. Jointly owned by the Kappert and the Van der Linden families, it offers complete peace and quiet and some excellent walking and cycling opportunities in the local area. A variety of more strenuous activities such as zip wire and abseiling are also possible. Children will enjoy the playground and can paddle safely in the river. There are 170 pitches in total, 120 for tourers, 50 of these with electricity (6-10A). There are five cabins and two tents for hire.

Facilities	Directions
One sanitary block is clean and well maintained with hot showers. Washing machine. Shop sells basics. Fresh bread daily. Bar/snack bar. Play area. Sports field. Boules. Free fishing (licence required; available at post office). Off site: Bicycle hire 1 km. Riding and golf 10 km.	From E42 exit junction 15 and follow E421 south, taking left turn for Lieler. Follow signs to Ouren and site is in the village. GPS: 50.141971, 6.142125

Charges guide

Per unit incl. 2 persons and electricity	€ 15.00 - € 23.00
extra person	€ 4.50

Open: 31 March - 30 October.

Sart-lez-Spa

Camping Spa d'Or

Stockay 17, B-4845 Sart-lez-Spa (Liège) T: 087 474 400. E: info@campingspador.be

alanrogers.com/BE0700

Camping Spa d'Or is set in a beautiful area of woodlands and picturesque villages, 4 km. from the town of Spa (Pearl of the Ardennes). The site is on the banks of a small river and is an ideal starting point for walks and bicycle trips through the forests. With 310 pitches in total, 240 are for touring, and all have 10A electricity (40 places are reserved for tents). The touring pitches have an open aspect, most are slightly sloping and all have 10A electricity connections.

Facilities	Directions
One new large, bright and cheerful sanitary block and one new smaller block (Portacabin-style) both with all the usual facilities. Room for visitors with disabilities. Laundry. Shop. Bar, restaurant (weekends only in low season) and takeaway. Outdoor heated swimming pool (1/5-15/9). Play area with good equipment. TV in bar. Goal posts and two boules courts. Entertainment during July/Aug. Mountain bike hire. Maps for mountain biking and walking on sale at reception. WiFi over site (charged). Off site: Fishing 2 km. Golf and riding 5 km. Spa 4 km.	From E42 take exit 9 and follow the signs to Spa d'Or. GPS: 50.50758, 5.91952

Charges guide

Per unit incl. 2 persons and electricity	€ 20.00 - € 31.50
extra person	€ 4.25 - € 5.50
dog	€ 4.00 - € 5.00

Camping Cheques accepted.

Open: 1 April - 7 November.

Spa

Camping Parc des Sources

Rue de la Sauvenière 141, B-4900 Spa (Liège) T: 087 772 311. E: info@campingspa.be

alanrogers.com/BE0683

Parc des Sources is a small, quietly situated site, close to the town of Spa (Pearl of the Ardennes). It is on the outskirts of a large nature reserve and close to the starting point of the famous Promenade des Artistes and many other interesting walks. There are 155 grassy pitches (60-70 sq.m), of which 110 are for touring; 70 of these have electricity (6A) and there are 13 hardstandings. The site does not have a wide range of amenities, but there is a small shop, and a bar, restaurant and takeaway are available daily in high season. The nearby resort town of Spa has shops, bars and restaurants, parks and museums, as well as the Thermes de Spa, where a wide range of treatments are offered. Parc des Sources is conveniently situated for the Francorchamps racing circuit.

Facilities	Directions
One heated toilet block is clean and well maintained, with hot showers (on payment), open style washbasins and baby changing facilities. Facilities for disabled visitors. Washing machine. Motorcaravan service point. Small shop, bar, restaurant and takeaway (open daily July/Aug). Fresh bread can be ordered (July/Aug). Outdoor swimming pool (July/Aug). Playground (under 5s). Bicycle hire. Torches useful. Free WiFi in reception area.	From E42, take exit 11 and site is 1.5 km from Spa on N62 towards Malmedy. GPS: 50.485284, 5.883828

Charges guide

Per unit incl. 2 persons and electricity	€ 20.00 - € 22.00
extra person	€ 3.00 - € 3.50
child (4-15 yrs)	€ 2.50 - € 3.00

Open: 1 April - 31 October.

For latest campsite news, availability and prices visit

alanrogers.com

Stavelot

Camping l'Eau Rouge

Cheneux 25, B-4970 Stavelot (Liège) T: 080 863 075. E: fb220447@skynet.be

alanrogers.com/BE0740

A popular, lively and attractively situated site, l'Eau Rouge is in a sheltered valley close to Spa and the Grand Prix circuit. There are 140 grassy pitches of 110 sq.m. on sloping ground either side of a central road (speed bumps) – 120 for touring units, 80 with 10A electricity (70 with water and waste water), the remainder for static units. The main building houses the busy reception, shop, bar and the main sanitary facilities. There are plenty of sporting activities in the area including skiing and luge in winter. The site is close to the motor race circuit at Spa-Francorchamps and is within walking distance for the fit. The site's Dutch owners have completed a five year programme upgrading the infrastructure and have other ideas in the pipeline. This is an excellent site, planned and run with passion by the owners.

Facilities

A brand new environmentally friendly toilet block has showers (on payment), private cubicles, and facilities for babies and children. Motorcaravan service point. Washing machine. Shop. Baker calls daily at 08.30 (in season). Takeaway (in summer). Bar. Boules. Archery (free lessons in high season). Playground. Entertainment in season. Free WiFi over site. Max. 2 dogs. Off site: Bicycle hire 1.5 km. Riding 10 km. Spa-Francorchamps motor racing circuit.

Open: All year.

Directions

Site is 1 km. east of Stavelot on the road to the race circuit. Leave E42 exit 11 Malmédy, at roundabout follow signs for Stavelot. At end of road at T-junction turn right, then first right. Do not follow sat nav, which will take you down narrow roads. GPS: 50.41203, 5.95317

Charges guide

Per unit incl. 2 persons and electricity	€ 20.00
extra person	€ 3.00
child (4-15 yrs)	€ 2.50
dog	€ 1.00

Camping L'eau Rouge On the shores of a small river in the valley of l'Eau Rouge
- Beautiful green family site
- Only 2 km from the centre
- Separate area for tents

Cheneux 25, 4970 Stavelot • +32 80 863 075 • E.mail: fb220447@skynet.be • www.eaurouge.eu

Waimes

Camping Anderegg

Bruyères 4, B-4950 Waimes (Liège) T: 080 679393. E: campinganderegg@skynet.be

alanrogers.com/BE0632

Camping Anderegg is an attractive, family owned site in village of Bruyeres in the Belgian Ardennes, close to the picturesque towns of Malmedy and Waimes. The 50 grassy touring pitches are well laid out, separated by low hedges, and have 6A electricity. Some are shaded by trees, others more open. A shallow, unfenced stream runs through the site, where children can play under supervision. There are miles of cycle routes in the area including the Ravel Routes, extending 150 km. along the former railway line. Road, mountain and electric bikes can be hired locally. This lovely, rural site is ideal for families who enjoy the great outdoors.

Facilities

The modern, heated sanitary building is clean and has showers (coin operated), washbasins in cubicles and baby changing facilities. Situated by the entrance it may be a distance from some pitches. Small shop for basics (bread can be ordered July/Aug). Snack bar with terrace. Takeaway. Adventure play area and a smaller play area for younger children. Football field. Badminton court. WiFi over site (charged). Off site: Bicycle hire 1 km. Fishing 1.5 km. Robertville reservoir (swimming, small beach and pedalo hire) 3 km. Riding and golf 10 km. Rail biking on the High Fens 15 km.

Open: All year.

Directions

From Waimes take the N676 towards Robertville. The site is well signed on the left. GPS: 50.43916, 6.11793

Charges guide

Per unit incl. 2 persons and electricity	€ 18.75
extra person	€ 4.25
child (2-12 yrs)	€ 2.50
dog	€ 1.00

FREE Alan Rogers Travel Card
Extra benefits and savings - see page 12

Hiking, biking, horse riding... there is a surprise around every corner of Belgian Limburg. Its rich cultural heritage dominates the region, each with its own landscape and character.

CAPITAL: HASSELT

In Haspengouw you can picnic beside the orchards, cycle through countryside dotted with fairytale castles, and enjoy the delicious regional cuisine. Borgloon is an attractive town, ideal for an afternoon stroll, and the 17th-century abbey tower of St Truiden offers a splendid view of this fertile region. The Voerstreek is a lush walker's paradise with six picturesque villages. The undulating hills, hollows and varied topography are a feast for the eyes, and it is an ideal base for cultural excursions with Liège, Aachen and Maastricht all being close by.

The Limburg Kempen comprises the sands of the Lommel Sahara, vast pine forests, babbling brooks, lakes and waterways. An area with a rich industrial heritage, it is also famed for its beer and cheese. The Meuse runs like a glittering blue thread through The Maasland, connecting Belgian and Dutch Limburg. Hop on one of the small ferries and observe the contrasting styles on either bank as you sail through the enchanting, waterside villages with their floral displays.

Places of interest

Hasselt: shopping streets, market places, historical buildings and striking, modern architecture; National Genever Museum and fashion museum.

Maaseik: cultural pearl of the Maasland, renaissance architecture, birthplace of the Van Eyck brothers, Museactron – three museums under one roof.

Tongeren: Roman and Middle Ages history; Benelux's largest antiques and brocante market (Sundays).

Borgloon: a charming town combining 13 former communities, with orchards, castles, cloisters and churches; good hiking country.

Attractions

Cosmodrome, Genk: gigantic dome with full dome projection system showing astronomical projections, nature and cultural films.

Bokrijk: step back in time in the Open Air Museum, with more than 100 historic buildings rebuilt in their original condition.

De Blauwe Kei (Lommel): idyllic village near the historic 'blue boulder' lock and canals, with cosy pub terraces.

The markets of St Truiden: landmark market square with its many cafés, monuments, events and a range of different markets.

Have fun, go camping ...
that is what we do in Limburg

Limburg
inviting enchanting

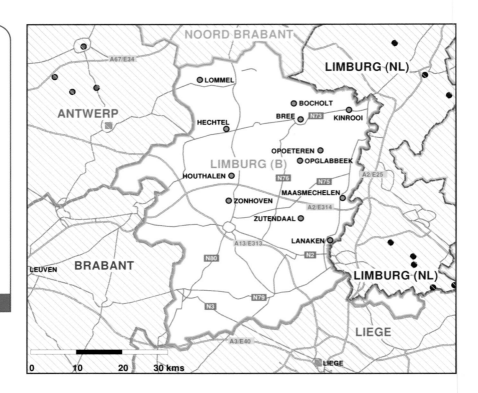

Bree

Camping De Kempenheuvel

Heuvelstraat 8, B-3960 Bree (Limburg) T: 089 462135. E: de.kempenheuvel@telenet.be

alanrogers.com/BE0781

Kempenheuvel is located around 2 km. from the bustling Limburg town of Bree (with an excellent Friday morning market). This is a friendly, family site with a heated outdoor swimming pool and a children's pool. It is a popular choice with anglers, thanks to a large well stocked carp pond. Other amenities include a tennis court and a boules pitch. Cycling is popular and Kempenheuvel is linked to the Limburg cycling route network. Pitches are of a good size and are supplied with 6A electricity. Many activities are on offer in peak season, including darts tournaments and line dancing.

Facilities

Two toilet blocks, both with good, clean facilities including free, preset showers and facilities for babies. The older one has facilities for disabled visitors, the new Portacabin style block is on the touring field. Bar/restaurant. Takeaway. Outdoor heated swimming pool and paddling pool (May-Sept). Tennis. Play area. Fishing lake. Activity and entertainment programme. WiFi over site (charged). Tourist information. Mobile homes for rent. Off site: Shops and restaurants in Bree, 2 km. Bicycle hire 2 km. Hasselt 30 km. Cycle tracks through the Limburg countryside.

Open: 1 March - 31 October.

Directions

Approaching from the north use E314 as far as Genk. Then take northbound N76 to Bree, by-passing Meeuwen. The site can be found (on left) before reaching the town centre. GPS: 51.137261, 5.568301

Charges guide

Per unit incl. 2 persons	
and electricity	€ 20.00 - € 22.50
extra person	€ 3.00
dog	€ 3.00

For latest campsite news, availability and prices visit

alanrogers.com

Bocholt
Goolderheide Vakantiepark

Bosstraat 1, B-3950 Bocholt (Limburg) T: 089 469 640. E: info@goolderheide.be
alanrogers.com/BE0760

A large family holiday site with 900 individual pitches, Goolderheide has been owned and operated by the same family for many years and has an excellent pool complex and playgrounds. There are many seasonal and rental units, plus around 300 tourist pitches with 4/6A electricity, all in a forest setting. The pitches are of variable size and access roads are quite narrow. The outdoor pool complex has two large pools (one of Olympic size), a slide and a paddling pool. There is also a fishing lake, and a lake with a small sandy beach. An enormous area is devoted to a comprehensive play area with a vast range of equipment. During the main season there is also a weekly supervised assault course with aerial ropeways etc, a soundproofed over-16s disco, plus a younger kids' disco and an extensive programme of varied activities to keep children and adults occupied. There are no extra charges for most of these activities.

Facilities

Four sanitary buildings provide an ample supply of WCs and washbasins in cabins, but rather fewer preset showers. Baby areas. Two en-suite units for disabled visitors (key access). Laundry facilities. Shop, bar and takeaway (daily in July/Aug, w/ends and public holidays in low season). Takeaway. Swimming pools. Tennis. Fishing. Boules. Minigolf. Play area and assault course. Children's discos. Programme of activities (July/Aug). Night security staff (main season). Off site: Bicycle hire 1 km.

Open: 1 April - 30 September.

Directions

From A13 (E313, Antwerp-Liege) take exit 25 and N141 to Leopoldsburg, then N73 through Peer, to outskirts of Bree (35 km). Take N76 north for 3 km, turn left at large roundabout into Bocholt, and towards Kaulille. Site road is on left towards edge of town. GPS: 51.17343, 5.53902

Charges guide

Per unit incl. 2 persons and electricity	€ 31.20
extra person	€ 5.80
child (under 12 yrs)	€ 3.30 - € 5.00
dog	€ 5.00
No credit cards.	

Delightful pitches,
comfort and high comfort.
Spacious mobile homes and luxurious tents for rent.

Bosstraat 1 Bocholt (België) tel: 0032 (0)89/46 96 40 www.goolderheide.be

Hechtel
Vakantiecentrum De Lage Kempen

Kiefhoekstraat 19, B-3941 Hechtel-Eksel (Limburg) T: 011 402 243. E: info@lagekempen.be
alanrogers.com/BE0796

This is a small, good quality site of which the owners are rightly proud. There are 100 pitches with 70 available for touring units. The pitches are large, all with electricity (6/10A) and are laid out in rows. A pleasant swimming pool complex has three heated pools, two for children and one with a large slide, and they are supervised in high season. A new bar and restaurant building opened in July 2012 and a shop opens in high season. Entertainment is provided daily in high season. This is a friendly and welcoming site with a good atmosphere. The owners have found the right balance of entertainment and time for relaxation.

Facilities

Single, high quality toilet block providing very good facilities including hot showers, washbasins in cabins and good facilities for babies and disabled visitors. Laundry facilities. Motorcaravan services. Shop, bar/restaurant and takeaway (all 15/5-1/9). Outdoor heated pool complex (May-Sept). Large adventure playground. Bicycle hire. WiFi over most of site (charged). Max. 1 dog. Off site: Riding 3 km. Fishing 5 km.

Open: Easter - 30 October.

Directions

From the E314/A2 motorway take exit for Houthalen and follow signs to Hechtel. Shortly after passing through Hechtel look for campsite signs on the left. GPS: 51.16092, 5.31433

Charges guide

Per unit incl. 2 persons and electricity	€ 24.00
extra person	€ 4.00
child (0-2 yrs)	free
dog (max. 1)	€ 2.00

Houthalen
Camping De Binnenvaart

Binnenvaartstraat 49, B-3530 Houthalen-Helchteren (Limburg) T: 011 526 720. E: info@debinnenvaart.be
alanrogers.com/BE0793

De Binnenvaart is a well equipped family site north of Hasselt, open all year. This is a very well equipped holiday centre with a good range of leisure amenities including minigolf and a sports field. The site has been developed alongside a small lake, with its own sandy beach, and is surrounded by woodland. Of the 180 pitches, 34 are for touring, all are of a good size and equipped with electricity (16A Europlug). Many pitches here are reserved all year. The site is part of the same group as BE0792 and BE0780, both of which are nearby, and guests are able to use amenities at these sites too.

Facilities	Directions
Two sanitary blocks, one being upgraded, have facilities for disabled visitors. Motorcaravan service point. Cafeteria and bar. Lake (swimming, fishing and windsurfing) with sandy beach. Tennis. Sports field. Minigolf. Play area. Animal park. Tourist information. Activity and entertainment programme. Free WiFi over site. No charcoal barbecues. Off site: Walking and cycle routes. Hot-air ballooning. Riding. Paintball. Golf 5 km.	Leave the A2 motorway at the Houthalen - Helchteren exit (number 29) and join the northbound N715 to the town. The site is clearly signed from here. GPS: 51.032158, 5.415949

Charges guide

Per unit incl. 2 persons and electricity	€ 24.00
extra person	€ 8.00
child	€ 4.00
dog	€ 4.00

Open: All year.

Houthalen
Camping Molenheide

Molenheidestraat 7, B-3530 Houthalen-Helchteren (Limburg) T: 070 222 034. E: info@molenheide.be
alanrogers.com/BE0794

In the centre of a naturally beautiful area, Park Molenheide is predominantly a high class bungalow park. However, it does have 30 large touring pitches which are located in a flat, grassy field with easy access. All the pitches have electricity (6-10A). What sets this site aside from others in the area is its amazing range of activities and high class facilities. All manner of recreational activities are housed indoors with a large tropical-style swimming pool with slides and an excellent Disney themed children's pool, all supervised. There are numerous high quality bars and restaurants, all housed under the same roof.

Facilities	Directions
One single well equipped, modern toilet block (bring your own paper) with large free controllable showers. Fully equipped en-suite unit for disabled visitors. Excellent bars and restaurants. Outstanding leisure facilities with tropical indoor heated swimming pool, bowling, incredible children's indoor play area, unique indoor crazy golf course. Bicycle hire. Max. 1 dog – allowed on the campsite but not in the facilities. WiFi (charged). Off site: Golf 5 km. Riding 10 km.	Follow the E314 motorway towards Aken and take exit 29. Follow the N74 for 8 km. and site well signed on the right. GPS: 51.0791, 5.3955

Charges guide

Per unit incl. up to 4 persons and electricity	€ 16.00 - € 90.00
extra person	€ 19.00
dog	€ 4.00

Open: All year.

Houthalen
Oostappen Vakantiepark Hengelhoef

Tulpenstraat 141, B-3530 Houthalen-Helchteren (Limburg) T: 089 382 500. E: info@hengelhoef.be
alanrogers.com/BE0788

This attractive and well cared for site would suit families with younger children. Situated in a forest it has 478 pitches of which 368 are for touring units. The pitches are large and laid out in avenues with plenty of shade and all have 10A electricity, water and drainage. At the centre of the site is a large, man-made lake surrounded by sand which is safe for children. A good sub-tropical style pool complex offers a range of slides and water based activities. With a range of activities on offer there is little need to leave the site. There is a large supermarket and a good restaurant and bars.

Facilities	Directions
Several good quality toilet blocks throughout the site provide very good facilities including hot showers, washbasins in cabins and good facilities for babies and disabled visitors. Laundry facilities. Motorcaravan services. Supermarket. Restaurant. Bar. Takeaway. Lake with beach. Indoor pool complex. Multisports court. Max. 1 dog, accepted in certain areas. Off site: Bicycle hire 1 km. Riding 3 km.	From the E314/A2 motorway take exit towards Houthalen Centrum Zuid. The site is well signed from the centre. GPS: 51.01439, 5.46655

Charges guide

Per unit incl. 2 persons and electricity	€ 16.00 - € 32.00

Open: All year.

For latest campsite news, availability and prices visit
alanrogers.com

Kinrooi

Camping Nieuw Geerensheide

Steyvershofstraat 14, B-3640 Kinrooi (Limburg) T: 089 702 751. E: geerensheide@belgacom.net

alanrogers.com/BE0789

This 8.5-hectare site has a rural feel and is located on the northeast border between Belgium, the Netherlands and Germany. Pitches and amenities are arranged around a small lake complex, which offers swimming in one section and a separate area for fishing. The bar/brasserie with its terrace overlooks a beach and a diving area. The sanitary building is modern and there are spacious pitches, some with electricity, water and drainage. Fishing on site sees the chance to net a variety of freshwater fish including carp, pike and roach. Both walking and cycling routes start near the site.

Facilities

Sanitary block with showers and baby room. Laundry facilities. Bar/brasserie with terrace. Snack bar and takeaway. Swimming in pond. Fishing. Pets' corner. WiFi (charged) Small children's playground. Multisports field. Recharging point for electric bicycles. Trampoline. Children's entertainment twice weekly (July/Aug). Off site: Public transport within 50 m. Shopping outlet village at Maasmechelen. Hasselt has a reputation for good food and Maastricht is within reach.

Open: All year.

Directions

From Kinrooi centre take N762 south in the direction of Maaseik. After 1.5 km. the site is signposted with small sign at the right side of the road. GPS: 51.132748, 5.754462

Charges guide

Per unit incl. 2 persons and electricity	€ 23.50 - € 25.00
extra person	€ 6.00
child (3-6 yrs)	€ 3.00

Lanaken

Camping Jocomo Park

Maastrichterweg 1a, B-3620 Lanaken (Limburg) T: 089 722 884. E: info@jocomo.be

alanrogers.com/BE0782

Situated in dense pine forest this is a peaceful site but lively enough to keep young children happy. There are 127 pitches with 37 available for touring units, all with 4A electricity and water. The touring pitches are arranged around an open field in the middle of the site. Children's entertainment is provided in high season and is centred around a small lake. A pleasant heated outdoor pool also has a separate pool for children (fenced).

Facilities

One modern toilet block serves the touring pitches. Preset showers with controllable hot and cold water to open washbasins. Baby bath. No facilities for disabled visitors. No shop but basics are available in reception. Small taverna type bar with simple takeaway menu (all year). Several small playgrounds throughout site. Max. 1 dog. Off site: Riding 1 km. Fishing and bicycle hire 1.5 km.

Open: 1 April - 1 October.

Directions

From Lanaken follow the N77 towards Zutendaal. 2.5 km. after leaving Lanaken look for a small gravel road on the right. The site is not signed and is very difficult to find. GPS: 50.90638, 5.62817

Charges guide

Per unit incl. 2 persons	€ 23.00 - € 24.00
extra person	€ 2.00 - € 3.00
dog	€ 1.00

Lommel

Oostappen Vakantiepark Blauwe Meer

Kattenbos 169, B-3920 Lommel (Limburg) T: 011 544 523. E: info@blauwemeer.be

alanrogers.com/BE0785

Surrounded by woodland, and with shade from tall pines, this large site has 976 pitches, of which 277 are for touring units. The touring pitches are attractively arranged around a large, man-made lake with a fence surrounding it. Each pitch has 10A electricity, water, drainage and television connections. There is a whole range of activities including a disco and a heated outdoor pool with slide. There are two additional small pools for children. A bar offers takeaway food and a good supermarket is on the site. This is a popular and lively site with an extensive entertainment programme which is varied to suit all age groups.

Facilities

Good clean toilet blocks are located throughout the site. Free hot showers, washbasins in cabins. Facilities for babies and children. Good facilities for disabled visitors. Laundry room. Supermarket, bar and takeaway (all July/Aug; weekends in low season). Heated outdoor swimming pool, two smaller ones for children (May-Aug). Several adventure style playgrounds. Children's zoo. Minigolf. Bicycle hire. WiFi over most of site (charged). Max. 1 dog. Off site: Forest Park adjacent. Riding 7 km.

Open: Easter - 30 October.

Directions

Lommel is 35 km. north of Hasselt. From the N71 at Lommel, turn south at lights on N746 (Leopoldsburg), for 2 km. to Kattenbos, and site entrance is on southern side of village on left. GPS: 51.19407, 5.30322

Charges guide

Per unit incl. up to 4 persons	€ 31.00 - € 33.00
Minimum stays apply (1 week in high season, 3 or 4 nights on public holidays).	

FREE Alan Rogers Travel Card

Extra benefits and savings - see page 12

Lommel
Oostappen Vakantiepark Parelstrand

Luikersteenweg 313A, B-3920 Lommel (Limburg) T: 011 649 349. E: info@vakantieparelstrand.be
alanrogers.com/BE0798

This large, attractive site is situated alongside the Bocholt - Herentals canal and the Lommel yacht marina. It has 800 pitches of which 250 are for touring units. Each pitch has 10A electricity, water and drainage. The site fronts onto a large lake with a safe beach and there are three smaller lakes within the site, one of which is used for fishing (well stocked but all fish must be returned). There is an Olympic-size, outdoor pool with a large slide and a small pool for children (not supervised). Several good quality play areas are spread throughout the site. This site is ideal for relaxing or enjoying the canal and other water-based activities.

Facilities	Directions
All the facilities that one would expect from a large site are available. Free hot showers, some washbasins in cabins. Facilities for babies and children. Good facilities for disabled visitors. Laundry room. Supermarket. Bar. Takeaway. Outdoor swimming pools (July/Aug), one for children. Bicycle hire. Fishing. WiFi over part of site (charged). Max. 1 dog per pitch. Off site: Boat launching 1 km. Riding 5 km.	Take the N712 from Lommel and after 3 km. turn left on the N715. After a further 3 km. the site is on the right hand side. It is well signed from Lommel. GPS: 51.2431, 5.3791

Charges guide

Per unit incl. 2 persons and electricity	€ 13.00 - € 25.00

Open: Easter - 30 October.

Maasmechelen
Recreatieoord Kikmolen

Kikmolenstraat 3, B-3630 Opgrimbie/Maasmechelen (Limburg) T: 089 770 900. E: info@kikmolen.be
alanrogers.com/BE0784

This is a large and very lively site situated around a large, man-made lake which also serves as the site swimming pool. The site is very much targeted at a family clientele. Large pitches are spread throughout the site, with the 120 for touring separate from the 680 seasonal and rental units. The pitches are on grass and all have 6A electricity and water. Dogs are officially not accepted but when we visited there were many dogs on the site. Two water slides run into the large artificial lake (not fenced and unsuitable for young children).

Facilities	Directions
Eight modern blocks are spread throughout the site, and one was rebuilt for 2012. All have good facilities with some washbasins in cabins, and hot water is charged through a prepaid SEP key system. One disabled toilet per block (unlocked and used by all). Two restaurants and bars. Takeaway. Well stocked shop. Games room. Lake swimming with water slides. Sports field. Lively activity and entertainment programme. Bicycle hire. Off site: Bus stop at site entrance. Fishing 1 km. Sailing 3 km. Golf and riding 15 km.	From A76 Antwerpen-Koln motorway take exit 33 towards Maasmechelen. Follow the N78 from 1 km. and the site is well signed on the right. GPS: 50.95387, 5.66198

Charges guide

Per unit incl. 2 persons and electricity	€ 17.00 - € 19.00
extra person	€ 5.00 - € 5.50
child (4-15 yrs)	€ 3.00 - € 3.50

Open: 1 April - 31 October.

Opoeteren
Camping Zavelbos

Kattebeekstraat 1, B-3680 Opoeteren (Limburg) T: 089 758 146. E: receptie@zavelbos.com
alanrogers.com/BE0792

Camping Zavelbos lies between woodland and moorland in a 2,000-hectare nature park. It is a pleasant spot for nature lovers and those who love peace and quiet. There are many cycling and walking routes to enjoy in this beautiful region, alternatively you can simply relax in the peaceful campsite grounds complete with a fishpond. There is no swimming pool here but guests have free use of the pool complex at Wilhelm Tell Holiday Park (6 km). The 45 touring pitches (80-100 sq.m) all have 16A electricity (Europlug) and water. Bungalows and chalets are available to rent.

Facilities	Directions
New sanitary facilities include family bathrooms, baths with jacuzzi and jet stream. Provision for disabled visitors. Laundry facilities. Motorcaravan service point. Bar and snack bar. Tavern. Fishpond. Playground. Boules. Bicycle hire. WiFi over site. No charcoal barbecues. Off site: Shops. Cycling and walking routes. Riding 6 km. Golf 10 km. National Park Hoge Kempen. Bobbejaanland.	Take Maaseik exit from A2 (Eindhoven - Maastricht) motorway and drive via Neerpoeteren to Opoeteren. The site is on the right heading to Opglabbeek. GPS: 51.0583, 5.6288

Charges guide

Per unit incl. 2 persons and electricity	€ 30.00
extra person	€ 8.00

Open: All year.

For latest campsite news, availability and prices visit
alanrogers.com

Opglabbeek
Family Camping Wilhelm Tell

Hoeverweg 87, B-3660 Opglabbeek (Limburg) T: 089 810 014. E: receptie@wilhelmtell.com
alanrogers.com/BE0780

Wilhelm Tell is a family run site that caters particularly well for children with its indoor and outdoor pools and lots of entertainment throughout the season. There are 128 pitches with 70 available for touring units, some separated, others on open fields and 60 electricity connections (10A). The bar/restaurant has access for wheelchair users. M. Lode Nulmans has a very special attitude towards his customers and tries to ensure they leave satisfied and want to return. For example, in his restaurant he says 'it serves until you are full'. The Limburg region is a relaxing area with much to do, including shopping or touring the historic towns with a very enjoyable choice of food and drink!

Facilities
Toilet facilities are adequate, but might be under pressure in high season. Facilities around the pool supplement at busy times. Baby room in reception area. Two en-suite units for disabled visitors. Laundry facilities. Motorcaravan service point. Fridge hire. Bar/restaurant and snack bar (times vary acc. to season). Outdoor heated pool with slide and wave machine (1/7-31/8) and indoor pool (all year), both well supervised. Play area. WiFi. No charcoal barbecues. Off site: Riding 1 km. Fishing 6 km. Golf 10 km.

Open: All year.

Directions
From E314 take exit 32 for Maaseik and follow 730 road towards As. From As follow signs to Opglabbeek. In Opglabbeek take first right at roundabout (Weg van Niel) then first left (Kasterstraat) to site. GPS: 51.02852, 5.59813

Charges guide
Per unit incl. 2 persons and electricity	€ 32.00
extra person	€ 8.00
child (0-12)	€ 4.00
dog	€ 4.00

Less 30% in low season.

Zonhoven
Camping Heidestrand

Zwanenstraat 105, B-3520 Zonhoven (Limburg) T: 011 520 190. E: info@heidestrand.be
alanrogers.com/BE0787

Heidestrand is a large family site of 30 hectares with a broad range of facilities. The site can be found north of Hasselt in the Flemish province of Limburg. There are over 600 seasonal pitches here and around 90 touring pitches, all with electricity and water. The site boasts an excellent outdoor swimming pool with a separate paddling pool, slides, diving tower and diving pool, as well as a large shallow swimming pond with a sandy beach. A separate fishing pond is well stocked with a wide variety of coarse fish.

Facilities
Two toilet blocks have free showers and facilities for disabled visitors, but may be stretched in peak season. Laundry in one block (some distance from touring field). Swimming pool complex. Supermarket. Bar. Restaurant. Snack bar. Disco. Sports fields. Play area. Leisure pavilion for children. Entertainment for children. Dance evenings. Boat hire. Fishing ponds. WiFi in reception (charged). Off site: Motor racing circuit at Zolder. Hasselt. Nature reserve at De Bolderberg. Flemish Mine museum.

Open: Easter - 1 October.

Directions
Zonhoven is located 8 km. north of Hasselt close to the N74. From Zonhoven take N72 towards Beringen. After 2 km, just after the railway, turn left to Wijvestraat. The site is 2.5 km. on the right. GPS: 50.98668, 5.31342

Charges 2013
Per unit incl. 2 persons and electricity	€ 24.75
extra person	€ 3.85
dog	€ 2.80

FREE Alan Rogers Travel Card
Extra benefits and savings - see page 12

Zonhoven

Camping Holsteenbron

Hengelhoefseweg 9, B-3520 Zonhoven (Limburg) T: 011 817 140. E: camping.holsteenbron@telenet.be

alanrogers.com/BE0786

Situated in the heart of the Park Midden-Limburg, this is a delightful site. There are 91 pitches with 60 for touring units, numbered and arranged in rows that are separated by hedges. All have easy access and 6A electricity. Water is provided by a single supply at the toilet block, but being such a small site, this is not a problem. A pretty lake is at the centre of the site and is well stocked with fish for the exclusive use of the camping guests. The site is situated only 500 m. from the start of a network of cycle tracks that stretches for 1,600 km. throughout the National Park.

Facilities	Directions
One single well equipped toilet block with large token operated showers. Laundry room. Excellent bar and restaurant with limited but good menu (all season). Playground. Sports field. Fishing. TV in bar. Free WiFi over site. Off site: Riding 3 km.	Site is on N29 Eindhoven-Hasselt road and is well signed from Zonhoven. GPS: 50.99826, 5.42451

Open: 1 April - 11 November.

Charges guide

Per unit incl. electricity	€ 18.00 - € 23.00
dog	€ 1.00

Zutendaal

Camping 't Soete Dal

Molenblookstraat 64, B-3690 Zutendaal (Limburg) T: 089 611 811. E: info@soetedal.com

alanrogers.com/BE0791

Camping 't Soete Dal is beautifully situated amongst mature trees, and is an oasis of tranquillity, nature and beauty. The area, Hoge Kampen, is ideally suited for cycling, walking and horse riding. A nearby gravel and sand fringed lake offers opportunities for sailing. Places for caravans, motorcaravans and tents are spacious and have all utilities and modern plumbing. The site also boasts a 60 metre swimming pool (supervised). Offering family camping where children are of paramount importance, the site has a varied summer programme for children up to 12 years, for teenagers and adults. The entertainment begins during the Easter holidays and continues throughout the summer.

Facilities	Directions
Shop. Bar/restaurant. Swimming pool on opposite side of camp entrance with additional play area, and café/terrace. Multisports court. Pirate ship-themed play area. Football. WiFi (free in reception, tavern and terrace). Activity programme in high season. Off site: Riding 2 km. Bicycle hire and karting 8 km. Hoge Kampen National Park.	Take exit 32 (Genk East) merging onto Europalaan/N75 direction Maaseik, Dilsen-Stokkem, Axle, Zutendaal 1.4 km. Turn right into the Wiemesmeerstraat/N744 follow N744 for 3.2 km. Continue onto Kempenseweg/N730 following N730. Go straight over a roundabout and site is on the right. GPS: 50.926193, 5.552224

Open: 1 April - 30 September.

Charges guide

Per unit incl. 2 persons and electricity	€ 23.30 - € 26.50
extra person	€ 6.40 - € 8.00

Zutendaal

Vakantiepark Mooi Zutendaal

Roelerweg 13, B-3690 Zutendaal (Limburg) T: 089 715 527. E: info@mooi-zutendaal.be

alanrogers.com/BE0778

This family site in Belgian Limburg is situated at the edge of the National Park Hoge Kempen which offers 6,000 hectares of nature. The beautiful landscape of valleys, moors and pine forests provides an ideal opportunity for walking or cycling tours. There are 130 serviced pitches available for touring on flat grass and separated by good hedges. A wide range of bungalows (6-12 persons) are available to rent. Swimming is possible all year as there are both outdoor and indoor pools. The interesting Dutch towns of Valkenburg and Maastricht are close by, as is the friendly Belgian town of Hasselt.

Facilities	Directions
The modern toilet block includes facilities for disabled visitors. Laundry. Supermarket. Restaurant. Café/bar. Snack bar. Takeaway. Outdoor and indoor swimming pools. Paddling pool. Entertainment programmes. Indoor playground. Play areas. Sports field. Boules. Bicycle and go-kart hire. Off site: National Park Hoge Kempen with many walking and cycle paths. Cities of Hasselt, Maastricht and Valkenburg.	From A2 take exit for Lanaken at Stein and follow direction Lanaken. Turn right at roundabout Rekem, after 6 km. at T-junction turn right and immediately left. Site is 1 km. and well signed. GPS: 50.91385, 5.59739

Open: 27 March - 8 November.

Charges guide

Per unit incl. up to 6 persons and electricity and water	€ 16.00 - € 29.00
extra person	€ 6.00
dog	€ 3.00

For latest campsite news, availability and prices visit

alanrogers.com

Belgian Luxembourg is a land of forests, rivers and deep valleys criss-crossed by a network of marked footpaths and cycling routes, a land of medieval castles and ancient hamlets.

CAPITAL: ARLON

The region of the rivers Ours and Aisne in the north is made up of many small villages, the little medieval town of Durbuy and a very interesting cave. Dominated by the ruins of a medieval castle, La Roche-en-Ardenne is an important tourist resort nestling in a meander of the River Ourthe and surrounded by forests. Houffalize, higher up in the Ourthe valley, is an attractive town famous for its colourful floral decorations and known worldwide as the Belgian mountain bike capital. The Land of Bastogne has several small towns and was the site of the Battle of the Bulge in 1944.

Bouillon is not only the historical site from where the First Crusade departed to Jerusalem, but also the starting point for those wishing to explore the magnificent valley, by canoe for instance. The Land of the Anlier Forest is one of the largest and most beautiful forests of the Ardennes. A significant number of villages and hamlets remain, a testament to the area's agricultural history. The Land of the Val de Salm is a treasure trove of architectural and natural sites, signposted walks and mountain bike trails with an abundance of bilberries and raspberries, and a wealth of nature reserves and game parks.

Places of interest

Bastogne: Bastogne historical centre and war museum; historical museum within an old city gate, Saint Peter's church.

Durbuy: charming medieval town where attractions include a unique collection of pruned bushes, a diamond museum and a jam-maker.

The stones of the Liberty Way: one set every kilometre from Omaha beach to the Bastogne Historical Center tracing the route followed by General Patton's 3rd Army. The last three markers can be seen in Bastogne.

Attractions

Herbeumont: ruins of a 13th-century castle perched on a rocky spur dominating the river – one of Wallonia's exceptional sites (free entrance).

Nature Park of the Valley of the Attert: comprises 17 villages and is a paradise for hikers and cyclists. The village of Nobressart is designated one of 'The Most Beautiful Villages of Wallonia'.

Moulin de la Petite Strument, La Roche-en-Ardenne: 19th-century working water mill, a tribute to the miller's work.

Animal Park, Bouillon: 200 animals from the forest, including fallow deer, wild sheep, wild boar, bison, foxes and wolves.

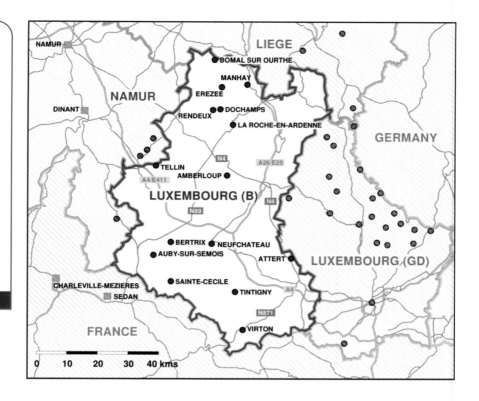

Attert

Camping Sud

Voie de la Liberté 75, B-6717 Attert (Luxembourg) T: 063 223 715. E: info@campingsudattert.com
alanrogers.com/BE0680

This is a pleasant, family run site which would make a good base for a short stay and is also well situated for use as an overnight halt. The 86 touring pitches are on level grass, all with 6A electricity. There are 11 drive-through pitches especially for stopovers, plus four hardstandings for motorcaravans and a tent area. The far end of the site is close to the N4 and may suffer from some road noise. On-site facilities include a small, but welcoming restaurant/bar with takeaway facility, a shop for basics, an outdoor swimming pool (12x6 m) with paddling pool and a sports field.

Facilities

A single building provides modern sanitary facilities including some washbasins in cubicles and baby areas. Showers are free in low season (€ 0.50 July/Aug). No facilities for disabled campers. Small shop (July/Aug). Pleasant bar/restaurant and takeaway (1/4-15/10). TV in bar. Swimming and paddling pools (June-Sept). Small playground. Children's entertainment (4-12 yrs) three afternoons per week during July/Aug. Free WiFi in reception area. Off site: Attert village has two churches and a museum and the Liberation Route passes the site. Internet café and Roman Museum in Arlon 8 km. Local nature parks. Supermarket, riding 5 km. Golf 8 km. Fishing 10 km. Bicycle hire 12 km.

Open: 1 April - 15 October.

Directions

Attert is 8 km. north of Arlon. From E25/E411 from Luxembourg take exit 31 and follow signs for Bastogne to join N4 north; take Attert exit, continue east for 1 km. to Attert village, site entrance is immediately on your left as you join the main street. GPS: 49.74833, 5.78698

Charges guide

Per unit incl. 2 persons and electricity	€ 14.50 - € 20.50
extra person	€ 4.50
child (2-11 yrs)	€ 2.25

No credit cards.

Amberloup
Camping Tonny

Tonny 35, B-6680 Amberloup (Luxembourg) T: 061 688 285. E: camping.tonny@skynet.be

alanrogers.com/BE0720

The new Dutch owners here are rightly proud of their site. With a friendly atmosphere, it is an attractive, small campsite in a pleasant valley by the River Ourthe. A family site, there are 75 grass touring pitches, with wooden chalet buildings giving a Tirolean feel. The pitches (80-100 sq.m) are separated by small shrubs and fir trees, electricity (4/6A) is available. Cars are parked away from the units and there is a separate meadow for tents. Surrounded by natural woodland, Camping Tonny is an ideal base for outdoor activities. In bad weather, the homely bar acts as a meeting place. There is a freestanding fireplace and a shady terrace for relaxing outside. The bar is open all year (according to demand). Nearby St Hubert has a Basilica, the St Michel Furnace Industrial Museum and a wildlife park, with wild boar, deer and other native species – all worth a visit.

Facilities

A new sanitary unit (heated in cool weather) includes showers (now free). Baby area and laundry. Freezer for campers use. Small shop. TV lounge and library. Sports field. Boules. Games room. Playgrounds. Bowling alley. Fishing. Cross-country skiing. WiFi (charged).

Open: 15 March - 15 November.

Directions

From N4 take exit for Libramont at km. 131 (N826), then to Amberloup (4 km) where site is signed just outside of the southwest town boundary. GPS: 50.02657, 5.51283

Charges guide

Per unit incl. 2 persons and electricity	€ 20.00 - € 22.00
extra person	€ 3.60 - € 4.00
child (0-12 yrs)	€ 2.25 - € 2.50

Off season discounts for over 55s and longer stays.

Auby-sur-Semois
Camping Maka

Route du Maka 100, B-6880 Auby-sur-Semois (Luxembourg) T: 061 411 148. E: info@campingmaka.be

alanrogers.com/BE0716

...mping Maka is a delightful, rural site on the banks of the River Semois, reputedly Belgium's clear... ...r. Thirty touring pitches, with 10A electricity and water, are sited close to the water, all ...yone access to the river and its banks and there are 15 tent pitches. Fifty-four private mobi... ...idden on two higher terraces. Two fully equipped wooden cabins and two tents are fo... ...s popular for swimming, fishing and canoeing. Canadian canoes, mountain bikes, b... ...or cooking equipment are available for hire. Facilities include a bar with a terrace... ...and a shop.

...es

...m, heated toilet block includes facilities for babies ...isabled campers (key). Pub/café/takeaway with ...hop (all season). Play area. Fishing. Games area. ...r access. Campfire area. Canoe and mountain ...Occasional activities and entertainment. Tents ...s for rent. WiFi throughout (charged). No electric ... Off site: Walking and cycle tracks. Golf. ...iking. Canoeing. Bouillon, Bertrix.

...ril - 23 September.

Directions

Site is close to the village ... of Bouillon. Approaching ... leave at N853 exit an... Before reaching the ...75 Auby-sur-Semois...

(45)

Bertrix

Ardennen Camping Bertrix

Route de Mortehan, B-6880 Bertrix (Luxembourg) T: 061 412 281. E: info@campingbertrix.be

alanrogers.com/BE0711

Bertrix is located at the heart of the Belgian Ardennes, between the towns of Bastogne and Bouillon and overlooking the hills of the Semois valley. Part of a Dutch chain, the site has 498 terraced pitches of which 303 are for touring, all with 10A electricity, and 43 also have water and drainage. A variety of seasonal caravans are sited among them and there is a friendly feel to the area. Some pitches are available with children's play huts on stilts! A wide range of imaginative activities are organised in the holidays, including some exciting excursions on horseback to the nearby working slate mine.

Facilities

Five well appointed toilet blocks, one with facilities for disabled visitors. The central one has a large laundry and a special, brightly decorated unit for children, with basins, toilets, showers of varying heights and baby baths in cubicles. Motorcaravan service point. Shop for basics and bread. Excellent restaurant and bar (closed low season on Tues. and Thurs) has satellite TV and Internet access and a terrace overlooking the large, heated swimming and paddling pools (27/4-16/9, supervised high season). Tennis. Bicycle hire. Children's games room. Woodland adventure trail. Ardennes chalets and holiday homes for rent. Off site: Shops, banks, bars and restaurants in Bertrix 1.5 km. Fishing and boat launching 6 km.

Open: 23 March - 12 November.

Directions

Bertrix is 90 km. south of Namur. Take exit 25 from the E411 motorway and take N89 towards Bertrix. After 6.5 km. join the N884 to Bertrix then follow yellow signs to site south of town.
GPS: 49.83861, 5.25122

Charges guide

Per unit incl. 2 persons and electricity	€ 20.00 - € 33.00
extra person (over 2 yrs)	€ 4.00 - € 5.50
dog	€ 4.00 - € 5.00

Camping Cheques accepted.

Bomal-sur-Ourthe

Camping International

Pré Cawai 3, B-6941 Bomal-sur-Ourthe (Luxembourg) T: 049 8629 079. E: info@campinginternational.be

alanrogers.com/BE0718

Camping International is a small site in the Belgian Ardennes, located on the banks of the River Ourthe. Although in a French-speaking area, it has a very Dutch ambience. The 60 pitches (20 for seasonal caravans) are of a good size and most have (metered) electrical connections. A central area is available for groups. The campsite tavern, which also houses reception, serves a selection of bar meals to eat in or take away. A wide range of activities are on offer in the area, including canoeing on the Ourthe, raft building, abseiling and mountain biking. There is occasional railway noise. A small collection of farm children, including discos, various sports, scavenger hunts and face painting. A small collection of farm animals can also be visited. The nearby village of Bornal-sur-Ourthe has shops and a choice of bars and restaurants, some just across the river, and a lively Sunday market. There is also a railway station there. This is excellent walking country and the site's friendly owners will be very pleased to recommend possible routes. School groups use the site in June and September and put the sanitary facilities under some pressure, but were well behaved when we visited.

Facilities

The basic sanitary facilities are adjacent to the tavern and have preset showers, cold water to washbasins (cabins in ladies'). No facilities for disabled visitors. Bar. Snack bar. Takeaway. Play area. Bicycle hire. Canoeing. Tourist information. Activity and entertainment programme. Direct river access. Fishing (licence needed). WiFi in reception area (charged). Off site: Adventure sports and canoeing 200 m. Bar and restaurants 200 m. Shops and bicycle hire in Bornal-sur-Ourthe 500 m. Walking and mountain biking. Riding and golf 8 km.

Open: 4 March - 13 November.

Directions

Bornal is 50 km. southeast of Namur. From the E411 Brussels/Luxembourg motorway leave at exit 18 for Assesse. Head south on N4 as far as Sinsin and turn east on N929 and N933 as far as le Petit Han. Then take N983 to Barvaux-sur-Ourthe and N86 to Bomal. Turn west on N683 to site on left after bridge. GPS: 50.374925, 5.519439

Charges guide

Per unit incl. 2 persons and electricity (plus meter)	€ 20
extra person	€
child (3-16 yrs)	€
dog	€

Small, friendly family campsite on the banks of the river Ourthe in Durbu Ideal for hiking and cycling along the Ravel 5, the GR 57 passes the sit Dogs are welcome. Of course you can participate in several outdoor activities directly from the site. Kayaking, mountain biking, rafting, swin in the river, fishing etc.

prices visit

Dochamps

Panoramacamping Petite Suisse

Al Bounire 27, B-6960 Dochamps (Luxembourg) T: 084 444 030. E: info@petitesuisse.be

alanrogers.com/BE0735

This quiet site is set in the picturesque countryside of the Belgian Ardennes, a region in which rivers flow through valleys bordered by vast forests where horses are still usefully employed. Set on a southerly slope, the site is mostly open and offers wide views of the surrounding countryside. The 193 touring pitches, all with 10A electricity, are either on open sloping ground or in terraced rows with hedges in between, and trees providing some separation. Gravel roads provide access around the site. To the right of the entrance barrier a large wooden building houses reception, a bar and a restaurant.

Facilities

All the facilities that one would expect of a large site are available. Showers are free, washbasins both open and in cabins. Baby room. Laundry room with washing machines and dryers. Shop, restaurant, bar and takeaway (2/4-5/11). Heated outdoor swimming pool (1/5-1/9), paddling pool and slide. Sports field. Tennis. Bicycle hire. Playground. Children's club. Entertainment programme in school holidays. Activity programme, including archery, canoeing, climbing, abseiling and walking. WiFi (charged).

Open: All year.

Directions

From E25/A26 autoroute (Liège-Luxembourg) take exit 50 then the N89 southwest towards La Roche. After 8 km. turn right (north) on N841 to Dochamps where site is signed. GPS: 50.23127, 5.62583

Charges guide

Per unit incl. 2 persons and electricity	€ 21.20 - € 42.20
extra person (over 4 yrs)	€ 4.25 - € 7.25
Camping Cheques accepted.	

Erezée

Camping le Val de l'Aisne

Rue du TTA 1 A, B-6997 Erezée (Luxembourg) T: 086 470 067. E: info@levaldelaisne.be

alanrogers.com/BE0725

From a nearby hill, Château de Blier overlooks Camping le Val de l'Aisne, a large site attractively laid out around a 1.5-hectare lake in the Belgian Ardennes. The site has 450 grass pitches with 150 for touring units, on level ground and with 16A electricity. Tarmac roads circle the site providing easy access. Trees provide some shade although the site is fairly open allowing views of the surrounding hills and the château. Activities play a large part on this site, ranging from quiet fishing in the lake to hectic quad bike tours in the hills. By the entrance a building houses reception and the bar/restaurant.

Facilities

Three toilet blocks provide showers (paid for by token) and mainly open washbasins. Facilities for disabled visitors. Baby room. Washing machines and dryers. Motorcaravan service point. Bar/restaurant and snack bar with takeaway. Bread can be ordered in reception. On the lake: fishing, swimming, kayaks (to hire). Quad bike hire and tours arranged. Mountain bike hire. Play area. Entertainment programme (summer). Activities team arrange a range of adventure activities including paintball, canyoning, etc. Off site: Riding, cycle and walking routes.

Open: All year.

Directions

From E411/A4 (Brussels-Luxembourg) take exit 18 (Courière, Marche), then southeast on N4 to Marche. At Marche head northeast on N86 to Hotton, crossing river bridge. In Hotton follow signs for Soy and Erezée. Just west of Erezée at roundabout follow signs for La Roche. Site is 900 m. on left. GPS: 50.2815, 5.5505

Charges guide

Per unit incl. 2 persons and electricity	€ 21.00
extra person (over 3 yrs)	€ 3.00
No credit cards.	

La Roche-en-Ardenne

Camping le Vieux Moulin

Petite Strument 62, B-6980 La Roche-en-Ardenne (Luxembourg) T: 084 411 380. E: info@strument.com

alanrogers.com/BE0770

Located in one of the most beautiful valleys in the heart of the Ardennes, le Vieux Moulin has 183 pitches and, although there are 127 long stay units at the far end of the site, the 60 touring pitches do have their own space. Some are separated by hedges, others for tents and smaller units are more open, all are on grass, and there are 50 electricity hook-ups (6A). The 19th-century watermill has been owned and operated by the owner's family for many years, but has now been converted into a small hotel and a fascinating mill museum.

Facilities

A new, centrally located toilet block is between the touring and long stay areas. It can be heated in cool weather and provides washbasins in cubicles and controllable hot showers on payment. Washing machine. No facilities for disabled campers. A further older unit is at the end of the mill building. Restaurant and bar with hotel. Mill museum.

Open: 1 April - 11 November.

Directions

From town centre take N89 towards St Hubert, turning right towards Hives (site signed). Site is 800 m. from town centre. GPS: 50.17362, 5.57750

Charges guide

Per unit incl. 2 persons and electricity	€ 16.40 - € 18.50

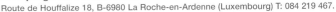

Luxembourg

La Roche-en-Ardenne

Camping Floréal La Roche

Route de Houffalize 18, B-6980 La Roche-en-Ardenne (Luxembourg) T: 084 219 467.
E: camping.laroche@florealclub.be alanrogers.com/BE0732

Maintained to very high standards, this site is set in a beautiful wooded valley bordering the Ourthe river. Open all year, the site is located on the outskirts of the attractive small town of La Roche-en-Ardenne, in an area understandably popular with tourists. The site is large with 587 grass pitches (min. 100 sq.m), of which 290 are for touring units. The pitches are on level ground and all have 10/16A electricity and water connections. Amenities on site include a well stocked shop, a bar, a restaurant and takeaway food. In the woods and rivers close by, there are plenty of opportunities for walking, mountain biking, rafting and canoeing. For children there is a large adventure playground which is very popular and during the summer entertainment programmes are organised. The Ardennes region is rightly proud of its cuisine in which game, taken from the forests that cover the area, is prominent; for those who really enjoy eating, a visit to a small restaurant should be planned. English, French, Dutch and German are spoken in reception.

Facilities

Six modern, well maintained sanitary blocks provide washbasins (open and in cabins), free preset showers. Facilities for disabled visitors. Baby room. Washing machines and dryers (token). Motorcaravan service point. Well stocked shop (with fresh bread, pastries and newspapers in July/Aug). Bar, restaurant, snack bar and takeaway. At Camping Floréal 2: heated outdoor swimming pool. New wellness facilities with sauna and jacuzzi. Professional entertainment team (during local school holidays). Sports field. Volleyball. Tennis. Minigolf. Pétanque. Dog shower. WiFi. Mobile homes to rent.

Open: All year.

Directions

From E25/A26 take exit 50 and follow N89 southwest to La Roche. In La Roche follow signs for Houffalize (beside Ourthe river). Floréal Club Camping 1 is 1.5 km. along this road. Note: go to camping 1 not 2. GPS: 50.17600, 5.58600

Charges guide

Per unit incl. 2 persons and electricity	€ 14.45 - € 22.85
extra person	€ 3.60
child (3-11 yrs)	€ 2.60
dog (max. 1)	€ 4.95

Manhay

Domaine Moulin de Malempré

1 Malempré, B-6960 Manhay (Luxembourg) T: 086 455 504. E: info@camping-malempre.be
alanrogers.com/BE0730

This pleasant countryside site, very close to the E25, is well worth a visit and the Dutch owners will make you very welcome (English is spoken). The reception building houses the office and a small shop, above which is an attractive bar and restaurant with open fireplace. The 140 marked touring pitches are separated by small shrubs and gravel roads on sloping terrain. All have 10A electricity, 40 have water and drainage as well and the site is well lit. There is a little traffic noise from the nearby E2.

Facilities

Modern toilet facilities include some washbasins in cubicles and family bathrooms on payment. The unisex unit can be heated and has a family shower room. Unit for disabled visitors. Baby room. Laundry. Motorcaravan services. Shop for basic provisions (15/5-31/8). Baker calls daily 08.30-09.15. Restaurant and bar (15/5-15/9 and weekends). Takeaway (15/5-15/9). Heated swimming and children's pools (15/5-15/9). TV. Boules. Playground. Off site: Bicycle hire 3 km. Riding 6 km. Fishing 10 km.

Open: 1 April - 31 October.

Directions

From E25/A26 (Liege-Bastogne) exit 49. Turn onto N651 (southwest) towards Manhay. After 220 m. turn sharp left (east) towards Lierneux. Follow signs for Malempré and site. GPS: 50.29498, 5.72317

Charges guide

Per unit incl. 2 persons	€ 18.50 - € 22.00
extra person	€ 4.00
child (3-12 yrs)	€ 2.75
electricity	€ 2.85

Neufchâteau
Camping Spineuse

Rue de Malome 7, B-6840 Neufchâteau (Luxembourg) T: 061 277 320. E: info@camping-spineuse.be
alanrogers.com/BE0675

This delightful Dutch-owned site lies about 2 km. from the town centre. It is on low lying, level grass, bordered by a river, with trees and shrubs dotted around the 87 pitches. Seasonal units take just 14 pitches leaving 73 for touring units, all with 10/16A electricity. One corner of the site is particularly secluded, but the whole place has the feel of a peaceful garden. There is unfenced water on site and a footbridge over the river with no guard rails. The attractive main building houses reception, and a pleasant bar/bistro with a friendly, family atmosphere.

Facilities	Directions
Toilet facilities in the central building and in a new block (open mid May to Sept) are neat and clean with preset showers, open washbasins in main block, cubicles with shower and washbasin in new block. Very limited facilities for disabled campers (none for wheelchair users). Washing machine and dryer. Motorcaravan service point. Small shop for basics (July/Aug). Bistro/bar and takeaway (April-Oct). Large inflatable pool (June-Sept). Tennis. Boules. Two playgrounds and playing field with volleyball court. Fishing. Mobile homes to rent. Free WiFi over part of site. Off site: Shops, bars and restaurants in Neufchâteau 2 km. Riding 10 km. Golf 30 km.	Neufchâteau is just off E25/E411 (Luxembourg, Liège, Brussels) at exits 26-28. Site is 2 km. southwest of Neufchâteau on the N15 towards Florenville. There are three sites fairly close together, this is the last one on the left hand side. GPS: 49.83287, 5.41743

Open: All year.

Charges guide

Per unit incl. 2 persons and electricity	€ 19.00
extra person	€ 3.50
child (0-6 yrs)	€ 2.00
dog	€ 1.25

Sainte Cécile
Camping de la Semois

Rue de Chassepierre 25, B-6820 Sainte Cécile (Luxembourg) T: 061 312 187.
E: info@campingdelasemois.com **alanrogers.com/BE0714**

La Semois is an attractive family site, located on the banks of the Semois River at the heart of the Belgian Ardennes. This is a tranquil spot and an ideal base for walking, mountain biking and canoeing. The 110 touring pitches are grassy with good shade, but not always level. They are unmarked, but all have 10A electricity. Motorised vehicles are parked at the site entrance to create a tranquil and safe environment. A shallow brook runs through the site and forms a popular play area for children, along with a well equipped playground. The site is most suited to tents and small motorcaravans as the entry road is narrow and steep. Canoeing is very popular and the site owners rent canoes and will undertake to collect canoeists from points along the river. Mountain bikes are also for rent and maps are available. Children will enjoy the children's farm with donkeys, goats and Vietnamese pot-bellied pigs. Accommodation to rent on site includes three yurts, two teepees, two large Sahara tents and a new Moroccan tent. There are three sanitary blocks, two of which are basic portacabins. The third unit is new and adjoins the reception/bar area. A pleasant terrace from the bar overlooks the site. The villages of Saints Cecile and Chassepierre are both within walking distance. Chassepierre has attracted many artists over the years, thanks to its Baroque church and attractive setting.

Facilities	Directions
A new unit has been added (with a family room), in addition to the three clean toilet blocks, a tiled one by the main entrance, and two basic Portacabin-style units. Covered dishwashing area with hot water. Café/snack bar. Canoe and bicycle hire. Play area. Trampoline. Children's zoo. Games room. Activity programme. Tourist information. Mobile homes for rent. WiFi in bar area (free). Off site: Villages of Chassepierre and Sainte Cécile. Orval Monastery. Walking and cycling trails. Fishing. Riding 2 km. Sedan (Europe's largest castle) 28 km.	Approaching from Brussles (A4), take exit 23A and head for Transinne, Maissin and Paliseul on N899. Continue as far as Menuchenet and then take N89 to Bouillon. Beyond Bouillon take N83 to Florenville and Sainte Cécile is 20 km. The site is well signed from here. GPS: 49.723073, 5.25625

Open: 1 April - 31 October.

Charges guide

Per unit incl. 2 persons and electricity	€ 24.00 - € 27.00
extra person	€ 4.00
child (3-17 yrs acc to age)	€ 2.50 - € 3.50
dog (max. 1)	€ 2.50

Rendeux

Camping Floréal Le Festival

89 route de la Roche, B-6987 Rendeux (Luxembourg) T: 084 477 371. E: camping.festival@florealgroup.be

alanrogers.com/BE0733

Floréal le Festival is a member of the Floréal group, attractively located in the wide wooded valley of the River Ourthe. There are 360 pitches here and the site is open all year. Pitches are of a good size and each is surrounded by hedges. Most have electrical connections. On-site amenities include a small supermarket, a bar (which also provides takeaway meals) and a restaurant. Sports amenities are good and include a football field, volleyball and tennis. Furthermore, the region is ideal for walking and mountain biking, and the site's managers will be pleased to recommend routes.

Facilities

Three traditional toilet blocks have washbasins (open style and in cabins), free showers, baby bath and facilities for disabled visitors. Washing machines and dryers. Supermarket. Bar. Takeaway meals. Restaurant. Play area. Tennis. Volleyball. Football. Tourist information. Mobile homes for rent. WiFi. Off site: Walking and cycle tracks. Riding 0.5 km. Bicycle hire 1 km. Grottes de Hotton. La Roche-en-Ardennes.

Open: All year.

Directions

Approaching from Namur, head south on N4 as far as Marche-en-Famenne. Here, join the westbound N86 to Hotton and then the southbound N822 to Rendeux. From here follow signs to the site. GPS: 50.22469, 5.52603

Charges guide

Per unit incl. 2 persons	
and electricity	€ 14.45 - € 22.85
extra person	€ 3.60
child (3-11 yrs)	€ 2.60
dog	€ 3.00

Tellin

Camping Parc La Clusure

Chemin de la Clusure 30, B-6927 Bure-Tellin (Luxembourg) T: 084 360 050. E: info@parclaclusure.be

alanrogers.com/BE0670

A friendly and very well run site, Parc La Clusure is highly recommended. Set in a river valley in the lovely wooded uplands of the Ardennes, known as the l'Homme Valley touring area, the site has 438 large marked, grassy pitches (350 for touring). All have access to electricity, cable TV and water taps and are mostly in avenues off a central, tarmac road. There is some noise from the nearby railway. There is a very pleasant riverside walk; the river is shallow in summer and popular with children (caution in winter). The site's heated swimming pool and children's pool have a pool-side bar and terrace. The famous Grottoes of Han are nearby, also the Euro Space Center and Lavaux-Saint Anne castle. Those preferring quieter entertainment might enjoy the Topiary Park at Durbuy.

Facilities

Three excellent sanitary units, one new and one heated in winter, include some washbasins in cubicles, facilities for babies and family bathrooms. Facilities for disabled campers. Motorcaravan services. Well stocked shop, bar, restaurant, snack bar and takeaway (all 27/4-1/11). Swimming pools (25/4-13/9). Bicycle hire. Tennis. New playgrounds. Organised activity programme including canoeing, archery, abseiling, mountain biking and climbing (summer). Caving. Fishing (licence essential). Free WiFi over site. Barrier card deposit (€ 20). Max. 1 dog in July/Aug. Off site: Riding 7 km. Golf 25 km.

Open: All year.

Directions

Site is signed north at the roundabout off the N803 Rochefort-St Hubert road at Bure, 8 km. southeast of Rochefort with a narrow, fairly steep, winding descent to site. GPS: 50.09647, 5.2857

Charges guide

Per unit incl. 2 persons	
and electricity	€ 20.00 - € 36.00
extra person (over 2 yrs)	€ 4.00 - € 6.00
dog	€ 4.00 - € 5.00
Camping Cheques accepted.	

or latest campsite news, availability and prices visit

alanrogers.com

Tintigny

Camping De Chênefleur

Norulle 16, B-6730 Tintigny (Luxembourg) T: 063 444 078. E: info@chenefleur.be

alanrogers.com/BE0715

This is a comfortable site with 223 pitches (196 for touring units), set beside the Semois river, close to Luxembourg and France. All pitches have 6A electricity and are separated by young trees. On the whole, the site is open but there is some shade. One of the guests we spoke to, a first time visitor, was very pleased with the spacious pitches and the peace and quiet on site. The site is still being developed, but Fred, the owner, is very enthusiastic and hard working. It has a swimming pool (also used by the locals) and in high season, entertainment is organised.

Facilities

Two new fully refurbished sanitary blocks, one with facilities for children. Washing machine and dryer. Shop. Bar. Restaurant. Heated outdoor swimming pool (30/4-15/9). Two new play areas. Full entertainment programme in season. Bicycle hire. Max. 2 dogs. Off site: Riding 4 km. Luxembourg City 40 km.

Open: 1 April - 1 October.

Directions

From Luik follow E25 towards Luxembourg and continue on E411. Take exit 29 Habay-La-Neuve and continue to Etalle. From Etalle follow N83 to Florenville. Drive through Tintigny and follow site signs. GPS: 49.68497, 5.52050

Charges guide

Per unit incl. 2 persons and electricity	€ 18.50 - € 31.00
extra person (over 3 yrs)	€ 4.30 - € 5.40
dog	€ 4.00 - € 5.00

Camping Cheques accepted.

Virton

Camping Colline de Rabais

Rue de Bonlieu, B-6760 Virton (Luxembourg) T: 063 571 195. E: info@collinederabais.be

alanrogers.com/BE0710

Colline de Rabais is a large site on a hill top looking out over the surrounding wooded countryside. The Dutch owners offer a warm welcome and are slowly making improvements to the site while maintaining its relaxed atmosphere. There are around 280 pitches for touring units, all with 16A electricity (some long leads needed), plus 69 mobile homes and bungalows for rent and a few tour operator tents. Various activities are organised throughout the season. The adjacent forest is open to walkers and cyclists alike – you can just keep on going without seeing another person. The French border is only 10 km. to the south if you fancy a taste of France, whilst the Duchy of Luxembourg is about 30 km. to the east and its capital city is less than an hour's drive away. A similar distance to the northwest along country roads is the town of Bouillon, which has an interesting ruined castle and from where you can explore the green hillsides and valleys of the Ardennes and perhaps take a canoe trip along a section of meandering river.

Facilities

Three toilet blocks, one modernised with shower and washbasin cubicles and an en-suite room for disabled visitors. Cleaning and maintenance can be variable and not all blocks are open in low season. Washing machines and dryers. Shop (1/5-15/9). Bar/restaurant and takeaway (July/Aug and weekends). Small outdoor swimming pool (May-Oct) with wood decking for sunbathing. Bicycle hire. Free WiFi over site. Off site: Fishing 1 km. Shops, bars and restaurants in Virton 2 km. Riding 3 km.

Open: All year.

Directions

Virton is 39 km. southwest of Arlon on E25/E411 Luxembourg-Brussels/Liège motorway. From exit 29 head for Virton. After Etalle, turn west for Vallée de Rabais, right at sports complex and at crossroads turn right up hill to site at end of road. From exit 31 take N82 for 22 km, then turn right for Vallée de Rabais and left to site. GPS: 49.58015, 5.54773

Charges guide

Per unit incl. 2 persons	€ 18.50 - € 25.00
extra person (over 2 yrs)	€ 3.00 - € 4.50
dog	€ 4.00 - € 5.00

FREE Alan Rogers Travel Card
Extra benefits and savings - see page 12

The province of Namur is known as The Land of the Valleys and visitors delight in its beautiful gardens, historic caves and two citadels.

CAPITAL: NAMUR

The province is divided by the many waterways, including the Meuse, Lesse, Rocq, Semois, Samson and Sambre, which carve the landscape into a series of extraordinary valleys and feed its lush hillsides. Namur's legendary caves are both a testament to prehistoric times and a focus of more recent archaeological interest. The region is a paradise for nature lovers with its leafy forests, nature and animal parks, and evidence of the past in the form of medieval castles, monasteries and citadels.

The beautiful water gardens of the Château d'Annevoie are a 20-minute drive along the River Meuse, and there are many more parks and gardens: Frewr, Chevetogne, Bambois, where you can enjoy a relaxing stroll and admire the fauna. The Brasserie du Bocq in Purnode has been brewing beer since 1858, and visitors can sample a glass after their guided tour. The Meuse, whose banks are populated with local fishermen, meanders through hamlets of modest cottages and is shaded by dramatic overhanging rocks, while further downstream, heavy barges line the basins near the barrages.

Places of interest

Han-sur-Lesse: world famous caves, wild animal park and Museum of the Subterranean World.

Rochefort: Gallo-Roman villa Malagne, ruins of the Castle of the Counts, abbey brewery, two tourist trains.

Philippeville: star-shaped landscaped streets around a central square; 10 km. of subterranean passageways, some open to the public.

Dinant: citadel via cable-car, abbey, imposing rock and cave, La Merveilleuse.

Namur: citadel de Namur, home of L'Impériale mustard, textiles, several good museums.

Attractions

Vents d'Houyet: not-for-profit initiative with an educational programme at L'Académie du Vent (The Wind Academy), teaching children about the benefits of sustainable wind energy.

Architectural Route of Hamois, Natoye: use the superbly illustrated guide to discover the vernacular architecture of the Condroz region, by bicycle or by car.

Ciney: railroad Bocq, a museum tourist train linking the cities of Ciney and Yvoir (Purnode) via the Valley of Bocq, tributary of the Meuse.

Auvelais: weekend barge cruises on the Sambre.

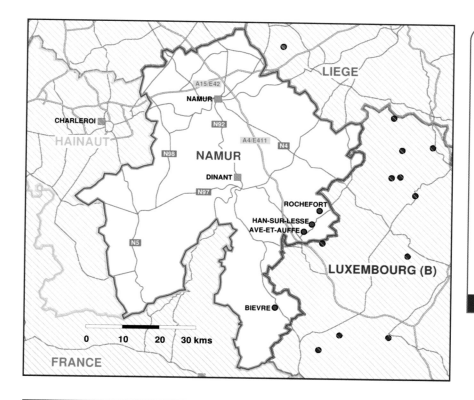

Bièvre

Camping les 3 Sources

Rue de la Wiaule 20, B-5555 Bièvre (Namur) T: 061 730 051. E: info@3sources.be

alanrogers.com/BE0713

Les 3 Sources can be found between the pilgrimage village of Beauraing and Bouillon. The campsite is run by a Dutch family and is well located for exploring the Belgian Ardennes. The site boasts a number of springs, three of which feed some large ponds, which are well stocked with carp and other coarse fish. A small fee is charged for fishing, and this is used to fund the addition of fresh fish stock. The site extends over 2.5 hectares and has 150 pitches. A number of these are occupied by seasonal units, or by mobile homes, chalets and fully equipped tents (many available for rent). The popular bar/restaurant provides breakfast and meals throughout the day (as well as takeaway food). This is the focal point of the site, and evening entertainment is organised here in peak season. This includes barbecues, dances and themed meals. There are over 1500 km. of marked walks through the surrounding hills, and the site's owners will be pleased to recommend suitable routes.

Facilities

New sanitary building (with heating and air conditioning). Play area. Three fishing ponds (small charge). Tourist information. Activity and entertainment programme. Accommodation for rent. Off site: Supermarkets, shops, post office etc. less than 1 km. Cycle and mountain bike trails. Riding. Bison ranch 10 km. Caves of Han-sur-Lesse. Castles, fortresses, charming villages.

Open: All year.

Directions

The campsite is close to N95, which runs parallel to the Brussels-Luxembourg motorway. Take the exit from N95 just north of Bièvre and the site is well indicated. GPS: 49.944925, 5.011002

Charges guide

Per unit incl. 2 persons and electricity	€ 15.00 - € 19.00
extra person	€ 3.00 - € 4.00
child (4-11 yrs)	€ 2.00 - € 2.50

Camping Les 3 Sources

Uniquely situated at the edge of the forest with several hiking and bikingfacilities. Near Bouillon and Han-sur-Lesse. Small campsite with about 100 pitches. Several facilities : Pub with small menu, animation, animal farm, playground, several playfields; soccer, basketball, volleyball, badminton and ping-pong. Presence of 3 fishponds.

WWW.3SOURCES.BE   TEL: 0032 61 73 00 51

FREE Alan Rogers Travel Card
Extra benefits and savings - see page 12

Ave et Auffe

Camping le Roptai

Rue Roptai 34, B-5580 Ave et Auffe (Namur) T: 084 388 319. E: info@leroptai.be

alanrogers.com/BE0850

This family site in the heart of the Ardennes, within easy reach of Dinant and Namur was established in 1932. In a rural wooded setting with its own adventure playground in the trees, it is a good site for an active holiday, especially in high season when there is a weekly programme, including rock climbing, abseiling, mountain biking and potholing. There are 108 good sized, grassy, touring pitches on sloping ground, most with 6A electricity. A programme of activities is organised for adults and children in high season. Other amenities include a swimming pool, a well stocked shop and a bar/snack bar. There are excellent footpaths around the site and the owner and staff will be pleased to recommend routes. The pretty little village of Ave is just 1 km. from le Roptai, and the larger village of Han-sur-Lesse is around 4 km. away. There is an evening market at Han, as well as world famous caves. The village is also home to the interesting Maison de la Vie Paysanne.

Facilities

Sanitary facilities below reception include an excellent suite for babies and disabled visitors. Five other blocks of varying styles are kept clean and offer basic facilities. Shop (9/7-20/8). Bar/snack bar with takeaway (27/6-2/9). Swimming pool and paddling pool (mid May-Aug). Play area. Tourist information. Activity programme (July/Aug). Bicycle hire. WiFi over part of site (charged). Mobile homes for rent. Off site: Riding 4 km. Fishing 6 km. Golf 15 km. Skiing 25 km. Cycling and walking tracks. Canoeing. Caves at Han-sur-Lesse.

Open: 1 February - 31 December.

Directions

From E411 (Brussels-Luxembourg) motorway take exit 23 (Wellin-Han-sur-Lesse) and follow signs for Han-sur-Lesse. Continue 1 km. to Ave and turn left at the church, following signs to the site (1 km. further). GPS: 50.11128, 5.13376

Charges guide

Per unit incl. 2 persons	
and electricity	€ 20.00 - € 26.00
extra person	€ 3.50 - € 4.50
child (5-15 yrs)	€ 2.50 - € 3.50
dog	€ 3.00

Han-sur-Lesse

Camping le Pirot

rue de Charleville, B-5580 Han-sur-Lesse (Namur) T: 084 377 280. E: han.tourisme@skynet.be

alanrogers.com/BE0860

Le Pirot is an attractive, rather basic site on an island in the River Lesse, on the edge of the pleasant village of Han. Because of the access, it is more suitable for small caravans, motorcaravans and tents. Camping de La Lesse, its sister site nearby, caters for larger units. Bars, restaurants and shops are within walking distance of both sites. There are just 18 grass pitches for touring units, 17 with electric hook-ups, and two areas for tents. There are views across both branches of the river.

Facilities

A fairly old but characterful wooden building at the end of the camping area houses adequate sanitary facilities, including washbasins in cabins with hot and cold water and controllable showers. There are no facilities for disabled visitors, no chemical disposal and no on-site motorcaravan services. Communal barbecue area (no barbecues on pitches). Off site: Bicycle hire 200 m. Shops, bars, restaurants and small supermarket, 'tram safari', caves and museums all within walking distance.

Open: 1 April - 30 September.

Directions

From E411 Brussels - Luxembourg motorway take exit 23 (Wellin/Han-sur-Lesse) and follow signs for Han-sur-Lesse. Site is on left immediately before main river bridge. Camping de La Lesse is signed about 100 m. further along on right. GPS: 50.125693, 5.186678

Charges guide

Per unit incl. 2 persons	
and electricity	€ 15.00 - € 17.00
extra person	€ 3.50 - € 4.00

Rochefort

Camping les Roches

Rue du Hableau, 26, B-5580 Rochefort (Namur) T: 084 211 900. E: campingrochefort@lesroches.be
alanrogers.com/BE0845

Camping les Roches has been recently renovated and can be found close to the centre of Rochefort, in the heart of the Ardennes. Despite its proximity to the town centre, this is a tranquil site, close to the large Parc des Roches. The 76 grassy touring pitches all have 16A electricity, water and drainage. They are of a good size on sloping ground. The adjacent tennis courts and municipal swimming pool are free to campers. During peak season, an entertainment team organises a range of activities for adults and children, including archery and accompanied cycle tours. Rochefort is hard to beat as a base for exploring the Ardennes, and is maybe best known (along with Han-sur-Lesse) for its ancient limestone caves. The red marble quarries of St Remy are close at hand, along with an imposing monastery, renowned for its strong, dark beers. Mountain biking and hiking are very popular throughout the region, and the site's friendly manager will be pleased to recommend routes.

Facilities

Two modern, well maintained toilet blocks, heated when required, have washbasins in cabins and preset showers. Family room with shower, children's bath and WC. Excellent unit for disabled visitors. Bar with basic snacks (July/Aug). Games/TV room. Children's playground. Activity and entertainment programme (July/Aug). Tourist information. Free Internet access and WiFi (charged) in reception. Off site: Swimming pool and tennis (free). Minigolf. Bicycle hire, shops and restaurants in Rochefort 500 m. Caves at Han-sur-Lesse 6 km. Golf 20 km. Walking and cycle tracks.

Open: Easter - All Saints' week.

Directions

Rochefort is 50 km. southeast of Namur. From E411 motorway leave at exit 22 for Rochefort and continue east on N911 to Rochefort. Cross the river and take the first road on the left (rue au Bord de l'Eau) and follow signs to the site.
GPS: 50.159585, 5.226185

Charges guide

Per unit incl. 2 persons and electricity	€ 22.50 - € 25.00
extra person	€ 4.00
child (4-11 yrs)	€ 3.00

LES ROCHES CAMPING ★★★★
www.lesroches.be

5580 Rochefort
rue du Hableau 26
tel.+32(0)84 2119 00
campingrochefort@lesroches.be

FREE Alan Rogers Travel Card
Extra benefits and savings - see page 12

Belgium's only coastal province with 67 km. of coastline. In the west, the river IJzer meets the sea at Nieuwpoort, while the north is characterised by its flat polders and to the south lie the West Flemish hills.

CAPITAL: BRUGES

Farming, fishing and bustling city centres; sea, hills and forest; industry and handicrafts, art and religion, gastronomy and provincial dishes – all are found in abundance in the land of contrasts that is the Westhoek region. The popular seaside town of De Panne is a coastal gem; its beach is the widest on the Flemish Coast and its many attractions are a magnet for visitors in high season. The region of the Leie marries a fascinating industrial heritage with contemporary living. Whether you prefer to cycle or walk, you can look forward to a world of discovery.

Oostende is a cosmopolitan city with a rich past where you can shop to your heart's content. It boasts a harbour and marina, international airport, numerous hotels, casino and busy nightlife. Sights include: the Earth Explorer science theme park, three-mast sailing ship Mercator, Fort Napoleon, the Japanese Garden and James Ensor House. Bruges, one of the most beautiful cities in Europe, was classed as a UNESCO World Heritage Centre in 2000. As you weave your way along winding alleys and over romantic canals, it isn't difficult to imagine yourself here in medieval times.

Places of interest

Koekelare: the Fransmansmuseum about Belgian seasonal workers in France, and the Käthe Kollwitz gallery.

Het Zwin, Knokke-Heist: bird and nature reserve with unaccompanied or guided walks in the salt marshes.

The river Leie: 150 km. of navigable waterways meandering between Northern France and Gent, perfect for a cruise or a shorter trip by hired craft.

Castle of Loppem: neo-gothic monument with original architecture and interiors, features a rich art collection, a romantic park and a labyrinth.

Kortrijk: many monuments and historic buildings, including World Heritage Sites the Belfort and the Begijnhof; museums, parks, gardens and modern architecture.

Attractions

Boudewijn Seapark: zoo, dolphinarium and amusement park; seals, sea lions and birds of prey will keep you entertained.

Museum Constant Permeke, Jabbeke: more than 150 works by the great Flemish expressionist.

Butterfly Garden, Knokke-Zoute: 350 specimens of 35 different species of tropical butterflies, exhibited in their various life stages.

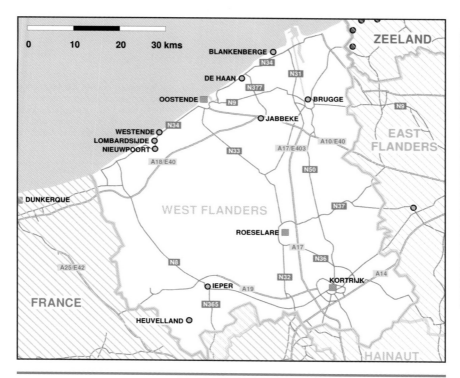

Blankenberge

Camping Bonanza 1

Zeebruggelaan 137, B-8370 Blankenberge (West Flanders) T: 050 416658. E: info@bonanza1.be

alanrogers.com/BE0546

Camping Bonanza 1 is a modern, family site within walking dist~~~
centre of the important resort of Blank~~~
and are genera~~~

Wendunsesteenweg 143 - B-8421 De Haan - Tel.+32-50-413593

www.campingterduinen.be

De Haan is situated on~~~ at the Belgian coast. The historical city of Bruges and the scenic city of Damme are on only 15 km distance. The adjacent leisure park offers you a subtropical pool complex and a covered play area, a true paradise for children. For internet access there is a separate building with pc's, also for use of your own notebook.

Brugge
Camping Memling

Veltemweg 109, B-8310 Brugge (West Flanders) T: 050 355 845. E: info@campingmemling.be

alanrogers.com/BE0580

This traditional site is ideal for visiting Brugge (or Bruges). The 100 unmarked pitches (69 for touring units) are on slightly undulating grass, with gravel roads and trees and hedges providing some shade. Electricity (6/10A) is available to 40 pitches. There is a separate area for 20 tents. Bars, restaurants, local shops and supermarkets are within walking distance. Brugge itself has a network of cycle ways and for those on foot, a bus runs into the centre from the campsite. Reservation in June, July and August is necessary. Visitors with large units should always telephone in advance to ensure an adequate pitch.

Facilities

Heated toilet facilities are clean and tidy, including some washbasins in cubicles. Limited facilities for disabled visitors (none for children). Laundry with washing machine and dryer. Freezer. Bread can be ordered from reception. Small, rather old bar with TV for 30 persons. Internet access (charged). Dogs are not accepted in July/Aug. Off site: Municipal swimming pool (open all year) and park nearby. Supermarkets 250 m. Fishing, bicycle hire and golf 2 km. Maldegem Steam Centre and narrow gauge railway 12 km. Boudewijn park and Dolphinarium southwest of town.

Open: All year.

Directions

From R30 Brugge ring road take exit 6 onto N9 towards Maldegem. At second set of traffic lights (opposite McDonald's), turn right, then immediately left. Site is 400 m. on the right.
GPS: 51.20692, 3.26294

Charges guide

Per unit incl. 2 persons and electricity	€ 22.50 - € 26.00
extra person	€ 5.00
child (3-15 yrs)	€ 4.00
dog	€ 3.00

De Haan
Camping Ter Duinen

Wenduinsesteenweg 143, B-8421 De Haan (West Flanders) T: 050 413 593.
E: infolawrence.sansens@scarlet.com **alanrogers.com/BE0578**

Ter Duinen is a large, seaside holiday site with 120 touring pitches and over 700 privately owned static holiday caravans. The pitches are laid out in straight lines with tarmac access roads and the site has three immaculate toilet blocks. Other than a bar and a playing field, the site has little else to offer, but it is only a 400 m. walk to the sea and next door to the site is a large sports complex with a sub-tropical pool and several sporting facilities. Opportunities for riding and golf (18-hole course) are close by. It is possible to hire bicycles in the town. The best places to visit for a day trip are Ostend with the Atlantic Wall from WWII, Knokke (which holds many summer festivals) and Bruges.

Facilities

Three modern toilet blocks have good fittings, washbasins in cubicles (hot and cold water) and showers (€ 1.20). Baby bath. Facilities for disabled visitors. Laundry facilities with two washing machines and a dryer, irons and ironing boards. Motorcaravan service point. Shop. Snack bar and takeaway. WiFi (charged). Off site: Bicycle hire and sea with sandy beach 400 m. Riding 1 km. Golf 3 km. Boat launching 6 km. A bus for Bruges stops 200 m. from the site, a tram for the coast 400 m.

Open: 16 March - 15 October.

Directions

On E40 in either direction take exit for De Haan/Jabbeke. 3 km. south of De Haan, turn at signs for campsites. GPS: 51.28318, 3.05753

Charges guide

Per unit incl. 2 persons and electricity	€ 17.00 - € 24.00
extra person	€ 2.50
child (under 10 yrs)	€ 2.00
dog	€ 3.00

Camping Cheques accepted.

Campsite Ter Duinen
De Haan - Belgian Coast

a true paradise for all ages, situated

Heuvelland

Camping Ypra

Pingelaarstraat 2, Kemmel, B-8956 Heuvelland (West Flanders) T: 057 444631. E: camping.ypra@skynet.be

alanrogers.com/BE0573

This is a peaceful, rural site less than a kilometre walk from a pretty Flemish village with cafés, bars, shops and a tourist information office. The site extends up the slopes of Kemmelberg, the highest point in West Flanders. The 230 seasonal pitches are on the upper part of the site, while 50 grass touring pitches are by the site entrance on firm, level ground. There are an additional 20 hardstandings for motorcaravans, and a separate tent field. All the pitches have 6A electricity hook-up available. English, Dutch, French and German are spoken.

Facilities

The sanitary facilities are located in five traditional blocks across the site (two can be heated) and have modern showers and toilets. Those by the touring area have facilities for disabled campers. Laundry with washing machines and dryers. Shop for basics. Bar and snack bar. Minigolf. Fishing. Tennis courts. Play area. Children's entertainment (July/Aug). WiFi. Off site: Bus stop at site entrance for Ieper and Poperinge. Kemmel village with banks, shops, cafés and restaurants 1 km. Bicycle hire 1 km. Riding 5 km. Walking and cycling.

Open: 1 March - 30 November.

Directions

From N33 Poperinge by-pass turn south onto N304 at roundabout (direction Reningelst). Pass through Reningelst and Klyte towards Kemmel. Turn right at site signpost at edge of Kemmel. GPS: 50.78477, 2.81958

Charges guide

Per unit incl. 2 persons and electricity	€ 22.00
extra person	€ 4.00
child (4-12 yrs)	€ 1.90
dog	€ 1.90

Ieper

Camping Jeugdstadion

Bolwerkstraat 1, B-8900 Ieper (West Flanders) T: 057 217 282. E: info@jeugdstadion.be

alanrogers.com/BE0570

Jeugdstadion is a small municipal site close to the historic old town. There are 22 caravan pitches, all with 6A electricity, plus a separate area for 70 tents. At the end of Leopold III Laan (ten minutes walk) is the Menin Gate built in 1927, which bears the names of British and Commonwealth soldiers who lost their lives between 1914-1918. The last post is sounded beneath the gate at 20.00 every evening in their honour. The Flanders Experience, an interactive museum in the Cloth Hall is a moving experience. The Commonwealth War Graves Commission is a little further away in Elverdingestraat.

Facilities

The modern, heated, but fairly basic toilet block can struggle to cope in busy periods. It has cold water to washbasins and three sinks for dishwashing outside. Bicycle hire. Off site: Sports complex adjacent. Indoor and outdoor swimming pools 500 m. Very large comprehensive playground. Minigolf. During school holidays these facilities are extensively used by local children and can therefore be fairly busy and lively.

Open: 1 March - 12 November.

Directions

From N336 (Lille) at roundabout by Lille Gate, turn left on Picanolaan and first right into Leopold III Laan. Jeugdstadion entrance is on right. Use roadside parking and book in at the Kantine inside the gates. Alternatively go to the vehicle gate and walk through site to reception. GPS: 50.84682, 2.89748

Charges guide

Per person	€ 4.00
child (6-12 yrs)	€ 2.50
caravan pitch incl. electricity	€ 6.00
dog	€ 1.00
tent	€ 2.50

Jabbeke

Recreatiepark Klein Strand

Varsenareweg 29, B-8490 Jabbeke (West Flanders) T: 050 811 440. E: info@kleinstrand.be

alanrogers.com/BE0555

In a convenient location just off the A10 motorway and close to Bruges, this site is in two distinct areas divided by an access road. The touring section has 137 large pitches on flat grass separated by well trimmed hedges; all have electricity, cable TV point and access to water and drainage. Though surrounded by mobile homes and seasonal caravans, this is a surprisingly relaxing area and the ambience was further enhanced in 2011 when a small park was created at its centre. Some children's leisure facilities are provided here, and there is a spacious bar and a snack bar with takeaway. The main site with all the privately owned mobile homes is closer to the lake, so has most of the amenities. These include the main reception building, restaurants, bar, minimarket, and sports facilities. This is a family holiday site and offers a comprehensive programme of activities and entertainment in July and August. The lake is used for water skiing and has a supervised swimming area with waterslides (high season) and a beach volleyball area. Klein Strand is an ideal base for visiting Bruges (by bus) and Gent (by train from Bruges).

Facilities

A single modern, heated, toilet block provides the usual facilities including good sized showers (charged) and open washbasins. Basic facilities for disabled visitors. Baby room. Laundry. Dishwashing outside. Further toilet facilities with washbasins in cubicles are located behind the touring field reception building (July/Aug). Motorcaravan services. Bar and snack bar. Play area. Fun pool for small children. In main park: Restaurants, bar and snack bar, takeaways. Shop (Easter-end Aug). Tennis courts. Sports field. Water ski school. Bicycle hire. WiFi (charged, first hour free).

Open: All year.

Directions

Jabbeke is 12 km. southwest of Bruges. From A18/A10 motorways, take exit 6/6B (Jabbeke). At roundabout take first exit signed for site. In 650 m. on left-hand bend, turn left to site in 600 m. Main reception is on left but in high season continue to touring site on right. GPS: 51.18448, 3.10445

Charges guide

Per unit incl. up to 4 persons and electricity	€ 20.00 - € 36.00
dog	€ 2.00

nice reductions in low-saison!

Camping Klein Strand

in Jabbeke, Belgium (near Bruges, Ostend, Ghent & Ypres!)

Large well equiped pitches (10 amp, TV & Wifi!)

www.kleinstrand.be - Tel: 0032 50 811440

Lombardsijde

Camping De Lombarde

Elisabethlaan 4, B-8434 Lombardsijde Middelkerke (West Flanders) T: 058 236 839. E: info@delombarde.be

alanrogers.com/BE0560

De Lombarde is a spacious, good value holiday site between Lombardsijde and the coast. It has a pleasant atmosphere and modern buildings. The 380 pitches are set out in level, grassy bays surrounded by shrubs, all with electricity (16A), long leads may be needed. Vehicles are parked in separate car parks. There are many seasonal units and 21 holiday homes, leaving 170 touring pitches. There is a range of activities and an entertainment programme in season. This is a popular holiday area and the site becomes full at peak times. A pleasant stroll takes you into Lombardsijde. There is a tram service from near the site entrance to the town and the beach.

Facilities

Three heated sanitary units are of an acceptable standard, with some washbasins in cubicles. Facilities for disabled visitors (but not for children). Large laundry. Motorcaravan services. Shop, restaurant/bar and takeaway (July/Aug. plus weekends and holidays 1/4-31/8). Tennis. Boules. Fishing lake. TV lounge. Entertainment programme for children. Playground. Internet access (in the bar). ATM.

Open: All year.

Directions

From lights in Lombardsijde, turn left following tram lines into Zeelaan. Continue following tramlines until crossroads and tram stop, turn left into Elisabethlaan. Site is on right in 200 m. GPS: 51.15644, 2.75329

Charges guide

Per unit incl. 1-6 persons and electricity	€ 18.00 - € 32.50

No credit cards.

Nieuwpoort

Kompas Camping Nieuwpoort

Brugsesteenweg 49, B-8620 Nieuwpoort (West Flanders) T: 058 236 037. E: nieuwpoort@kompascamping.be
alanrogers.com/BE0550

Near Ostend and convenient for the A18 motorway, this large, well equipped and well run site with 1056 pitches caters particularly for families. There are many amenities including a heated pool complex, a range of sporting activities, and a children's farm. The 469 touring pitches, all with electricity (10A), are in regular rows on flat grass in various parts of the site; 120 also have a water point and waste water drainage. With many seasonal units and caravan holiday homes, the site becomes full during Belgian holidays and in July and August. A network of footpaths links all areas of the site. Gates to the rear lead to a reservoir reserved for sailing, windsurfing and canoeing (canoes for hire) during certain hours only. Although the site is vast, there is a sense of spaciousness thanks to the broad stretch of landscaped leisure areas. These house sophisticated playgrounds for children, sports facilities and a children's farm.

Facilities

Seven modern, clean and well maintained toilet blocks include washbasins in cubicles, controllable showers and excellent facilities for families, young children and disabled visitors. Dishwashing and laundry rooms. Washing machines and dryers. Motorcaravan service point. Supermarket, bakery, restaurant, takeaway and café/bar (all w/e low season, otherwise daily). Swimming pools (heated and supervised) with slide, children's pool and pool games (9/5-15/9). Bicycle hire. Tennis. Extensive adventure playgrounds. Multisports court. Entertainment programme in July/Aug. WiFi throughout (charged).

Open: 22 March - 12 November.

Directions

Nieuwpoort is 19 km. southwest of Ostend. From east on A18 (E40) take exit 4 (Middelkerke). Turn north towards Diksmuide on D369; in 2 km. turn right on N367 towards Nieuwpoort. Pass through Sint-Joris and the site is on the right. GPS: 51.12965, 2.77222

Charges guide

Per unit incl. 4 persons and electricity	€ 26.10 - € 38.00

Largest unit accepted 2.5x8 m.
Camping Cheques accepted.

Westende

Kompas Camping Westende

Bassevillestraat 141, B-8434 Westende (West Flanders) T: 058 223 025. E: westende@kompascamping.be
alanrogers.com/BE0565

Camping Westende is a large holiday site near the sea. Of the 435 pitches, half are taken by seasonal caravans plus 43 rental units, leaving about 100 touring pitches on grass and with 10A electricity, plus a group of 77 large (150 sq.m), serviced pitches with water and electricity. The site seems reasonably well cared for, but on a previous visit, some pitches were looking rather worn, perhaps partly because of the rigid pitching policy which dictates that caravans have to be placed on a specific side of the pitch. All the main services are grouped around reception which can be a fair walk from the more remote pitches. One end of the site is now leased to a firm providing rental accommodation in mobile homes. Adjacent are a large Kompas holiday rental complex and an automated motorcaravan park.

Facilities

Four toilet blocks were well cared for when we visited, but reportedly have suffered from heavy use and variable cleaning in high season. Good facilities for children and disabled visitors in furthest block but access difficult at time of visit. Shop, bar, restaurant and takeaway (Easter-Nov, but weekends only outside July/Aug). Play area. WiFi. Boules. Children's entertainment (July/Aug). Bicycle hire.

Open: 22 March - 11 November.

Directions

Westende is 15 km. southwest of Ostend. From the E40 take exit 4 to Middelkerke. At the church turn left to Westende. After Westende church take the fourth turn right to the site. GPS: 51.15787, 2.7606

Charges 2013

Per unit incl. 4 persons and electricity	€ 28.90 - € 38.00

Camping Cheques accepted.

The Grand Duchy of Luxembourg is a sovereign state, lying between Belgium, France and Germany. Divided into two areas, the spectacular Ardennes region in the north and the rolling farmlands and woodland in the south, it is bordered on the east by the wine growing area of the Moselle Valley.

CAPITAL: LUXEMBOURG CITY

Tourist Office

Luxembourg Tourist Office
122 Regent Street, London W1B 5SA
Tel: 020 7434 2800
Fax: 020 7734 1205
Email: tourism@luxembourg.co.uk
Internet: www.luxembourg.co.uk

From wherever you are in Luxembourg you are always within easy reach of the capital, Luxembourg-Ville, home to about one fifth of the population. The city was built upon a rocky outcrop, and has superb views of the Alzette and Petrusse Valleys. Those who love the great outdoors must make a visit to the Ardennes, with its hiking trails, footpaths and cycle routes that take you through beautiful winding valleys and across deep rivers, a very popular region for visitors. If wine tasting takes your fancy, then head for the Moselle Valley, particularly if you like sweet, fruity wines. From late spring to early autumn, wine tasting tours take place in cellars and caves. The Mullerthal region, known as the 'Little Switzerland', lies on the banks of the River Sûre. The earth is mostly made up of soft sandstone, so through the ages many fascinating gorges, caves and formations have emerged.

Population

492,000

Climate

A temperate climate prevails, the summer often extending from May to late October.

Language

Letzeburgesch is the national language, with French and German also being official languages.

Telephone

The country code is 00 352.

Money

Currency: The Euro
Banks: Mon-Fri 08.30/09.00-12.00 and 13.30-16.30.

Shops

Mon 14.00-18.30. Tues to Sat 08.30-12.00 and 14.00-18.30 (grocers and butchers at 15.00 on Sat).

Public Holidays

New Year; Carnival Day mid-Feb; Easter Mon; May Day; Ascension; Whit Mon; National Day 23 June; Assumption 15 Aug; Kermesse 1 Sept; All Saints; All Souls; Christmas 25, 26 Dec.

Motoring

Many holidaymakers travel through Luxembourg to take advantage of the lower fuel prices, thus creating traffic congestion at petrol stations, especially in summer. A Blue Zone area exists in Luxembourg City and various parts of the country (discs from tourist offices) but meters are also used.

Esch-sur-Alzette

Camping Gaalgebierg

Boite Postale 20, L-4001 Esch-sur-Alzette T: 541 069. E: gaalcamp@pt.lu

alanrogers.com/LU7700

Occupying an elevated position on the edge of town, near the French border, this site is run by the local camping and caravan club. On a hilltop and with a good variety of trees, most pitches have shade. Of the 150 grass pitches marked out by trees, 100 are for tourers, the remainder being occupied by seasonal units. There are some gravel pitches set aside for one night stays, plus four all-weather pitches for motorcaravans. All pitches have 16A electricity and TV points.

Facilities

The toilet block can be heated and includes some washbasins in cubicles, hot showers and separate facilities for disabled visitors and babies. Laundry. Key card entry system. Motorcaravan service point. Gas available. Small bar, snack bar and takeaway (all year; on demand in low season). Playground. Bicycle hire. Boules. Entertainment and activity programme in high season. WiFi over site (charged). Off site: Restaurant within walking distance. Swimming pool and tennis nearby. Shops, bars and restaurants in Esch 2 km.

Open: All year.

Directions

Esch is 18 km. southwest of Luxembourg city. Site is signed from centre of town. From motorways take exit 5 for Esch Centre but at T-junction in 1 km. avoid town centre by turning left (Schifflange) then right after railway crossing, ahead at traffic lights and follow signs to site at top of hill.
GPS: 49.48492, 5.98657

Charges guide

Per unit incl. 2 persons and electricity	€ 17.25
extra person	€ 3.75
child (3-12 yrs)	€ 1.75

Ettelbruck

Camping Kalkesdelt

Chemin du Camping 88, L-9022 Ettelbruck T: 812 185. E: kalkesdelt@ettelbruck-info.lu

alanrogers.com/LU7910

This agreeable, good value municipal site is situated on a hilltop overlooking the town. It is quietly located about 1 km. from the centre of Ettelbruck, with a nice atmosphere and well tended gardens and grass. The modern main building includes reception, an excellent restaurant and a 'salle de séjour' (with library and TV). The 136 marked pitches, 76 for touring, are accessed from tarmac roads and have electricity available (16A). Reception provides good tourist information and English is spoken.

Facilities

A new sanitary unit using solar energy provides washbasins in cabins and hot showers. Provision for disabled campers. Laundry. Motorcaravan services. Restaurant. Snack bar and takeaway open evenings. Breakfasts can also be served. A baker calls daily at 07.30. (order day before). Bicycle hire. Playground. Entertainment in season. Off site: Within walking distance of Ettelbruck 1 km. Luxembourg city by train.

Open: 1 April - 31 October.

Directions

Site is signed on the western outskirts of Ettelbruck off the N15 and approached via a short one-way system. GPS: 49.846073, 6.082022

Charges guide

Per unit incl. 2 persons and electricity	€ 22.90
extra person	€ 6.00
child (3-14 yrs)	€ 3.00
dog	€ 2.50

Heiderscheid

Camping Fuussekaul

4 Fuussekaul, L-9156 Heiderscheid T: 268 8881. E: info@fuussekaul.lu

alanrogers.com/LU7850

This site lies in the rolling wooded hills of central Luxembourg, not far from the lakes of the Sûre river dam. Of the 370 pitches, 220 of varying sizes are for touring units, all with a 6A electricity connection. There are some super pitches with private electricity and water. The site consists of winding roads, some sloping, along which the pitches are set in shaded areas. The touring area (separate from the chalets and seasonal pitches) is well endowed with modern facilities, although there is no provision for visitors with disabilities.

Facilities

Four excellent sanitary blocks provide showers (token € 0.75), washbasins (in cabins and communal) and children and baby rooms with small toilets, washbasins and showers. Laundry. Parking and service area for motorcaravans. Well stocked shop. Bar. Restaurant and takeaway. Swimming pools. Suite with sauna and sun beds. Beauty salon. Playgrounds. Cross-country skiing when snow permits. Bicycle hire. Children's club. Bowling centre. WiFi (charged). Off site: Castles, museums and walks all within a reasonable distance. Riding 500 m.

Open: All year.

Directions

Take N15 from Diekirch to Heiderscheid. Site is on left at top of hill just before reaching the village. Motorcaravan service area is signed on the right. GPS: 49.87750, 5.99283

Charges guide

Per unit incl. 2 persons and electricity	€ 18.50 - € 38.00
extra person	€ 3.00
child	€ 1.00 - € 2.00
dog	€ 2.00

FREE Alan Rogers Travel Card
Extra benefits and savings - see page 12

Heiderscheid

Naturistencamping de Reenert

4 Fuussekaul, L-9156 Heiderscheid T: 268 888. E: info@fuussekaul.lu

alanrogers.com/LU7860

Naturistencamping de Reenert is located at Heiderscheid, in the natural park of the Haute-Sûre. Visitors report to the reception at Camping Fuussekaul opposite, where they are given the code to enter the site. There are 70 large flat pitches, all with electricity (6/10A). Amenities include a newly built, heated swimming pool with lounge area and meeting rooms for campers, and a small children's outdoor play area. An extensive entertainment programme including sports, games, body painting and many other activities is run during the high season. Visitors are welcome to use the bar, restaurant, sauna, tennis court and shop at Fuussekaul (where fresh bread is baked daily).

Facilities

One modern and one Portacabin-style unit provide excellent facilities, including one family shower and three low level showers. Heated indoor swimming pool. Play area. Entertainment/meeting room. Shop, bar, restaurant, sauna, tennis, bicycle hire at Fuussekaul. Caravan holiday homes for rent. Off site: Riding 500 m. Fishing 3 km. Supermarket and shops in Ettelbruck 7 km. Castles, museums and walks all within a reasonable distance.

Open: All year.

Directions

Take the N15 from Deikirch to Heiderscheid. Site is on right at top of hill just before reaching the village – check in at Fuussekaul on left.
GPS: 49.87788, 5.99364

Charges guide

Per unit incl. 2 persons and electricity	€ 16.00 - € 23.00
extra person (over 14 yrs)	€ 3.00

Camping Cheques accepted.

Kautenbach

Camping Kautenbach

An der Weierbach, L-9663 Kautenbach T: 950 303. E: info@campingkautenbach.lu

alanrogers.com/LU7830

Kautenbach is situated in the heart of the Luxembourg Ardennes and was established over 50 years ago. Although in an idyllic location, it is less than a mile from a railway station with regular trains to Luxembourg city to the south. There are 135 touring pitches here, mostly of a good size and with reasonable shade. Most pitches have electrical connections (10A). This is excellent walking country with many tracks around the site. The site managers are happy to recommend walks for all abilities. Kautenbach has an attractive bistro style restaurant, specialising in local cuisine, as well as a large selection of whiskies!

Facilities

Two toilet blocks with open style controllable washbasins and showers, baby changing. Facilities for disabled visitors (key). Laundry. Shop for basics (1/4-31/10, bread to order). Restaurant, bar/snack bar (all season). Direct river access. Fishing. Play area. Tourist information. Mobile homes for rent. Internet café. Off site: Walking and cycle trails. Railway station 500 m. Caves at Consdorf. Cathedral at Echternach.

Open: 20 January - 20 December.

Directions

Head south from Namur on the A4 and then join the N4 (junction 15). Continue on the N4 to Bastogne and then join the N84 towards Wiltz. Follow signs to Kautenbach on the CR331 and the site is well signed from here. GPS: 49.95387, 6.0273

Charges guide

Per unit incl. 2 persons and electricity	€ 20.05 - € 21.60
extra person	€ 5.90

Larochette

Camping Auf Kengert

Kengert, L-7633 Larochette-Medernach T: 837186. E: info@kengert.lu

alanrogers.com/LU7640

A friendly welcome awaits you at this peacefully situated, family run site, 2 km. from Larochette, which is 24 km. northeast of Luxembourg City, providing 180 individual pitches, all with electricity (16A Europlug). Some in a very shaded woodland setting, on a slight slope with fairly narrow access roads. There are also eight hardened pitches for motorcaravans on a flat area of grass, complete with motorcaravan service facilities. Further tent pitches are in an adjacent and more open meadow area. There are also owned wooden chalets for rent. This site is popular in season, so early arrival is advisable.

Facilities

The well maintained sanitary block includes a modern, heated unit with some washbasins in cubicles, and fully equipped cubicles for disabled visitors. Showers, facilities for babies, additional WCs and washbasins, plus laundry room are below the central building housing the shop, bar and restaurant. Motorcaravan services. Gas. Solar heated swimming pool (Easter-30/9). Paddling pool. WiFi (free).

Open: 1 March - 8 November.

Directions

From Larochette take the CR118/N8 (towards Mersch) and just outside town turn right on CR119 towards Schrondweiler, site is 2 km. on right. GPS: 49.79992, 6.19817

Charges guide

Per unit incl. 2 persons and electricity	€ 22.00 - € 32.00
extra person	€ 10.00 - € 15.00

For latest camp site news, availability and prices visit

alanrogers.com

Larochette

Camping Birkelt

1 Um Birkelt, L-7633 Larochette T: 879 040. E: info@camping-birkelt.lu

alanrogers.com/LU7610

This is very much a family site, with a great range of facilities provided. It is well organised and well laid out, set in an elevated position in attractive, undulating countryside. A tarmac road runs around the site with 427 large grass pitches (280 for touring), some slightly sloping, many with a fair amount of shade, on either side of gravel access roads in straight rows and circles. Two hundred pitches have electricity, 134 serviced ones have 16A, the remainder 10A. An all-weather swimming pool complex is beside the site entrance (free for campers) and entertainment for children is arranged in high season. The site is very popular with tour operators (140 pitches).

Facilities	Directions
Three modern heated sanitary buildings well situated around the site include mostly open washbasins (6 cabins in one block). Baby baths. Facilities (including rental accommodation) for wheelchair users. Washing machines and dryers. Motorcaravan service point. Shops. Coffee bar. Restaurant with terrace. Swimming pool with sliding cupola (heated 15/5-15/9). Outdoor pool for toddlers. Sauna. Play areas. Trampolines. Volleyball. Minigolf. Tennis. Bicycle hire. Riding. Free WiFi over site.	From N7 (Diekirch-Luxembourg City), turn onto N8 (CR118) at Berschbach (just past Mersch) towards Larochette. Site is signed on the right 1.5 km. from Larochette. Approach road is fairly steep and narrow. GPS: 49.78508, 6.21033

Open: 16 March - 3 November.

Charges 2013

Per unit incl. 2 persons and electricity	€ 19.50 - € 36.00
with water and drainage	€ 22.50 - € 39.00
Camping Cheques accepted.	

Luxembourg

Camping Kockelscheuer

22 route de Bettembourg, L-1899 Luxembourg T: 471 815. E: caravani@pt.lu

alanrogers.com/LU7660

Camping Kockelscheuer is 4 km. from the centre of Luxembourg City and quietly situated (although there can be some aircraft noise at times). On a slight slope, there are 161 individual pitches of good size, either on flat ground at the bottom of the site or on wide flat terraces with easy access, all with 16A electricity. There is also a special area for tents, with picnic tables and, in the reception building, a tent campers' lounge. For children there is a large area with modern play equipment on safety tiles and next door to the site is a sports centre. There is a friendly welcome, charges are reasonable and English is spoken.

Facilities	Directions
Two fully equipped, identical sanitary buildings, both very clean. Washing machines. Motorcaravan services. Shop (order bread the previous day). Snack bar. Restaurant in adjacent sports centre also with minigolf, tennis, squash etc. Rest room. No entry or exit for vehicles (reception closed) 12.00-14.00. WiFi (charged). Off site: Bus 200 m. every 10 minutes to Luxembourg. Swimming pool and bicycle hire 5 km. Fishing 20 km.	Site is SSW of Luxembourg City on the N31 to Bettembourg. From the south, exit A4 at junction signed Kockelscheuer onto N4. In 2 km. turn right (Kockelscheuer and campsite) and continue to follow the signs. GPS: 49.57180, 6.10900

Open: Easter - 31 October.

Charges guide

Per unit incl. 2 persons and electricity	€ 15.50
extra person	€ 4.00
No credit cards.	

Maulusmühle

Camping Woltzdal

Maison 12, L-9974 Maulusmühle T: 998 938. E: info@woltzdal-camping.lu

alanrogers.com/LU7780

Set by a stream in a valley, Camping Woltzdal is one of the many delightful sites in the Ardennes, a region of wooded hills and river valleys that crosses the borders of Belgium, France and Luxembourg. The site has 79 flat touring pitches, set on grass amongst fir trees; all with 4A electricity and 20 of which also have water and waste water. They are fairly open and have views of the surrounding wooded hills. A railway passes the site on the far side of the stream, but there are only trains during the day and they are not disturbing.

Facilities	Directions
The site boasts a new state-of-the-art toilet block with solar-powered water heating (smart key access with deposit). Large family bathrooms and facilities for disabled visitors. Laundry room. Motorcaravan services. Reception, a small shop, a bar and restaurant/snack bar are in the large house at the entrance. Play area. Boules. Children's entertainment (high season). WiFi over site (charged).	Site is 6 km. north of Clervaux on CR335. Leave Clervaux towards Troisvierge (N18). After 1 km. take right fork to Maulusmühle on CR335. Site is signed on right just before Maulusmühle village. Steep turn onto campsite road. GPS: 50.091283, 6.027833

Open: All year.

Charges guide

Per unit incl. 2 persons and electricity	€ 20.00 - € 23.20

Mersch

Camping Krounebierg

12 rue du Camping, L-7572 Mersch T: 329 756. E: contact@campingkrounebierg.lu

alanrogers.com/LU7580

Situated on a hillside with views over the Mersch valley this is an attractive site for stopovers or longer stays. It is close the town of Mersch with good facilities and transport links but the site has a pleasant rural ambience. There are 177 pitches, 137 for touring, including 12 hardstandings. All are level, grassy and of a good size, with 10A electricity, and separated by hedges. A stylish, modern building at the site entrance houses reception, shop, bar and restaurant and has an elevated terrace overlooking the open -air children's pool. Campers can also use the town's indoor pool, adjacent to the site, at a reduced rate.

Facilities

Five traditional, clean sanitary blocks are heated and have free hot showers. Facilities for disabled visitors. Well stocked shop. Modern bar and restaurant/takeaway. Outdoor paddling pool. Games room with TV, darts etc. Play area. Football field. Badminton. Daily activity programme (July/Aug). Internet and WiFi. Off site: Close Mersch with good transport links into Luxembourg City (15 km) and further afield. Riding 5 km. Bicycle hire 6 km.

Open: 1 April - 31 October.

Directions

From A7 motorway take exit 3. Turn left onto rue de la Chapelle and left again onto rue Quatre-Vents. Site is well signed from this point.
GPS: 49.743573, 6.089781

Charges guide

Per unit inc. 2 persons and electricity	€ 19.80 - € 30.80
extra person	€ 4.00

Nommern

Europacamping Nommerlayen

Rue Nommerlayen, L-7465 Nommern T: 878 078. E: nommerlayen@vo.lu

alanrogers.com/LU7620

Situated at the end of its own road, in the lovely wooded hills of central Luxembourg, this is a top quality site with fees to match, but it has everything! A large, central building housing most of the services and amenities opens onto a terrace around an excellent swimming pool complex with a large fun pool and an imaginative water playground. The 367 individual pitches (100 sq.m) are on grassy terraces, all have access to electricity (2/16A) and water taps. Pitches are grouped beside age-appropriate play areas and the facilities throughout the campsite reflect the attention given to families in particular. Interestingly enough the superb new sanitary block is called Badtemple (built in the style of a Greek temple). A member of Leading Campings group.

Facilities

A large, high quality, modern sanitary unit provides some washbasins in cubicles, facilities for disabled visitors, and family and baby washrooms. The new block includes a sauna. Twelve private bathrooms for hire. Laundry. Motorcaravan service point. Supermarket. Bar, restaurant, snack bar (all 1/4-1/11). Excellent swimming pool complex (1/5-15/9) and new covered and heated pool (Easter-1/11). Solarium. Fitness programmes. Bowling. Playground. Large screen TV. Entertainment in season. WiFi (charged).

Open: 1 March - 1 November.

Directions

Take the 118 road between Mersch and Larochette. Site is signed 3 km. north of Larochette towards the village of Nommern on the 346 road.
GPS: 49.78472, 6.16519

Charges guide

Per unit incl. 2 persons and electricity	€ 22.50 - € 43.75
extra person (over 2 yrs)	€ 5.50
No credit cards.	

Reisdorf

Camping de la Sûre

23 route de la Sûre, L-9390 Reisdorf T: 836 246. E: hientgen@pt.lu

alanrogers.com/LU7650

Camping de la Sûre is on the banks of the river that separates Luxembourg and Germany. It is a pleasant site close to Reisdorf with 180 numbered pitches (120 with 10A electricity). These are not separated but are marked with lovely beech and willow trees that provide some shade. There are caravan holiday homes in a fenced area towards the back of the site, leaving the prime pitches for touring units. The site is surrounded by trees on the hillsides and from Reisdorf visits can be made to Vianden Castle or Trier (oldest German city) just across the border.

Facilities

Modern, clean sanitary facilities which are in the process of being refitted and extended, including some washbasins in cubicles. Laundry. Small shop. Bar and restaurant. Takeaway. Playground. Minigolf. Sports field. Canoeing. Fishing. WiFi over site (charged). Off site: Town centre within easy walking distance. Cycle ways abound. Bicycle hire 200 m. Riding 5 km. Golf 8 km.

Open: 1 April - 30 October.

Directions

From the river bridge in Reisdorf, take the road to Echternach, de la Sûre is the second campsite on the left. GPS: 49.87003, 6.26750

Charges guide

Per unit incl. 2 persons and electricity	€ 19.50
extra person	€ 5.00
No credit cards.	

Borger
Recreatiepark Hunzedal

De Drift, NL-9531 Tk Borger (Drenthe) T: 0599 234 698. E: info@vakantiegevoel.nl
alanrogers.com/NL6145

Recreatiepark Hunzedal is a large park with holiday homes, touring pitches, rental units and seasonal guests. It is in beautiful natural surroundings, close to the moors of Drenthe. It has over 250 touring pitches, 80 with water, 6-16A electricity, waste water and cable. Pitches are laid out in circular bays, off hardcore access roads on grassy fields taking around ten units. Level pitches are numbered and with shade to the back from mature trees and shrubs. Close to the touring pitches is a large water area with play equipment and a sandy beach. The reception building houses a sub-tropical pool.

Facilities
Three fully equipped toilet blocks for tourers with toilets, washbasins (open style and in cabins) and preset showers. Family shower rooms. Baby room. En-suite facilities for disabled visitors. Laundry. Motorcaravan services. Shop. Bar/restaurant. Snack bar. Sub-tropical pool. Minigolf. Sun beds and sauna. Playgrounds. Adventure hall. WiFi (charged). Off site: Zoo in Emmen. Camp Westerbork

Open: 3 April - 31 October.

Directions
On A28 in either direction take exit 32 and continue East on N33. At the crossroads with the N34, turn South towards Borger. In Borger follow the site signs. GPS: 52.92322, 6.8034

Charges guide
Per unit incl. 5 persons and electricity	€ 18.00 - € 50.00
extra person	€ 4.00

Diever
Camping Diever

Haarweg 2, NL-7981 LW Diever (Drenthe) T: 0521 591 694. E: info@camping-diever.nl
alanrogers.com/NL6180

Camping Diever is just outside the quiet, rural village of Diever and close to the Drents-Friese Wold nature reserve. A special attraction in Diever is the open-air theatre where they perform a Shakespearean play all summer. Camping Diever has 210 touring pitches, all with 10A electricity, arranged informally around the site between the trees and separated by natural greenery. Some of the ground is sandy with some grass areas off sand access roads. The village is an easy 15 minute walk.

Facilities
Three toilet blocks (one heated) provide toilets, washbasins (open style and in cabins) and preset hot showers with key for hot water. Family shower. Baby room. Laundry facilities. Fresh bread and basics from reception. Recreation hall with games machine, billiards, library and fireplace. Playing field. Bicycle hire. Adventure play island (parents not allowed). No charcoal barbecues. Torch useful. WiFi (charged). Off site: Shakespeare Theatre, village of Diever 1 km.

Open: 1 April - 30 September.

Directions
On A28, take exit 31 and continue on N381 towards Drachten. At Hoogersmilde, turn south on N371 towards Meppel. Turn towards Diever and follow site signs. GPS: 52.86675, 6.32018

Charges guide
Per unit incl. 2 persons and electricity	€ 15.15
extra person (under 10 yrs)	€ 4.75
child	€ 2.50
dog	€ 2.45

Diever
Camping Wittelterbrug

Wittelterweg 31, NL-7986 PL Diever (Drenthe) T: 0521 598 288. E: info@wittelterbrug.nl
alanrogers.com/NL6148

Camping Wittelterbrug is a well established, family friendly site with a central location between the Drents-Friese Wold and the Dwingelderveld. This is excellent cycling and walking country (cycle hire is available on site). Pitches are in long lanes off paved access roads on good sized, grassy fields. All are equipped with electricity (10A), water and drainage (a small charge is made for hot showers). On-site amenities include two indoor heated pools and a café/snack bar serving takeaway meals. In peak season, there is a lively activity and entertainment programme, including special activities for children.

Facilities
Two blocks for tourers with controllable, hot showers and open style washbasins. Baby room. Facilities were not adequate for wheelchair users. Bar provides meals, takeaways, drinks and ice. Covered swimming pool and children's pool. Playground. Bowling alley. Bicycle hire. Tourist information. WiFi (charged). Accommodation for rent. Off site: Shops and restaurants in Dwingeloo and Diever. Fishing. Golf 8 km. Walking and cycle tracks across the Drenthe countryside.

Open: 1 April - 31 October.

Directions
Approaching from the south (Amersfoort and Zwolle), use A28 motorway and leave at Meppel. Continue north on N371 to Diever, and follow signs to the site. GPS: 52.824973, 6.318356

Charges guide
Per unit incl. 2 persons, electricity, water and waste water	€ 17.00 - € 21.00
extra person (over 1 year)	€ 3.25 - € 3.65
dog	€ 3.00 - € 3.60

FREE Alan Rogers Travel Card
Extra benefits and savings - see page 12

Dieverbrug
Landgoed 't Wildryck

Groningenweg 13, NL-7981 LA Dieverbrug (Drenthe) T: 0521 591 207. E: info@wildryck.nl

alanrogers.com/NL6139

Landgoed 't Wildryck offers camping on a large, 32 ha. estate in one of the most beautiful parts of Holland. Behind the site is the Drents-Friese Wold national park, with two others nearby (De Weerribben and the Dwingelderhei). 't Wildryck has just 59 touring pitches up to 140 sq.m, all with 10A electricity and private sanitary facilities (shower, toilet and washbasin) in attractively built little houses. The site is landscaped with low trees and pitches are on three level areas, some in the open, others with shade from mature trees and partly separated by fir trees. Site roads can become dusty in dry weather.

Facilities

Private sanitary facilities with basin, toilet and shower at each pitch. Baby room combined with toilet for disabled visitors. Small shop. Restaurant with bar for simple meals (closed Tues). Indoor heated pool with paddling pool. Tennis. Bicycle hire. Playground and indoor play attic. WiFi (charged). Torch useful. Barbecues are not permitted. Off site: Fishing 200 m. Lake beach and riding 5 km. Golf 9 km.

Open: All year.

Directions

Take exit 31 on A28 and continue west on N381 towards Drachten. At Hoogersmilde, turn south on N371 towards Meppel. Site is signed on this road. GPS: 52.863493, 6.353008

Charges guide

Per unit incl. 2 persons and electricity	€ 15.00 - € 29.00
extra person (over 3 yrs)	€ 4.00

Dwingeloo
Camping Meistershof

Lheebroek 33, NL-7991 PM Dwingeloo (Drenthe) T: 0521 597 278. E: info@meistershof.nl

alanrogers.com/NL6147

Meistershof is a small, interesting site with only 157 pitches, all for tourers. Developed on a former farm, the buildings have retained their original style, which gives the site a rustic look and feel. This, and the fact that the site is partly car free, ensures a relaxing holiday in beautiful, natural surroundings. The numbered pitches are all level and arranged on grassy fields with paved access lanes. They are separated by a variety of hedges and have shade from mature trees, and 10A electricity. There are 40 pitches with electricity, water and drainage; some have hardstandings or private sanitary facilities.

Facilities

New, stylish toilet block at the centre of the site with superb facilities. Toilets, washbasins (open style and in cabins) and controllable hot showers (charged). Toilets and basins for children. Facilities for disabled visitors. Family shower room. Baby room. Laundry. Shop for basics. Snack bar. Playing field. Playground and covered play area. Minigolf. Boules. WiFi (charged).

Open: 1 April - 30 September.

Directions

From the A28 take exit 29 (Dwingeloo) and continue towards town. Site is signed before Dwingeloo and is in the village of Lheebroek. GPS: 52.845746, 6.427469

Charges guide

Per unit incl. 2 persons and electricity	€ 24.15
extra person	€ 4.10
child (1-10 yrs)	€ 3.50

Dwingeloo
Camping Torentjeshoek

Leeuweriksveldweg 1, NL-7991 SE Dwingeloo (Drenthe) T: 0521 591 706. E: info@torentjeshoek.nl

alanrogers.com/NL6141

Camping Torentjeshoek is situated next to the Planetron attraction in the Dwingelderveld National Park. The partly car-free site is attractively landscaped with trees and shrubs and has 260 pitches, with 160 for tourers. The numbered and level touring pitches are well laid out and well spaced on circular, grassy fields between mature fir and spruce trees. There is shade around the fields and all pitches have 10A electricity, water, waste water and cable. An open-air, heated public pool adjacent to the site has free entry for campers. In high season an entertainment team provides various activities.

Facilities

Two toilet blocks (main block to the front and a smaller block to the back) with toilets, washbasins (open style and in cabins) and free, preset hot showers. Toilets for children. Family shower room. Baby room. Facilities for disabled visitors. Laundry. Motorcaravan service. Basics from reception. Bar with terrace and TV. Snack bar (weekends). Boules. Bicycle hire. Animal farm. Playground. Recreation hall with entertainment team in high season. WiFi. Off site: Riding 1 km. Lake beach and fishing 2.5 km. Golf 10 km.

Open: 1 April - 31 October.

Directions

On A28, take exit 29 for Dwingeloo and follow signs for the town. Site is signed in Dwingeloo and is next to the Planetron. GPS: 52.819048, 6.360644

Charges guide

Per unit incl. 2 persons and electricity	€ 18.70 - € 27.10
extra person	€ 1.30 - € 1.50
dog	€ 3.00

For latest campsite news, availability and prices visit

alanrogers.com

Dwingeloo
RCN Camping De Noordster

Noordster 105, NL-7991 PB Dwingeloo (Drenthe) T: 0521 597 238. E: noordster@rcn.nl

alanrogers.com/NL6158

RCN de Noordster can be found in the Dutch National Park Dwingelderveld, a beautiful expanse of moorland in the northern Netherlands. Hours of long walks though fields of purple heather and deep into ancient forests are possible here. All the pitches are well shaded, under large trees and surrounded by colourful shrubs. A range of mobile homes and chalets is available for rent, including some units specially adapted for visitors with disabilities. There are several children's playgrounds here, including a skate board park. Other leisure amenities include an outdoor pool (with waterslide), children's and toddlers' pools and various water games.

Facilities	Directions
Five clean, modern toilet blocks. Launderette. Restaurant, bar, café and takeaway. Bakery and supermarket. Fun paddling pool. Evening entertainment. Play area. Minigolf. Sports hall. Multisports field. Bicycle and go-kart hire. Skateboard track with half pipe. WiFi. Off site: Heated outdoor pool (adjacent). Planetron (planetarium) at Dwingeloo 3 km.	Site is 3 km. south of Dwingeloo, reachable from A28 (via N855) and A32 (via N371). In town centre follow the camping signs. GPS: 52.81337, 6.378926

Charges guide

Per unit incl. 2 persons and electricity	€ 16.50 - € 24.00
dog	€ 4.95 - € 7.50

Open: All year.

Gasselte
Camping de Berken

Borgerweg 23, NL-9462 RA Gasselte (Drenthe) T: 0599 564 255. E: info@campingdeberken.nl

alanrogers.com/NL6128

De Berken is an established site with well laid out pitches on grass fields with some trees. The site has 161 pitches of which 95 are for touring units. All have electricity, water and a drain, and there are 18 with private sanitary facilities. On site you will find a small shop for basic supplies, a recreation hall with an indoor playground and boules. A restaurant is 200 m. from the entrance. A countryside site, there are many possibilities for walking and cycling through nature reserves. In high season, an entertainment team keeps everyone busy.

Facilities	Directions
Two heated modern toilet blocks with toilets, preset hot showers, family shower rooms and baby room. Shop for basics. Indoor playground. Full entertainment programme in high season. Internet access. Off site: Bar and restaurant 200 m. Nije Hemelriek for swimming 2 km. Pool complex 5 km.	From the N33 Groningen-Emmen take exit for Borger. Continue to Drouwen and site is on the right just after Drouwen and well signed. GPS: 52.96476, 6.78934

Charges guide

Per unit incl. 2 persons and electricity (plus meter)	€ 19.00 - € 21.00
with own sanitary unit	€ 25.00 - € 27.50
extra person	€ 3.50
dog	€ 3.00

Open: 1 April - 23 October.

Gasselte
Camping De Lente van Drenthe

Houtvester Jansenweg 2, NL-9462 TB Gasselte (Drenthe) T: 0599 564 333. E: info@delentevandrenthe.nl

alanrogers.com/NL6124

De Lente van Drenthe is located on the edge of the Gieten-Borger forest. Along with its attractive situation amidst forests and moorland, it is also just a short walk (200 m.) from 't Nije Hemelriek. This is a large lake, with a maximum depth of 1.3 m, crystal clear water and a fine sandy beach. There is direct access to the many cycle, mountain bike and walking routes in the area. There are around 100 pitches for touring units here, all with 6A electricity and cable TV connections. The pitches are of a good size (a minimum of 100 sq.m). Electricity, water and drainage are available on 25 touring pitches.

Facilities	Directions
Good modern toilet blocks, including a family shower room. Basic essentials from reception. Small restaurant, bar, snack bar (1/4-15/9). Playground. Sports field. Tennis. Minigolf. Bicycle and go-kart hire. Nordic walking classes. Games room. Internet corner. Entertainment for children (high season). Max. 2 dogs. Off site: Beach 200 m. Riding 3 km. Golf 4 km. Drouwenerzand adventure park. Boomkroonpad (tree top walkway).	Site is 3 km. west of Gasselte. From the N34 (Borger-Gieten) take exit for Gasselte and follow signs to Nije Hemelrijk and site. GPS: 52.97652, 6.75608

Charges guide

Per unit incl. 2 persons and electricity	€ 17.50 - € 20.50

Open: 29 March - 25 October.

FREE Alan Rogers Travel Card
Extra benefits and savings - see page 12

Klijndijk

Vakantiecentrum De Fruithof

Melkweg 2, NL-7871 PE Klijndijk (Drenthe) T: 0591 512 427. E: info@fruithof.nl

alanrogers.com/NL6131

Vakantiecentrum de Fruithof is an immaculately kept site that is attractively landscaped with different varieties of shrubs and trees. The site is fairly open and has attractive pitches on well kept grassy lawns with access from tarmac roads. They are separated by fir trees and low hedges, providing lots of privacy. De Fruithof has 450 level, numbered pitches (250 for tourers), all with 6A electricity, water, cable and drainage. At the centre of the site is a large lake with sandy beaches and some play equipment.

Facilities

Four toilet blocks, well placed around the site, have toilets, washbasins (open style and in cabins) and free, preset hot showers. Washbasins for children. Family shower room. Baby room. Facilities for disabled visitors. Laundry. Motorcaravan services. Shop (bread to order; open daily). Bar, restaurant and snack bar. Open-air swimming pool (heated) with water slide and paddling pool. Lake with sandy beach. Playing field. Tennis. Bicycle hire. Playground. Entertainment team (high season and school holidays). WiFi (free). Off site: Emmen zoo.

Open: 8 April - 26 September.

Directions

On N34 take the exit for Emmen-Noord and turn immediately left towards Klijndijk. Follow site signs from there. GPS: 52.828868, 6.857342

Charges guide

Per unit incl. 2 persons and electricity	€ 19.50 - € 29.50
extra person (over 2 yrs)	€ 4.65
dog (max. 1)	€ 2.75

Meppen

Vakantieoord De Bronzen Emmer

Mepperstraat 41, NL-7855 TA Meppen (Drenthe) T: 0591 371 543. E: info@bronzenemmer.nl

alanrogers.com/NL6129

De Bronzen Emmer is in the centre of three nature reserves, close to the German border in the southwestern part of Drenthe. Level and grassy pitches are attractively laid out and average 100 sq.m. in size. All have 4/10A electricity and are shaded by mature trees. There are 38 full service pitches. To the front of the site are a heated indoor pool, a paddling pool with a small slide and an open-air paddling pool. Here also are a sauna, sun beds, recreation hall, small café and a playground.

Facilities

Two well placed, traditional style toilet blocks (one heated) with toilets, washbasins (open style and in cabins) and free, preset hot showers. Laundry. Motorcaravan services. Small shop for basics (high season only). Small restaurant with bar and open-air terrace (weekends and high season). Indoor swimming pool (20x10 m) with paddling pool and open air paddling pool. Sauna and sun beds. Bicycle hire. Playing field. Fishing. Tennis. Playground. Activity team in high season. WiFi. Off site: Riding 150 m.

Open: 2 April - 30 October.

Directions

On A28, take exit 31 (Beilen) and continue east on N381 road towards Emmen. Before Emmen turn south towards Meppen and follow site signs. GPS: 52.778987, 6.686323

Charges guide

Per unit incl. 2 persons	€ 17.20 - € 28.70
extra person (over 3 yrs)	€ 3.60
dog (max. 2)	€ 4.00
electricity (per kWh)	€ 0.40

Nietap

Wastersportcamping Cnossen Leekstermeer

Meerweg 13, NL-9312 TC Nietap (Drenthe) T: 0594 512 075. E: info@cnossenleekstermeer.nl

alanrogers.com/NL6185

Camping Cnossen Leekstermeer is a great site for nature lovers and watersports enthusiasts. There is a very extensive fleet of canoes, sailing boats, motorboats and rowing boats with windsurfing and sailing schools available. There are 140 touring pitches (125-175 sq.m), 110 with 6-16A electricity, water and drainage, and 30 tent pitches on the nature camping field. All pitches are on level, grassy fields with shade from mature trees and bushes, and there are three hardstandings. The site is situated in the centre of a nature reserve, which is still being extended, offering opportunities for walking and cycling.

Facilities

Two toilet blocks, one central and CO_2 neutral, a smaller one to the back, with underfloor heating, toilets, washbasins in cabins and preset hot showers. Extra services at the marina. Facilities for children and disabled visitors. Family shower rooms. Baby room. Laundry. Motorcaravan services. Bar/restaurant. Sailing boats, canoes and rowing boats for hire. Windsurfing and sailing schools. Play area. WiFi (charged).

Open: 1 April - 1 November.

Directions

From the A7 take exit 34 (Leek) and continue south towards Leek, then Nietap. Site is signed Leekstermeer. GPS: 53.175752, 6.423177

Charges guide

Per unit incl. 2 persons and electricity	€ 19.75 - € 27.50
extra person (over 4 yrs)	€ 4.25
dog	€ 3.40

For latest campsite news, availability and prices visit

alanrogers.com

Rolde
Camping De Weyert

Ballo'rstraat 2, NL-9451 AK Rolde (Drenthe) T: 0592 241 520. E: info@deweyert.nl
alanrogers.com/NL6144

Camping De Weyert is located within the Drentsche Aa National Park. This is a good choice for nature lovers, close to the holiday village of Rolde. There are 70 good sized touring pitches on two level, grassy fields (the larger one used as an ice-skating rink in winter). All have water, electricity (4/6A), drainage and cable TV connections. Alternatively, it is possible to rent a Hooiberghut (Hay store), a delightful traditional chalet, unique to this area, which can accommodate up to four people. On-site amenities include a café and well designed children's playgrounds, in addition to a large indoor playroom.

Facilities	Directions
Two modern, heated toilet blocks with controllable hot showers, open style washbasins and a baby room. Cafeteria. Covered playground. WiFi over part of site (charged). Activities and entertainment. Mobile homes and Hooiberghuts for rent. Off site: Zoo at Emmen. Theme park at Slagharen. Excellent cycle routes. Shops 1 km.	Take N33 from Assen to Gieten/Veendam. Then take the exit to Rolde. In Rolde follow signs to Balloo and site is on the right. GPS: 52.99081, 6.641711

Open: 1 April - 31 October.

Charges guide

Per unit incl. 2 persons and electricity	€ 18.20 - € 21.70
extra person	€ 3.80

Ruinen
Camping Ruinen

Oude Benderseweg 11, NL-7963 PX Ruinen (Drenthe) T: 0522 471 770. E: info@camping-ruinen.nl
alanrogers.com/NL6160

Camping Ruinen is a large, spacious site with 299 pitches in the woods of Drenthe. All 276 touring pitches have electricity (4/10A) and include 105 serviced pitches with water, drainage, cable TV and electricity connections. The numbered pitches are over 100 sq.m. in size and are on large, grassy fields. They are separated by hedges and in the shade of trees, and there are five hardstandings for motorcaravans. At this comfortable site you can relax by cycling or walking through the woods or over the moors, or join organised trips in groups on a regular basis.

Facilities	Directions
Four well spaced toilet blocks provide washbasins (open style and in cabins), child size toilets, bathrooms, child size baths and a baby room. Facilities for disabled visitors. Laundry. Motorcaravan services. Shop. Restaurant with children's menu. Pancake restaurant. Play areas between the pitches. Giant chess. Boules. Minigolf. Bicycle hire. Full entertainment programme in high season. WiFi. Dogs are allowed on certain pitches only. Off site: Riding 400 m. Fishing 3 km. Golf 18 km.	From Zwolle follow A28 north and take Ruinen exit. Follow site signs from there. GPS: 52.77492, 6.36993

Open: 1 April - 1 October.

Charges guide

Per unit incl. 2 persons and electricity	€ 22.25 - € 27.55
extra person	€ 3.35 - € 4.25
serviced pitch, plus	€ 6.30

No credit cards.
Camping Cheques accepted.

Schipborg
Camping De Vledders

Zeegserweg 2a, NL-9469 PL Schipborg (Drenthe) T: 0504 091 489. E: info@devledders.nl
alanrogers.com/NL6130

Camping De Vledders is set in the centre of one of the most beautiful nature reserves in Holland, between the Drentse Hondsrug and the Drentsche Aa river. This attractive site is landscaped with many varieties of trees and shrubs. There are 150 touring pitches (all with 6A electricity) on rectangular, grassy fields, separated by well kept hedges. The level pitches are around 100 sq.m. in size with some shade provided at the back from mature trees and hedges. Static units and seasonal pitches are on separate fields. In one corner of the site there is an attractive lake with sandy beaches.

Facilities	Directions
Two refurbished, heated sanitary blocks with some washbasins in cabins and controllable hot showers. Family shower rooms. Baby room. En-suite facilities for disabled visitors. Motorcaravan service point. Shop for basics. Snack bar. TV in reception. Lake with fishing, boating, windsurfing. Football field. Riding. Nordic walking. Playground. Some entertainment for children (high season). Bicycle hire. Torch useful. WiFi over site. Off site: Golf 10 km. Sub-tropical pool in Zuidlaren.	From the A28 take exit 35 and continue towards Zuidlaren. Just before Zuidlaren follow signs for Schipborg and then site signs. GPS: 53.079267, 6.665617

Open: April - October.

Charges guide

Per unit incl. 2 persons and electricity	€ 19.15 - € 22.95
extra person (over 1 yr)	€ 3.25
dog	€ 2.85

Vledder
Recreatiecentrum De Adelhof

Vledderweg 19, NL-8381 AB Vledder (Drenthe) T: 0521 381 440. E: info@adelhof.nl
alanrogers.com/NL6125

With a fine location close to the large nature reserves of the Drents-Friese Wold and Het Land van Oost, Recreatiecentrum De Adelhof is an ideal base for a cycling holiday in Drenthe, with miles of cycle tracks in the area. This is also a good site for anglers with a well stocked fishing lake. De Adelhof has 140 spacious touring pitches spread over several fields. The pitches are surrounded by bushes and shrubs to ensure privacy. They are generally around 100 sq.m. and all have electricity.

Facilities

Four toilet blocks (one open in winter, cleaning can be variable). Small shop (end April-end Aug). Café/restaurant and snack bar (April-Nov). Large fishing lake with carp. Children's farm. Play areas. All-weather tennis. Minigolf. Bicycle and go-kart hire. Football field. Internet access. WiFi in some areas (charged). Professional entertainment team (spring holidays and high season). Off site: Municipal outdoor swimming pool (end April-beginning Sept, charged). Miramar Museum. Dwingelerveld National Park.

Open: All year.

Directions

Vledder is 10 km. northeast of Steenwijk. From A38 motorway take the Steenwijk exit and follow N855 north to Frederiksoord and Vledder. The site is just before the village to the right. GPS: 52.85178, 6.19845

Charges guide

Per unit incl. 2 persons and electricity	€ 23.00
extra person	€ 3.50

Wateren
Camping d'Olde Lantschap

Schurerslaan 4, NL-8438 SC Wateren (Drenthe) T: 0521 387 244. E: info@oldelantschap.nl
alanrogers.com/NL6152

D'Olde Lantschap is ideal for those who enjoy peace and relaxation, although there are plenty of activities available too. There are facilities for several sports, minigolf and an open-air theatre. In good weather, swimming is possible in the three-hectare lake with its sandy beaches and an island. Alternatively, in poor weather there is an indoor, heated swimming pool. The 200 touring pitches are spacious, all with 6A electricity (some with 10A), TV connections and water (shared between two).

Facilities

Toilet block with WCs, showers (on payment) and washbasins in cabins. Baby room. Well stocked shop. Bar. Restaurant. Snack bar with takeaway. Heated indoor swimming pool with paddling pool. Play area, bouncy castle and a few climbing frames. Sports field. Horse and pony riding. Minigolf. Boules. Lake swimming. Fishing. Bicycle and tricycle hire. Mountain bike hire. Entertainment team in high season. Miniclub. Walking and cycling routes. WiFi (charged). Off site: Riding 1 km. Golf 4 km.

Open: 21 March - 31 October.

Directions

From Diever follow signs for Zorgvlied. The site is on the right immediately before Zorgvlied. GPS: 52.92227, 6.26731

Charges guide

Per unit incl. 2 persons and electricity	€ 17.50 - € 25.00
serviced pitch	€ 6.00
dog (max. 2)	€ 4.35

Wezuperbrug
Rekreatiepark 't Kuierpadtien

Oranjekanaal NZ 10, NL-7853 TA Wezuperbrug (Drenthe) T: 0591 381 415. E: info@kuierpad.nl
alanrogers.com/NL5790

Professionally run, this all year round site is suitable as a night stop, or for longer if you wish to participate in all the activities offered in July and August. The site itself is in a woodland setting on the edge of the village. The 525 flat and grassy pitches for touring units (with 653 in total) are of reasonable size. All have 4/6/10A electricity and 32 are fully serviced with electricity, TV aerial point, water and drainage. On-site activities include canoeing, windsurfing, water chutes and the dry ski slope, which is also open during the winter. A member of the Holland Tulip Parcs group.

Facilities

Eight quite acceptable sanitary blocks, including a new one, with hot showers (07.30-10.00 in July/Aug). Facilities for disabled visitors. Laundry. Motorcaravan services. Supermarket (1/4-15/90; bread all year). Restaurant and bar with TV. Takeaway. Indoor pool (all year). Outdoor heated pool (1/5-15/9). Sauna, solarium and whirlpool. Internet access. Dry ski slope. Play areas. Minigolf. Lake with beach. Boat rental. New High Rope Adventure Parc. WiFi. Off site: Fishing 500 m. Riding 1 km. Golf 1.5 km.

Open: All year.

Directions

From N34 Groningen-Emmen road exit near Emmen onto N31 towards Beilen. Turn right into Schoonord where left to Wezuperbrug. Site is at beginning of village on the right. GPS: 52.84005, 6.72593

Charges guide

Per unit incl. 2 persons and electricity	€ 20.00 - € 36.20
extra person	€ 6.00

No credit cards.
Camping Cheques accepted.

For latest campsite news, availability and prices visit
alanrogers.com

Zeewolde

Camping Het Polderbos

Groenewoudse Weg 98, NL-3896 LS Zeewolde (Flevoland) T: 036 523 6366. E: info@hetpolderbos.nl
alanrogers.com/NL6214

Het Polderbos is a pleasant rural site, located at the edge of a vast forest, the Horsterwold, in the province of Flevoland. There is a real sense of space and nature here. This immaculately kept site has 80 large, grassy touring pitches (well distributed over the site and up to 200 sq.m) most with 6-10A electricity. The forest is ideal for walking, cycling and riding, with many miles of marked tracks. Unusually, it's possible to bring your own horse to the site and then discover the Zeebodemtrail, a route of over 80 km. with facilities for horses along the way.

Facilities	Directions
One central, modern toilet block has preset hot showers, family rooms, baby room and facilities for disabled visitors. Play area. Giant chess. Bar with library, TV and children's games. Boules. Children's farm. Stabling for horses. Bicycle and go-kart hire. Tourist information. WiFi (charged). Off site: Golf (18 holes) 1.5 km. Zeewolde with all usual facilities, beaches and a marina 3 km. **Open:** 1 April - 20 October.	The site is located just west of Zeewolde. Leave the A28 Amersfoort-Zwolle motorway at exit 9 and follow the signs Zeewolde. The campsite is well signed. GPS: 52.340118, 5.505473

Charges guide

Per unit incl. 2 persons and electricity	€ 16.90 - € 20.90
extra person	€ 3.50

Zeewolde

Erkemederstrand Camping Horeca Jachthaven & Dagrecreatie

Erkemederweg 79, NL-3896 LB Zeewolde (Flevoland) T: 0365 228 421. E: info@erkemederstrand.nl
alanrogers.com/NL6200

Erkemederstrand (Erkemede beach) is a leisure park in Flevoland with direct access to the Nuldernauw where there is a sandy beach, a lake and a forest. It provides a campsite for families, a marina, an area for youngsters to camp, a camping area for groups and a recreation area for day visitors. The campsite itself is divided into two areas: one before the dyke at the waterfront and one behind the dyke. The pitches are spacious (around 125 sq.m) and all have electricity, water and drainage.

Facilities	Directions
Six neat, clean and heated toilet blocks (access by key; exclusively for campers). Washbasins in cabins, showers and family bathrooms (some charges for hot water). Laundry facilities. Shop for basic provisions, bar, restaurant and takeaway. Several play areas and children's farm. Watersports facilities and lake swimming. Fishing. Football pitch. Minigolf. Bicycle hire. Extended entertainment programme. WiFi (charged). Beach and shower for dogs. Off site: Golf and riding 11 km. **Open:** 29 March - 27 October.	From A28 (Utrecht-Zwolle) take exit 9 (Nijkerk, Almere) and follow N301 to Zeewolde. Cross bridge and turn right following signs to site. From Amsterdam/Almere, take exit 5 and follow N27 (becomes N305) to Zeewolde. Then take N301 to Nijkerk. From bridge turn right and follow signs to site. GPS: 52.27021, 5.48871

Charges guide

Per unit incl. 2 persons and electricity	€ 18.90 - € 33.50
extra person	€ 3.00

Zeewolde

RCN Camping Zeewolde

Dasselaarweg 1, NL-3896 LT Zeewolde (Flevoland) T: 0365 221 246. E: zeewolde@rcn.nl
alanrogers.com/NL6215

This site, a member of the RCN group, has been developed on reclaimed land in the Polderland in the province of Flevoland. There is direct lake access, and the site is split into inner and outer dykes. In the outer dyke area, there are grassy, sunny touring pitches (most with 10A electricity, water and drainage) close to the lake and its sandy beach, as well as Zeewolde's marina. The marina is a great centre for sailing, fishing and windsurfing. It also has a friendly beach bar. The inner dyke pitches are also grassy but are enclosed by hedges and have mature trees to provide more shade.

Facilities	Directions
Modern sanitary block at the beach pitches with facilities for disabled visitors and children. Launderette. Restaurant. Bar. Beach bar. Bakery and supermarket. Beach with swimming area for toddlers. Play areas. Open-air and covered pools (heated). Multisports field. Mountain bike track. Tennis. Bicycle hire. Go-kart hire. Jetty and beach for catamarans. 5-a-side football. Climbing wall. WiFi over site (charged). Accommodation to rent. Off site: Sailing boat hire (adjacent). Riding 5 km. **Open:** All year.	Take the Zeewolde exit from A28 and follow the road for 5 km. crossing a bridge. After crossing the bridge, at the roundabout take the N701 to Zeewolde. Follow this road for 6 km. The campsite will be on your right. GPS: 52.31167, 5.54356

Charges guide

Per unit incl. 2 persons and electricity	€ 18.50 - € 29.50
extra person	€ 3.90

FREE Alan Rogers Travel Card
Extra benefits and savings - see page 12

Friesland is a unique province where Frisian is spoken and written widely, alongside Dutch. The many lakes are a Mecca for tourists and not just lovers of watersports.

CAPITAL: LEEUWARDEN

Friesland has a strong agricultural history, with a vast network of canals, ditches and streams dividing the fields and pastures. These lead not only to magnificent Frisian lakes, picturesque villages and beautiful countryside vistas but also to the 11 Frisian cities with designated historical status. Typical of the Frisian landscape are its strong vertical elements – steeples, windmills, masts and sails; the vast tracts of land and enormous skies are among its main attractions, together with the forests of Gaasterland and the cliffs of the IJsselmeer. But do not forget the four islands in the Waddenzee that also belong to this province: Vlieland, Terschelling, Ameland and Schiermonnikoog, all accessible by ferry from the mainland.

The 11 Frisian cities are all worth a visit. The historic Hanseatic Bolsward, the pilgrimage town of Dokkum, the former university city of Franeker, the fishing town of Harlingen, the picturesque Hindeloopen, the canal city IJlst, the capital Leeuwarden, small Sloten, bustling lakeside Sneek, the old Stavoren and the picturesque town Workum. Moving from city to city you will take in the many cultural and historical sights while being captivated by some of the most beautiful corners of the Frisian countryside.

Places of interest

Leeuwarden: city with 575 national monuments, home to 'De Elfstedentocht' the traditional 200 km. skating tour – there is also an alternative route for cyclists.

Schiermonnikoog: island and national park, with only a few areas closed to the public. Feel the wind in your hair and savour the tang of the tidal flats.

Hindeloopen: city surrounded by water on three sides, with charming narrow streets, bridges, shops, canals and a popular marina.

Makkum: known worldwide for its pottery – the oldest in the Netherlands.

Moddergat: 50 small fishermen's cottages are a feature of this picturesque town.

Attractions

The Fries Museum, Leeuwarden: the largest regional museum in the Netherlands, combining art, culture and history under one roof.

Fries Scheepvaart Museum, Sneek: maritime museum tracing the history of Frisian shipping from the 17th to the 20th century.

Sneekweek: home to the country's largest watersport event, with the famous race of the 'skûtsjes', a week-long regatta with historic sailing ships representing the different towns of Friesland.

Bolsward: visit the distillery of Sonnema and sample the national drink 'Berenburg'.

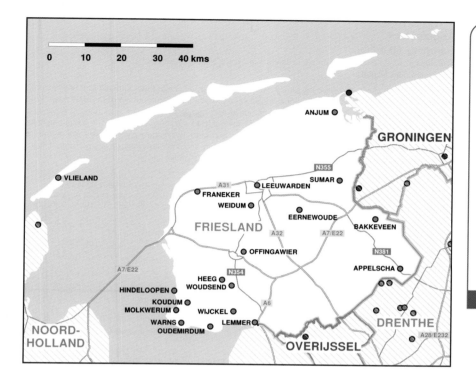

Anjum
Landal Esonstad

Oostmahorn 29B, NL-9133 DT Anjum (Friesland) T: 0519 329 555. E: esonstad@landal.nl

alanrogers.com/NL6051

Esonstad is a member of the Landal group and is attractively located on the Lauwersmeer, close to the Schiermonnikoog ferry. There is an impressive range of facilities, including an all-weather tennis court, indoor pool and indoor play barn. This open site is situated on the edge of the National Park, in a landscape of lakes, forests and dykes – ideal for wildlife and watersports enthusiasts. It extends over five hectares and comprises 129 spacious pitches (100 sq.m), including a number occupied by mobile homes. Many pitches are close to the water and have 16A electricity and a private water supply. There are some tent pitches on a separate field and a few hardstandings.

Facilities

The modern, clean toilet block has vanity type basins, preset hot showers, a baby room and facilities for disabled visitors. Swimming pool with separate paddling pool. Whirlpool. Solarium. Sauna and Turkish bath. Indoor play barn. Games room. Tennis. Golf. Mobile homes for rent. Tourist information. Site ferry to Schiermonnikoog. Off site: Old windmill at Anjum. Nature museum at Dokkum.

Open: 30 March - 5 November.

Directions

Follow A28 motorway to Meppel and then A32 towards Heerenveen and Drachten (A7). On A7 take the exit to Buitenpost (N358). In Buitenpost follow signs to Lauwersoog as far as Anjum. In Anjum turn right to Oostmahorn and follow signs to Landal Esonstad. GPS: 53.37909, 6.162332

Charges guide

Per unit incl. 2 persons and electricity	€ 18.00 - € 34.00
extra person	€ 4.75
dog	€ 4.75

Appelscha

Camping Alkenhaer

Alkenhaer 1, NL-8426 EP Appelscha (Friesland) T: 0516 432 600. E: info@campingalkenhaer.nl

alanrogers.com/NL6085

Alkenhaer is a pleasant and peaceful family campsite near Appelscha in the southeast part of Friesland, and close to the province of Drenthe. Located between the beautiful natural parks of Drents-Friese Wold and Fochteloërveen, the focus is very much on space and nature. The 65 touring pitches at Alkenhaer are dispersed over spacious marked fields and are all equipped with 10A electricity. The fields only take a few units, making camping here cosy. Shade is provided by mature trees. There are separate hardstanding areas for mobile homes and large caravans. On-site amenities include a large football field, a volleyball court, a well equipped playground and a children's pool.

Facilities

Two modern toilet blocks have open style washbasins and preset hot showers. Children's facilities and a baby room. Bar, restaurant and snack bar (1/4-30/9). Children's pool. Play equipment. Football. Volleyball. Off site: Open-air swimming pool. National parks. Hiking, mountain biking and riding. Appelscha.

Open: 1 April - 31 October.

Directions

From A28 take exit 31 and follow N381 towards Drachten/Appelscha. Take the exit for Appelscha, then follow signs to site. GPS: 52.94579, 6.362007

Charges guide

Per unit incl. 2 persons and electricity	€ 17.50 - € 20.50
extra person	€ 2.50
dog (max 1)	€ 3.00

Bakkeveen

Camping de Ikeleane

Duerswâldmer Wei 19, NL-9243 KA Bakkeveen (Friesland) T: 0516 541283. E: info@ikeleane.nl

alanrogers.com/NL6021

Camping de Ikeleane (Frisian for Oak Lane) has a rural setting, 14 km. southeast of the pleasant town of Drachten. This is a much loved part of Friesland, where forests alternate with dunes and heathland. De Ikeleane is a good base for exploring this Frisian countryside on foot or bicycle (bicycle and go-kart hire on site) and has wonderful views over the countryside. This is a well equipped site with 78 touring pitches, all with 10A electricity, and 63 with water and drainage. Children will enjoy the football and volleyball pitches and the indoor play barn. The entertainment team organises a variety of activities, including ballooning, cycling and volleyball matches. Campers have free access to the public swimming pool at Bakkeveen.

Facilities

Three toilet blocks with open style basins, controllable hot showers (card operated), family showers, baby room and facilities for disabled visitors. Bar, restaurant (small meals) and snack bar. Washing machine. Motorcaravan service point. Play barn. Football. Volleyball. Bicycle and go-kart hire. Entertainment and activities. WiFi. New luxury chalets and caravans for rent. Off site: Swimming pool, restaurants, shops and minigolf in Bakkeveen 1.5 km. Riding 2 km. Fishing 3 km. Golf 15 km. Nearby towns of Drachten and Assen.

Open: 1 April - 31 October.

Directions

From A7 Heerenveen-Groningen motorway, take exit 30 and follow N381 towards Oosterwolde. After 500 m. turn left to Ureterp and follow this road (N917) to Bakkeveen. In the village bear right to Wijnjewoude. Campsite is 1 km. to the left. GPS: 53.071158, 6.242742

Charges guide

Per unit incl. 2 persons and electricity	€ 17.50 - € 24.00
extra person	€ 3.00
dog (max. 1)	€ 2.50

For latest campsite news, availability and prices visit

alanrogers.com

Bakkeveen

Recreatiecentrum De Waldsang

Foarwurkerwei 2, NL-9243 JZ Bakkeveen (Friesland) T: 0516 541 255. E info@waldsang.nl

alanrogers.com/NL6035

Camping on the Waldsang is camping in the green heart of Friesland. Close to the site are numerous woodlands, dunes and moors, which makes it an ideal base for long walks and cycling tours. De Waldsang has 115 touring pitches (up to 120 sq.m) on separate fields from the static units. Pitching is on rectangular, level, grassy fields off gravel access lanes, partially shaded by mature trees. Most pitches have 16A electricity, and some 30 also have water and waste water. A canal runs alongside the site and some road noise can be heard.

Facilities	Directions
Two modern toilet blocks with toilets, washbasins and preset, hot showers (6 minutes free). Laundry. Motorcaravan services. Shop, bar/restaurant with snack bar and open-air terrace (all daily in season). TV and video room. Fishing. Entertainment team in high season. Canoe hire. Bicycle hire. Playground. WiFi throughout (charged). Off site: Open-air public pool in Bakkeveen.	On A28 in either direction, take exit Beilen-Noord and continue on N31 towards Drachten. Take the exit Wijnjewoude/Bakkeveen after 35 km. and then follow the site signs. GPS: 53.085483, 6.250033

Charges guide

Per unit incl. 2 persons and electricity	€ 18.50 - € 22.50

Open: 1 April - 1 October.

Bakkeveen

Molecaten Park 't Hout

Duurswouderweg 11, NL-9243 KA Bakkeveen (Friesland) T: 0516 541 287. E: info@thout.nl

alanrogers.com/NL6020

Camping 't Hout is a holiday paradise for children with its covered playground, indoor play paradise, open-air fun pool with paddling pool and animal farm. The site is in the woods, just outside the interesting village of Bakkeveen. It has 250 touring pitches on seven well cared for grassy fields, all with cable. Of these, 130 have 10A electricity, water, waste water and a numbered parking place. Other pitches have 4A electricity. The central building next to the pool also houses a bakery selling croissants, pizza and bread rolls, a shop and there is an open-air terrace for drinks.

Facilities	Directions
Four modern, heated toilet blocks have washbasins in cabins, and free, preset hot showers (6 min. hot water). Toilets, showers and basins for children. Family shower rooms. Baby room. Laundry. Shop for basics. Central building with snack bar, bread shop and terrace. Open-air fun pool (10x5 m) with water slide and paddling pool (heated July/Aug). Air cushions. Volleyball. Basketball. Skelter hire. Covered playground. Indoor play palace. Canoe hire. Children's theatre. Internet. WiFi (charged).	On A28 in either direction, take exit Beilen-Noord and continue on N31 towards Drachten. Take the exit Wijnjewoude/Bakkeveen after 35 km. and then follow the site signs. GPS: 53.078665, 6.252913

Charges guide

Per unit incl. 2 persons and electricity	€ 16.50 - € 27.50
extra person	€ 4.00
dog	€ 4.50

Open: 1 April - 30 September.

Eernewoude

Camping It Wiid

Koaidijk 10, NL-9264 TP Eernewoude (Friesland) T: 0511 539 223. E: info@wiid.nl

alanrogers.com/NL6055

Camping It Wiid is surrounded by water and has easy access to the famous Frisian lakes. On site, it is possible to rent sailing boats and motorboats or you can moor your own. The site has 300 touring pitches, all with 4–16A electricity. Of these, 90 have water, waste water and cable as well. Pitching is on level, grassy fields with shade from mature trees and hedges. To the far edge of the site is a spit of land where you can camp surrounded by water, and from where there are great views over the Fokkesloot water. Cars are parked away from pitches.

Facilities	Directions
Two new, heated toilet blocks with basins and preset, hot showers. Baby room. Facilities for children and disabled visitors. Laundry. Motorcaravan services. Well stocked shop. Bar/restaurant and takeaway. Open-air pool with 65 m. water slide and fun paddling pool. Boat rental. Sailing school. Football. Volleyball. Basketball. Fishing. Bicycle hire. Tennis. Playground. Entertainment programme in high season. WiFi (charged). Off site: Fishing 100 m. Bicycle hire 2 km.	From channel ports you can either go north from Amsterdam via A7/E22 through Leeuwarden towards Drachten, or east from Amsterdam via A6, onto A7 at sign for Leeuwarden/Groningen, then N31 at sign for De Haven/Drachten. On N31 take Earnewald exit and follow site signs. GPS: 53.1268, 5.946183

Charges guide

Per unit incl. 2 persons and electricity	€ 26.75 - € 28.25
extra person	€ 6.00

Open: 1 April - 1 October.

Franeker

Recreatiepark Bloemketerp

Bug. J. Dijkstraweg 3, NL-8800 AA Franeker (Friesland) T: 0517 395 099. E: info@bloemketerp.nl

alanrogers.com/NL6075

Camping Bloemketerp can be found within walking distance of the interesting and historic town of Franeker. There are 120 sheltered and good sized pitches here. These are dispersed around several camping fields. The park also has a range of holiday homes for rent. There is a well equipped sports centre adjacent, with sub-tropical indoor swimming pool, canoe rental and bicycle hire. Campers are allowed free access to this centre (fitness, tennis, squash, racquetball, sauna and massage). The park boasts an attractive, friendly restaurant (with sun terrace) offering both a set menu and buffet options.

Facilities	Directions
One large toilet block with controllable, hot showers (€ 0.50), open style washbasins and facilities for disabled visitors. Laundry. Motorcaravan services. Restaurant (with buffet option). Takeaway meals. Sports centre full facilities. Play area. Ten-pin bowling. Recreation team (high season). Canoe hire. WiFi over site (charged). Accommodation for rent. Off site: Adjacent sub-tropical swimming pool. Canoeing. Riding. Sneek. Planetarium. **Open:** All year.	Franeker is located near the A31 between the head of the Afsluitdijk and the capital of Friesland, Leeuwarden. Take exit 20 towards Franeker and then follow signs to Bloemketerp. GPS: 53.189683, 5.553333

Charges guide	
Per unit incl. 2 persons and electricity	€ 20.50 - € 23.45
extra person	€ 3.50

Heeg

Watersport Camping Heeg

De Burd 25A, NL-8621 JX Heeg (Friesland) T: 0515 442 328. E: wch@watersportcampingheeg.nl

alanrogers.com/NL6026

Watersport Camping Heeg is a welcoming and comfortable site, ten minutes walk from the centre of Heeg, an old fishing town that is now mainly a focus for watersports. Heeg is a bustling resort with many opportunities for dining and shopping. The campsite is on the lake and has a small sandy beach and a jetty for 90 boats with a trailer ramp. There are 200 attractive, level pitches on grass (with 4A electricity) off gravel access roads. With 120 numbered pitches for touring (100 sq.m.) and three hardstandings there are lovely views over the lake from the front rows.

Facilities	Directions
Two toilet blocks, one at the front, a second, newer one towards the back, with toilets, washbasins (open style and in cabins) and controllable, hot showers (€ 0.50). Baby room. Laundry with washing machines and dryers. Kiosk for basics. Playground. Dutch tub for hire. Small sandy beach. Lake for swimming and sailing. Canoe and sailing boat rental. Fishing. Off site: Riding 500 m. Golf 25 km. **Open:** 1 April - 1 October.	From the A6, take exit 17 (Lemmer) and continue west on the N359. At Balk, turn north on N928 towards Woudsend and turn north again on N354. Exit for Heeg and follow site signs. GPS: 52.967369, 5.594594

Charges guide	
Per unit incl. 2 persons and electricity	€ 22.70
extra person	€ 5.40
child (under 12 yrs)	€ 2.85
dog	€ 3.45

Hindeloopen

Camping Hindeloopen

Westerdijk 9, NL-8713 JA Hindeloopen (Friesland) T: 0514 521 452. E: info@campinghindeloopen.nl

alanrogers.com/NL6050

Hindeloopen is one of the 11 historic cities of Friesland and this site is nearby. The delightful city retains plenty of old maritime charm. Situated directly behind the embankment of the IJsselmeer, the site has 138 touring pitches (out of a total of 640), all of which have 6/16A electricity (Europlug), water and a drain. There are 15 hardstandings for motorcaravans and large caravans. The pitches are 90-100 sq.m. in size and are arranged in groups that are separated from each other by high hedges. The lake here is not deep and from its banks there are wonderful views of the town and the surrounding countryside.

Facilities	Directions
Two toilet blocks include showers and washbasins in cabins. Facilities for children. Baby room. Facilities for disabled visitors. Laundry. Motorcaravan service point. Shop (daily in July/Aug). Café/restaurant and snack bar (daily in July/Aug). Play area with bike course. Football pitch. Tennis. Bicycle hire. Fishing. Surfing school. Boat launching and boat rental. Activities for children (high season). WiFi (free). No dogs. Off site: Riding 5 km. **Open:** 31 March - 1 November.	From Lemmer follow the N359 northwest to Hindeloopen and from there, campsite signs. GPS: 52.93492, 5.40430

Charges guide	
Per unit incl. 2 persons, water, waste water and electricity	€ 18.50 - € 23.50
hiker pitch incl. 2 persons	€ 10.00
extra person	€ 3.00

For latest campsite news, availability and prices visit

alanrogers.com

Weidum

Camping WeidumerHout

Dekemawei 9, NL-9024 BE Weidum (Friesland) T: 0582 519 888. E: welkom@weidumerhout.nl

alanrogers.com/NL5715

Camping WeidumerHout is a member of the Kleine Groene Campings group, literally 'small green campsites'. It has a beautiful rural location, close to the historic village of Weidum. There are 48 well spaced pitches (150 sq.m) with 10A electricity and two with hardstanding. The owner makes sure that all visitors can enjoy the great views over either the countryside or the river that runs past the site. The site has been developed on a farm that dates back to 1867 and has a tranquil, historic atmosphere. The site's fully equipped sauna (on payment) will add to your relaxation – owner Eddy de Boer will describe the benefits of a good sauna. The campsite is combined with a comfortable hotel and welcoming, stylish restaurant. Try one of the daily, high quality meals created with local produce, maybe washed down with a glass of Us Heit Frisian beer. The site has its own water purifying system and tries to operate in an environmentally friendly way. The River Zwette running past the site is part of the famous 11 city skating tour and you are more than welcome to bring a boat.

Facilities

Heated sanitary block with toilets, showers and washbasins. Baby room. Washing machine and dryer. Bar and restaurant. Sauna. Solarium. Library. Bicycle hire. Beach access plus fishing and boat launching. Canoe hire. WiFi (free). Fitness equipment. Torch useful.
Off site: Shop and bus stop 800 m. Riding 5 km. Sailing 8 km. Golf 12 km.

Open: All year, excl. Christmas - 1 January.

Directions

From Leeuwarden head south on the A32 and follow signs for Weidum. Just before entering the village, the site is on the right. GPS: 53.14906, 5.76166

Charges guide

Per unit incl. 2 persons and electricity	€ 21.25
extra person (over 2 yrs)	€ 5.75
dog	€ 2.00

Dekemawei 9 - 9024 BE Weidum - tel +31 (0)58-2519888 - fax +31 (0)58-2519826

WeidumerHout

WeidumerHout, hard to find, easy to love!

WeidumerHout, a country estate with spacious pitches, beautiful hotel rooms and an excellent restaurant, in the middle of the splendid environment of Friesland.

welkom@weidumerhout.nl - www.weidumerhout.nl

Wijckel

Camping 't Hop

Meerenstein 1, NL-8563 AV Wijckel (Friesland) T: 0514 602 436. E: info@campingthop.nl

alanrogers.com/NL6044

Camping 't Hop, in addition to 60 seasonal pitches and 35 permanent pitches, provides 60 touring pitches, all with 4A electricity and of about 100 sq.m. There are a few hardstandings. The site is adjacent to the Menno van Coehoorn forest and only a few yards from Sloter lake with an open connection to it for boats. The site is divided into 11 areas, each with around ten pitches. The seasonal pitches are in a separate area. The focal point of the site is an adventure play area, together with the pride of the site, a café which offers a varied menu and is definitely recommended.

Facilities

The single toilet block near reception provides toilets, open style washbasins (cold water only) and controllable hot showers (€ 0.50). Baby room. Facilities for disabled visitors. Motorcaravan services. Laundry with washing machines and dryers. Café/bar for small meals. Tennis. Bicycle and canoe hire. Playground. Entertainment programme for youngsters in season. Off site: Boat launching, fishing, beach and sailing 500 m. Riding 3 km.

Open: 1 April - 30 September.

Directions

On the A6 from Joure travelling south towards Almere, take exit 17 (Lemmer, Balk) and follow the N359 to Balk. Following site signs, turn right then left after 1 km. GPS: 52.89361, 5.6224

Charges guide

Per person	€ 4.75
child (2-10 yrs)	€ 4.00
pitch	€ 3.50 - € 5.50

Woudsend

Recreatiecentrum De Rakken

Lynbaen 10, NL-8551 NW Woudsend (Friesland) T: 0514 591525. E: info@derakken.nl

alanrogers.com/NL6027

Located between the three largest Frisian lakes, Slotermeer, Heegermeer and Sneekermeer, De Rakken is a great choice for both nature and watersports enthusiasts. Just two minutes on foot from the site, Woudsend is a good watersports resort with a wealth of catering facilities and places of interest (including mills and churches). The site offers boat moorings as well as bicycle, electric boat and car hire. The 50 touring pitches are of a reasonable size and all have 6A electricity, with 15 on hardstanding. Accommodation for rent on site includes hikers' cabins and attractive chalets. De Rakken is open all year. Around Woudsend there is an abundance of unspoiled nature, woodland, meadows and polders.

Facilities

Four heated toilet blocks include preset hot showers, open style washbasins, a baby room and facilities for disabled visitors. Play area with volleyball. Petting zoo. Tennis. Fishing. Marina. Boat launching. Electric boats for rent. Hiker cabins and chalets for rent. Off site: The charming old town of Woudsend with good shops and restaurants. The Frisian lakes. Watersports.

Open: 15 March - 15 October.

Directions

Take A6 northbound (Heerenveen) and a few kilometres past Lemmer take the exit to Woudsend (N354). At the roundabout before Woudsend, go left (N928, Balk) then turn right at next roundabout. Follow signs to the site. GPS: 52.94651, 5.62768

Charges guide

Per unit incl. 2 persons and electricity	€ 17.15 - € 27.85
dog	€ 1.00

Want independent campsite reviews at your fingertips?

alan rogers

An exciting **FREE** app for both iPhone and Android

www.alanrogers.com/apps

For latest campsite news, availability and prices visit

alanrogers.com

Once the scene of heavy fighting during WWII, Gelderland is now a province with much to offer the tourist in Achterhoek, Veluwe, Rivierenland, Arnhem and Nijmegen.

CAPITAL: ARNHEM

The Achterhoek is a region of forests, estates, castles, streams and picturesque villages, a perfect destination for the cyclist and the hiker. De Hoge Veluwe National Park is one of the Netherlands' oldest and largest national parks with no less than 5,500 hectares of woodland, heathland, lakes and drift sands. Together with the Kröller-Müller Museum and the sculpture garden, it is a unique alliance of nature, art and architecture. Rivierenland (Riverland) is a rural area that has developed around the traditional activities of farming and handicrafts. Many of the old mills, castles, fortifications and art galleries are well worth a visit.

The cities of Arnhem and Nijmegen have evolved from a fascinating and occasionally turbulent history. While they are located only 20 km. from each other, their attractions, shops, landscapes, culture and gastronomy couldn't be more different. Not surprisingly, there is great rivalry too, as you can see when their football clubs meet! Arnhem is a very green city with several parks and the estate of the Rosendaal Castle (former residence of the dukes of Gelre), while Nijmegen is an ancient city where you can still glimpse remains dating from the Roman period to the Middle Ages.

Places of interest

Hanseatic cities: along a sparkling river, the IJssel, lie the beautiful medieval gems of Hasselt, Kampen, Zwolle, Hattem, Deventer, Zutphen and Doesburg.

Museum Castle Wijchen: an extensive archaeological collection is housed in Wijchen's picturesque castle.

Rural Cuijk: attractions include horse driving, vineyards, tea garden and even a home theatre in a hayloft; sample the delicious local produce at the farm shops.

Zutphen: a comprehensive selection of shops, markets, restaurants, pubs, museums and galleries.

Attractions

Koningin Julianatoren: family fun park in Apeldoorn.

Tivoli Amusement Park: a small park for younger children with magic shows, circus workshops and minigolf.

Dolfinarium Harderwijk: Europe's largest marine park with performing dolphins, sea lions and seals, enjoyed by 1 million visitors annually.

Kasteel Doorwerth: a 13th-century fairytale castle and museum, with its own moat and resident ghost.

The Liberation Route: follow the path of allied forces through the Arnhem/Nijmegen region in 1944 and 1945.

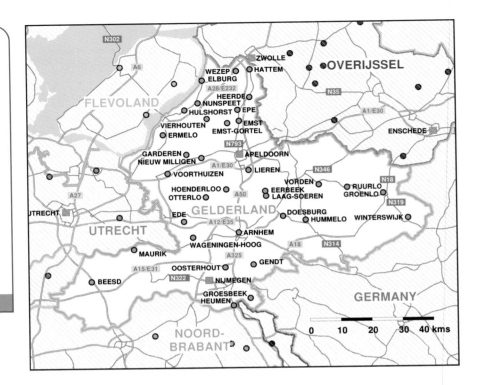

Beesd

Camping Betuwestrand

A Kraalweg 40, NL-4153 XC Beesd (Gelderland) T: 0345 681 503. E: info@betuwestrand.nl

alanrogers.com/NL5860

A pleasant site for a night stop or a longer stay, conveniently situated just off the A2/E25 motorway (Utrecht - 's Hertogenbosch, exit 14). It is a large site with 200 places for tourers on well cared for, grassy lawns (all with 6/10A electricity and drainage), in addition to its 450 well established permanent units. The touring pitches are in four distinct areas with many situated around the edges of an attractive lake with a large sandy beach and pleasant views. For families with young children there are various areas away from the water with play areas, as well as many facilities for older children. An area of the lake is cordoned off for swimming with a slide and diving boards and it is also suitable for windsurfing; mechanised water skiing is a new concept. The lake is also used by the public. Gelderland is the part of the Netherlands famous for fruit growing, situated between the rivers Maas and Waal and worthy perhaps of further consideration by British visitors.

Facilities

The toilet blocks are of a good standard and include family rooms and facilities for disabled visitors. Hot water is on payment in both showers and washbasins (in individual cabins). Laundry facilities. Motorcaravan service point. Shop. Restaurant. Bar/TV room. Room for young people. Play area. Lake fishing. Tennis. WiFi over site (charged). Dogs are permitted on a small field for tourers only. Off site: Bicycle hire 500 m. Golf 3 km.

Open: 28 March - 30 September.

Directions

Site is 25 km. SSE of Utrecht, clearly signed from both directions on the E25 road between Utrecht and 's Hertogenbosch. Take the exit 14 (Beesd) and site is 200 m. GPS: 51.898623, 5.184541

Charges guide

Per unit incl. up to 2 persons, electricity	€ 25.00 - € 32.50
extra person	€ 4.80

Less 20% in low season. No credit cards.

For latest campsite news, availability and prices visit

alanrogers.com

Arnhem

Oostappen Vakantiepark Arnhem

Kemperbergerweg 771, NL-6816 RW Arnhem (Gelderland) T: 0264 431 600. E: arnhem@holiday.nl
alanrogers.com/NL6310

Vakantiepark Arnhem is a wooded site in the Veluwe region of the Netherlands, close to the Hoge Veluwe National Park. The 750 pitches are partly in the sun and partly in the shade of tall trees and there are 500 for touring units, some with hardstanding. This is a perfect base for visiting the national park, the Kröller-Müller museum or the outdoor museum. You could also go riding or play golf nearby or experience the silence high up in the air in a glider from Terlet airport. There is also plenty to do on the site including tennis and minigolf. Expect some road noise from the motorway to the east of the site.

Facilities

Modern sanitary blocks (may be under pressure in high season) provide free hot showers, facilities for disabled visitors and a baby room. Launderettes. Motorcaravan services. Supermarket. Restaurant. Takeaway. Bar. Tennis. Minigolf. Sports field. Boules. Open-air theatre. Playgrounds. Adventure pond. Swimming pool and paddling pool. Entertainment programme in high season. Bicycle hire. Off site: Arnhem for shopping. Burgers Zoo. Kröller-Müller museum. Airborne museum. Riding and golf.

Open: 1 April - 26 October.

Directions

From the A50 take exit 21 for Schaarsbergen. Go to Schaarsbergen and follow the Recreatiepark Arnhem signs. GPS: 52.02428, 5.85874

Charges guide

Per unit incl. 2 persons
and electricity   € 15.00 - € 29.00

Doesburg

Camping IJsselstrand

Eekstraat 18, NL-6984 AG Doesburg (Gelderland) T: 0313 472 797. E: info@ijsselstrand.nl
alanrogers.com/NL6332

This campsite calls itself a recreation village on the river, and the name suits it perfectly. It has 700 pitches in total, with a mix of permanent and touring pitches. The 200 touring pitches are set on sunny, grassy fields and around the marina and beach area. There are about 30 hardstandings for motorcaravans. Central to the campsite is a new, covered water complex, including a pool, a jacuzzi and slide. This can be opened in summer. The extensive facilities include a marina, a sandy beach by the river, a riding school and a large, covered sports field.

Facilities

Modern sanitary facilities are plentiful. Supermarket. Covered swimming pool. Indoor and outdoor play areas. Riding. Sandy beach. Marina and floating restaurant. Pedaloes and canoes for hire. Professional entertainment team. Free WiFi over site. Chalets, lodges and tents for hire. Off site: Ancient, fortified town of Doesburg. Walking and cycling in the Achterhoek Châteaux countryside. The Veluwe forest is 30 mins. away by car.

Open: All year.

Directions

From A12 take exit 27 onto the A348 (Zutphen), then right onto N317 for 4 km. to Doesberg. Take third exit from the roundabout (Zomerweg) for 1.2 km. then the third exit again (Eekstraat) and site is 1 km. on the left. GPS: 52.02848, 6.16292

Charges guide

Per unit incl. 2 persons
and electricity   € 19.25 - € 31.75
extra person   € 4.00

Ede

Recreatiepark 't Gelloo

Barteweg 15, NL-6718 TH Ede (Gelderland) T: 0318 618 282. E: info@gelloo.nl
alanrogers.com/NL6340

Recreatiepark 't Gelloo is an attractive family park that is popular with nature lovers, young families and those looking for peace and quiet. This is a comfortable site where quality is a priority. There are 420 pitches, 150 for tourers (all with 6A electricity), and 55 of these have water and drainage. The recreational facilities are also very good and include an indoor swimming pool. The site is close to the town of Ede and in the area there are theme parks such as Pretpark Julianatoren and, as this is right in the centre of the Hoge Veluwe region, plenty of nature reserves. Member of the Topparken Group.

Facilities

One centrally located toilet block with good, clean facilities. Baby rooms in ladies' section. Two en-suite facilities for disabled visitors. Motorcaravan services. Shop. Restaurant (high season and weekends). Takeaway. Heated indoor swimming pool. Bicycle hire. Indoor and outdoor play areas. Tennis. Games room. Entertainment for children in high season. Free WiFi over site. Chalets to rent. Off site: Ede 4 km. Fishing and riding 5 km.

Open: 21 March - 25 October.

Directions

From the A30 take exit 3 (de Stroet, Lunteren) towards Lunteren, then signs towards Ede. Site is signed. GPS: 52.07451, 5.66816

Charges guide

Per unit incl. up to 4 persons
and electricity   € 17.00 - € 31.00
extra person   € 6.00
dog (max. 2)   € 5.00

FREE Alan Rogers Travel Card
Extra benefits and savings - see page 12

Eerbeek

Landal Coldenhove

Boshoffweg 6, NL-6961 LD Eerbeek (Gelderland) T: 0313 659 101. E: coldenhove@landal.nl

alanrogers.com/NL5827

Coldenhove is a member of the Landal group and is an attractive campsite within the acclaimed natural region of the Veluwe, some 20 km. from Arnhem. This is a well equipped site with a good range of on-site amenities. There are 180 marked and shady pitches of 100 sq.m, located in the woods, half a kilometre from the main activity centre, and providing a quiet, relaxing atmosphere. Leisure facilities are grouped together near the site entrance and include an indoor swimming complex, an indoor playground, minigolf and a mini-scooter track.

Facilities

Modern toilet blocks. Restaurant. Bar. Takeaway. Swimming complex. Beauty salon. Minigolf. Children's playgrounds. Boules. Basketball court. Activity and entertainment programme. WiFi over site (charged). Accommodation for rent. Dogs are not accepted. Off site: Open-air swimming pool at Apenheul. The sumptuous Paleis Het Loo. Apeldoorn and Arnhem.

Open: 18 March - 7 November.

Directions

Approaching on A50 motorway, between Arnhem and Apeldoorn, take the Loenen/Eerbeek exit. At the first roundabout follow directions to Dieren, and then signs to Coldenhove. GPS: 52.091692, 6.034281

Charges guide

Per unit incl. 2 persons and electricity	€ 26.00 - € 37.00
extra person	€ 4.75

Elburg

Recreatieoord Veluwe Strandbad

Flevoweg 5, NL-8081 PA Elburg (Gelderland) T: 0525 681 480. E: info@monda.nl

alanrogers.com/NL6325

Recreatieoord Veluwe Strandbad is beside the Veluwe lake and it makes an ideal base for an active holiday on the water, either here or on the larger IJsselmeer lake. The site has a few touring fields set amongst a large number of static units and from some there are views over the lake. The 110 touring pitches are all level and on grass, with tarmac access roads. Most have 6A electricity, water, waste water and cable connections. Central on the site is a welcoming bar/restaurant with a terrace from where there are views to the lake. An indoor pool (10x10 m) with a paddling pool is also here.

Facilities

Two good, modern toilet blocks (heated) with washbasins (open style and in cabins), baby room and facilities for disabled visitors. Laundry facilities. Motorcaravan service point. Beach shop. Indoor pool. Bar/restaurant with terrace. Games room. Tennis. Boat launching. Fishing. Children's activities. Bicycle hire. Skateboard park. Basketball. Boules. Playground. WiFi over site (charged). No dogs. Payment card required for toilet blocks, pool and laundry facilities. Off site: Riding 2 km.

Open: All year.

Directions

Via the N309 or N306 enter Elburg from the northwest and site is on the right. GPS: 52.455576, 5.821251

Charges guide

Per unit incl. 2 persons and electricity	€ 14.00 - € 23.50
extra person	€ 4.00 - € 5.00
No credit cards.	

Emst

Camping De Veluwse Wagen

Oranjeweg 67, NL-8166 JA Emst (Gelderland) T: 0578 661 628. E: info@veluwse-wagen.nl

alanrogers.com/NL6305

De Veluwse Wagen is attractively landscaped with different sorts of trees and bushes. This small, car-free site is behind a pancake restaurant of the same name. It has immaculately kept pitches on four level, grassy fields, taking 25 touring units in total. Electricity is available to all and the numbered pitches are level and with some hardstanding. With access from gravel roads, the camping areas are separated by mature trees on two fields which give shade to some pitches. The remainder of the site is occupied by privately-owned mobile homes. De Veluwse Wagen is in beautiful natural surroundings, near the Royal woodland and hunting grounds, the Vierhouterbos and the Gortel moors.

Facilities

The single toilet block is behind the restaurant with toilets, open style washbasins and controllable, hot showers (4 minutes free hot water). Washing machines and dryers. Bar/restaurant with small terrace. Playing field. Riding. Bicycle hire. Boules. Animal farm. Some play equipment. WiFi over site (charged). No cars allowed on site. Off site: Kievitsveld lake with sandy beach 2 km.

Open: 1 April - 1 November.

Directions

From A50, take exit 27 (Epe) and continue towards Emst. Site is signed from the roundabout in Emst, on the road towards Gortel. GPS: 52.322486, 5.958097

Charges guide

Per unit incl. 2 persons and electricity	€ 18.25 - € 20.25
extra person	€ 3.75
child (2-12 yrs)	€ 3.25

Heumen

Rekreatiecentrum Heumens Bos

Vosseneindseweg 46, NL-6582 BR Heumen (Gelderland) T: 0243 581 481. E: info@heumensbos.nl

alanrogers.com/NL5950

Heumans Bos covers 17 hectares of woodland and grassed fields providing 165 level touring pitches arranged in groups of ten or twelve. All pitches have electricity (6A) and cable connections, and cars are parked away from the units allowing plenty of recreational space. The site is situated beside miles of beautiful woods, criss-crossed by cycle paths, in a tranquil, rural setting. Heumans Bos is open over a long season for touring families and all year for bungalows. One small section for motorcaravans has some hardstandings.

Facilities

The main, good quality sanitary building, plus another new block, are modern and heated, providing showers on payment. Rooms for families and disabled visitors. Smart launderette. Motorcaravan services. Gas supplies. Shop. Bar, restaurant and snack bar. Heated outdoor swimming pool (1/5-30/9). Bicycle hire. Tennis. Boules. Glade area with play equipment on sand and grass. Activity and excursions (high season). Large wet weather room. WiFi over site (charged). Off site: Riding 300 m. Fishing 2 km.

Open: All year.

Directions

From A73 (Nijmegen-Venlo) take exit 3 (4 km. south of Nijmegen) and follow site signs.
GPS: 51.76915, 5.82050

Charges guide

Per unit incl. 2 persons	
and electricity	€ 18.00 - € 30.00
extra person (over 3 yrs)	€ 4.00
dog (max. 1)	€ 4.00

Hoenderloo

Veluwecamping De Pampel

Woeste Hoefweg 35, NL-7351 TN Hoenderloo (Gelderland) T: 0553 781 760. E: info@hetschinkel.nl

alanrogers.com/NL5840

Camping De Pampel has the most congenial atmosphere and caters both for families (great facilities for children) and for those seeking peace and quiet. This is enhanced by its situation deep in the forest, with nine hectares of its own woods to explore. There are 280 pitches (20 seasonal) with 6-16A electricity. You can choose to site yourself around the edge of a large, open field with volleyball in the middle, or pick one of the individual places which are numbered, divided by trees and generally quite spacious.

Facilities

Toilet facilities are excellent, and the new Sani Plaza has to be seen. Laundry. Shop (1/4-1/10). Restaurant. Snack bar (July/Aug, otherwise weekends only). Swimming pool and new fun paddling pool with water canon (heated by solar panels; open 1/4-31/10). Play area. Pets corner. Sports area. Indoor play area. Barbecues by permission only, no open fires. Dogs are not accepted. WiFi throughout (charged). Off site: Riding 1 km. Golf 10 km.

Open: All year.

Directions

From the A50 Arnhem-Apeldoorn road exit for Hoenderloo and follow signs.
GPS: 52.11885, 5.90569

Charges guide

Per unit incl. 2 persons	
and electricity	€ 20.00 - € 37.00
extra person	€ 4.25 - € 5.25
child (1-11 yrs)	€ 3.25 - € 4.25

Hulshorst

Droompark Bad Hoophuizen

Varelseweg 211, NL-8077 RB Hulshorst (Gelderland) T: 0341 451 353. E: m.budding@droomparken.nl

alanrogers.com/NL6343

Centrally located on the shores of Veluwemeer in the beautiful Veluwe region, between Harderwijk and Nunspeet, Camping Droompark Bad Hoophuizen is a good family site. There are currently 550 touring pitches, most with water, electricity (6-10A) and cable TV connections. This is a spacious site with a choice of pitches of varying sizes and locations. Several types of rented accommodation are also on offer, and from 2013 will include a number of new chalets overlooking the lake. The recently reconstructed café/restaurant has a conservatory and lakeside terrace.

Facilities

Eight well maintained, Portacabin-style sanitary blocks with modern facilities including baby rooms and facilities for disabled campers. Restaurant. Snack bar. Shop. Indoor pool planned for 2013. Bicycle hire. Canoes, kayaks, pedaloes and boats for hire. Tennis. Free WiFi over site. Indoor play area. Off site: Free entry to the sub-tropical swimming pool (De Brake) in Nunspeet. Walking and cycling. Theme parks. Ferry across the Veluwemeer.

Open: 25 March - 30 October.

Directions

From A28 motorway, take exit 13 towards Lelystad (N302). After 2 km. turn right towards Hierden and Hulshorst. In Hulshorst follow signs to the site (to the left). GPS: 52.382711, 5.708323

Charges guide

Per unit incl. 2 persons	
and electricity	€ 18.50 - € 35.50
extra person	€ 5.50
dog	€ 4.50

FREE Alan Rogers Travel Card
Extra benefits and savings - see page 12

Hummelo
Parkcamping De Graafschap
Loenhorsterweg 7C, NL-6999 DT Hummelo (Gelderland) T: 0314 343 752. E: info@camping-degraafschap.nl
alanrogers.com/NL5865

De Graafschap is an attractive, family friendly site located on the outskirts of the beautiful Kruisbergse forest between Doetinchem and Hummelo, a large green area perfect for hiking, mountain biking and cycling enthusiasts. Pitches here are all of a good size, on average 125-150 sq.m. There are 65 touring and 65 permanent pitches on several well kept grassy fields, all with electricity (6A), water, drainage and cable TV connection (charged). There is a canteen offering snacks and drinks and a small shop in the reception for daily essentials. Finnish Kotas and mobile homes are available to rent throughout the year.

Facilities
Two heated sanitary blocks with free hot water and baby room. Launderette. Motorcaravan service point. Small shop. Canteen. Playground. Boules. WiFi (charged). Off site: Shops and restaurants in Doetinchem 2 km. Bronckhorst, local historic village. House Verwolde Castle. Cycling and walking routes through the Kruisbergse forest.
Open: All year.

Directions
Take the A12 from Arnhem towards Oberhausen and exit at A348 to Zutphen. Continue to the end and then follow N317 towards Doesburg/Doetinchem into Laag Keppel. At the intersection turn left into Hummelo and first right towards Hengelo. Follow signs to the site. GPS: 51.9912, 6.27960

Charges guide
Per unit incl. 2 persons and electricty	€ 20.75
extra person	€ 4.00
No credit cards.	

Laag-Soeren
Vakantiedorp De Jutberg
Jutberg 78, NL-6957 DP Laag-Soeren (Gelderland) T: 0313 619 220. E: jutberg@ardoer.com
alanrogers.com/NL6344

What makes De Jutberg attractive is the relaxed atmosphere, the friendly staff and the natural setting of the site. This is a typical Dutch Veluwe campsite with curved paths and different types of pitches, 145 in total. They range from luxury pitches with water, drainage, electricity and cable TV, to rather more natural pitches without any services. Some are a distance from the toilet blocks and there is not much lighting. Almost all are sheltered by trees or hedges. There are several areas occupied by private chalets, all hidden in their own wooded glades. There are two wooden pods and two teepees for rent.

Facilities
Four modern toilet blocks include facilities for families and babies. No facilities for disabled visitors. Shop, restaurant and takeaway (1/4-31/10). Bar. Swimming pool with sliding roof (1/4-31/10). Bicycle hire. Play area. Nature hut. Sculpting workshop. Activities daily in high season. Football pitch. Free WiFi over site. Torches useful. Off site: Riding 1 km. Fishing 2 km. Golf 10 km.
Open: All year.

Directions
De Jutberg is 15 km. northeast of Arnhem, signed from the N786 between Dieren and Laag-Soeren. GPS: 52.07089, 6.0764

Charges guide
Per unit incl. 2 persons and electricity	€ 17.00 - € 33.00
extra person (over 2 yrs)	€ 2.50 - € 4.75

Lieren
Recreatiecentrum De Bosgraaf
Kanaal Zuid 444, NL-7364 CB Lieren (Gelderland) T: 0555 051 359. E: bosgraaf@ardoer.com
alanrogers.com/NL6338

With a real park-like feel, this green site has spacious grass pitches in wooded surroundings. It is a delightful site for quiet relaxation. There are 194 touring pitches (6/10A electricity), half of which have private sanitary facilities for rent. In addition, there are privately owned chalets and mobile homes, also set in the woods. In the summer months the site is mostly organised for campers with children. The large children's pool with its water slides is very popular, as is the paddling pool. The play areas are numerous and varied and in high season there are organised activities. A member of the Ardoer group.

Facilities
Four modern toilet blocks include facilities for families and babies. Private toilet facilities for 94 pitches are rather basic (extra charge). Launderette. Shop (10/4-15/9). Bar. Restaurant (3/4-20/9). Sauna. Large sports field with adventure playground. Small animal farm. Fishing. Bicycle hire. WiFi over part of site (charged). Accommodation for hire. Dogs are not accepted. Off site: Golf and fishing 1 km. Riding 2 km. Bus to Apeldoorn in summer.
Open: 21 March - 25 October.

Directions
From the A1 take exit for Apeldoorn-Zuid and Beekbergen and turn left towards Dieren. After 600 m. turn right towards Dieren and follow the canal for 5 km. to reach the site. GPS: 52.14842, 6.03828

Charges guide
Per serviced pitch incl. 2 persons and electricity	€ 24.00 - € 30.00
extra person	€ 5.00
No credit cards.	

For latest campsite news, availability and prices visit
alanrogers.com

Maurik

Camping De Loswal

Rijnbandijk 36, NL-4021 GH Maurik (Gelderland) T: 0344 692 892. E: info@camping-deloswal.nl
alanrogers.com/NL6280

De Loswal is a beautifully landscaped site with many fruit trees and a large marina. The 50 level touring pitches are spacious and sunny, with those close to the dyke being particularly spacious (up to 120 sq.m). All the pitches have 6A electricity and many great views over the lake. There are four sanitary buildings of which one is new, this one being located near the entrance and reception. All the buildings are heated, tiled and well maintained. This site is good for fishing and ideal for watersports enthusiasts as you can moor your own boat here. Boat hire is available within 2 km.

Facilities

Four sanitary buildings which are kept clean and well maintained. One modern but all tiled and neat. Facilities for disabled visitors. Launderette. Small bar/restaurant/takeaway. Boat launching and marina for various types of boats. Several sandy beaches and lake swimming. Adventure play area. Fishing. Off site: Shop. Restaurant. Bar. Bicycle hire 1 km. Golf 7 km.

Open: April - October.

Directions

From the A15 take exit for Tiel/Maurik and follow signs to Maurik. Site is well signed from here. From the A2 take Culemborg exit and follow N320 to Maurik (site well signed). GPS: 51.96328, 5.40657

Charges guide

Per unit incl. 2 persons and electricity	€ 17.60 - € 23.50
extra person	€ 3.00

Maurik

Camping Eiland van Maurik

Eiland van Maurik 7, NL-4021 GG Maurik (Gelderland) T: 0344 691 502. E: receptie@eilandvanmaurik.nl
alanrogers.com/NL6290

Camping Eiland van Maurik is beside a lake in the centre of an extensive nature and recreation park in the Nederrijn area. These surroundings are ideal for all sorts of activities – swimming, windsurfing, water-skiing or para-sailing, relaxing on the beach or fishing. There is even an animal farm for the children. The site has 265 numbered, flat pitches, all fully serviced (10A electricity). You could enjoy pancakes in the Oudhollandse restaurant with its views over the water. There is direct access from the site to the lakeside beach. This is a site for families.

Facilities

The three toilet blocks for tourers include washbasins (open style and in cabins), controllable showers and a baby room. Launderette with iron and board. Shop. Bar/restaurant/pizzeria (all season). Play areas (one indoors). Playing field. Tennis. Minigolf. Bicycle hire. Go-karts. Water-skiing. Sailing and motorboat hire. Para-sailing. Animal farm. Entertainment in high season (incl. riding). Max. 2 dogs. Off site: 18-hole pitch and putt 1 km.

Open: 1 April - 1 October.

Directions

From A2 (Utrecht-'s Hertogenbosch) take Culemborg exit (Kesteren). Follow signs for Eiland Maurik. From A15 (Rotterdam-Nijmegen) take exit 33 Tiel (Maurik) and follow signs as above. GPS: 51.97656, 5.43013

Charges guide

Per unit incl. 2 persons and electricity	€ 20.00 - € 35.00
extra person	€ 5.00

No credit cards.
Camping Cheques accepted.

Nieuw Milligen

Landal Rabbit Hill

Grevenhout 21, NL-3888 NR Nieuw Milligen (Gelderland) T: 0577 456 431. E: touroperators@landal.nl
alanrogers.com/NL5822

You will soon discover the reason for Landal Rabbit Hill's name. Wildlife abounds on this friendly site, which is a member of the Landal Group. It is located deep within the heavily forested Veluwe, close to Nieuw Milligen. The cities of Apeldoorn, Amersfoort and Arnhem are all within easy reach. There are 140 pitches. These are large and well shaded. All have electrical connections (10A) and cable TV connections. You will be impressed with its facilities, which include an excellent indoor swimming pool complex with water slides and other features. There is also a wonderful indoor children's play area.

Facilities

Two modern, heated sanitary blocks. Free controllable hot showers and some washbasins in cabins. Family room. Facilities for disabled visitors. Laundry facilities. Shop. Motorcaravan service point. Café/restaurant. Indoor and outdoor swimming pool complex. Playgrounds. Sports pitch. Free WiFi over part of site. Mobile homes and chalets for rent. No dogs. Off site: Shops and restaurants in Nieuw Milligen. Riding 1 km. Fishing 7 km.

Open: All year.

Directions

Approaching from the west (Amersfoort) use A1 motorway as far as the Nieuw Milligen exit, and then join the northbound N302. The site is signed to the right within the village. GPS: 52.218673, 5.785503

Charges guide

Per unit incl. 2 persons and electricity	€ 16.00 - € 42.00

Nunspeet

Molecaten Park De Hooghe Bijsschel

Randmeerweg 8, NL-8071 SH Nunspeet (Gelderland) T: 0341 252 406. E: dehooghebijsschel@molecaten.nl
alanrogers.com/NL6359

A family focused campsite with direct access to Lake Veluwe, this site is understandably popular with windsurfers, sailors and fishermen. The lake is shallow and therefore also ideal for younger children. The two large camping fields are car-free and are bordered by hedges and mature trees. The 123 grassy touring pitches all have 6/10A electricity. There is plenty of space for children to safely play in the middle of the fields. Two new chalets are for rent. There is a marina and pier (with a slipway) – ideal for boat launching, and also a lakeside beach.

Facilities

Two toilet blocks have facilities for babies and for disabled visitors. Restaurant and bar with terrace and lake view, takeaway food. Small shop. Heated outdoor swimming pool with children's pool (8/5-1/9), whirlpool. Direct lake access. Beach with play area. Volleyball. Tennis. Play areas. Bicycle and boat hire. Boat launching. Windsurfing and sailing tuition. In high season free courses for children (up to 12 yrs) to try watersports. Activities and entertainment. WiFi throughout (charged). Off site: Harderwijk. Walibi Holland theme park.

Open: 29 March - 30 September.

Directions

Take exit 14 from the A28 motorway and follow signs to Elspeet/Nunspeet on N310. Upon reaching Nunspeet, continue ahead onto Elspeterweg/N310. On the outskirts of Nunspeet, take first exit on Vreeweg. The site is signed from here.
GPS: 52.392054, 5.735056

Charges guide

Per unit incl. 2 persons and electricity	€ 18.50 - € 28.00
extra person	€ 3.90

No credit cards.

Oosterhout

Camping De Grote Altena

Waaldijk 39, NL-6678 MC Oosterhout (Gelderland) T: 0481 481 200. E: info@campingdegrotealtena.nl
alanrogers.com/NL6395

This campsite occupies a scenic location on the River Waal. It has 160 pitches in total, half of which are situated immediately beside the river with fabulous views. There are 25 permanent and 60 seasonal pitches, plus 75 for touring with 6A electricity. A separate field, with a fish pond, is available for short stays. The playground with open-air chess and trampoline is popular with children. De Grote Altena is ideal for nature lovers who enjoy peace and space. Arnhem and Nijmegen are both within easy reach.

Facilities

Three sanitary buildings are modern and well maintained with free hot showers and facilities for babies. Laundry facilities. Snack bar. Playground. Fishing. Direct river access. Open-air chess. Small, riverside beach. Boat launching. WiFi. Off site: Restaurant. Nearest shops in Oosterhout 1 km. Supermarket in Elst 4 km. Walking and cycle tracks. Excursions to Arnhem and Nijmegen.

Open: Easter - 9 October.

Directions

The site is 9 km. northwest of Nijmegen. From Arnhem or Nijmegen follow A325, and leave at Ressen Tiel/Rotterdam exit (A15). After 2.6 km. take exit 38 to Elst/Oosterhout. Turn left after 500 m. at petrol station, turn right, then follow signs to site.
GPS: 51.87585, 5.80752

Charges guide

Per unit incl. 5 persons and electricity	€ 25.00
extra person	€ 4.75

Otterlo

Camping De Wije Werelt

Arnhemseweg 100-102, NL-6731 BV Otterlo (Gelderland) T: 0318 591 201. E: wijewerelt@ardoer.com
alanrogers.com/NL6350

Camping De Wije Werelt offers all the facilities you need for a very comfortable holiday. The 170 touring pitches all have water and drainage, 10A electricity, cable, and WiFi. The site is surrounded by forest – the home of many wild animals and there are numerous good cycling and walking routes. This peaceful site is very child friendly and extremely popular with families during school holidays. There are plenty of activities for children on site including play areas. There is also a heated, outdoor swimming pool.

Facilities

Heated toilet block includes washbasins in cabins. Family wash cabins and facilities for children. Baby room. Launderette. Microwave. Shop. Bar. Restaurant. Snack bar and takeaway. TV room. Playground, bouncy castle and climbing frames. Sports field. Boules. Bicycle and tricycle hire. Entertainment in high season. Recreation area. Miniclub. Electronic games. WiFi over site (charged). Off site: Riding 500 m. Fishing 1 km. Golf 20 km.

Open: 21 March - 25 October.

Directions

The site is north of Arnhem. From the A1 take exit 17 south onto the N310 and the site is signed to the right after Otterlo and De Zanding.
GPS: 52.08656, 5.76945

Charges guide

Per serviced pitch incl. 2 persons, electricity, water and waste water	€ 22.00 - € 36.25
extra person	€ 5.00

For latest campsite news, availability and prices visit

alanrogers.com

Sellingen

Campingpark De Barkhoorn

Beetserweg 6, NL-9551 VE Sellingen (Groningen) T: 0599 322510. E: info@barkhoorn.nl

alanrogers.com/NL6115

Camping De Barkhoorn is located in the Westerwolde, southeast of Groningen. The campsite is surrounded by vast forests and heathland interspersed with beautiful ponds. It offers camping in a tranquil setting on spacious, verdant pitches with shade to the back provided by tall trees. A car-free site, there are 152 touring pitches (13 comfort pitches), all with 10A electricity, and hardstandings for motorcaravans outside the gate. This is a pleasant family campsite, ideal for families with children, and for those who enjoy walking and cycling. The German border is nearby.

Facilities

Four older style, but clean sanitary buildings including one without hot water have showers, open style washbasins and preset hot showers. Private facilities to rent. Facilities for disabled visitors. Launderette. Bar/restaurant and terrace (Fri-Sun). Snack bar also sells basics. Play areas. Recreation lake with beach. Sports field. Minigolf. Tennis. Bowling and other activities. Bicycle hire. Fishing. Canoeing. WiFi over site (charged). Cabins to rent. Off site: Swimming pool 200 m. Supermarket 1 km.

Open: 30 March - 27 October.

Directions

Follow signs from Zwolle, Hoogeveen and Emmen for Ter Apel. Sellingen is on the main road between Ter Apel and Winschoten, 2 km. from the centre of Sellingen. Follow site signs from the village. GPS: 52.946406, 7.131192

Charges guide

Per unit incl. 2 persons and electricity	€ 15.00 - € 25.50
extra person	€ 3.50

Wedde

Camping Wedderbergen

Molenweg 2, NL-9698 XV Wedde (Groningen) T: 0597 561 673. E: info@wedderbergen.nl

alanrogers.com/NL6100

Camping Wedderbergen is a well established, modern site. Its focus is being changed from seasonal to touring pitches. There are now 233 touring pitches, all with 10A electricity, water, waste water and cable. A separate area provides hardstandings for larger units and motorcaravans. This is supported by a toilet block in front of the touring fields. There are some views over the Westerwoldsche river and shade in some areas from mature trees. Pitches at the front of the site have a jetty for small boats. To the back of the site is a large expanse of water with a sandy beach.

Facilities

A toilet block for tourers with toilets, washbasins in cabins and preset hot showers (hot water with key). Family shower rooms. Baby room. Facilities for disabled campers. Laundry. Motorcaravan services. Well stocked shop. Bar, canteen and snack bar. Recreation lake with sandy beach. Playing field. Bicycle hire. Fishing. Tennis. Playgrounds. Bouncy cushion. WiFi (charged). Off site: Sub-tropical pool.

Open: April - October.

Directions

On A7 from either direction take exit 47 for Winschoten and continue towards Vlagtwedde. Passing through Wedde, follow the site signs. GPS: 53.08611, 7.08291

Charges guide

Per unit incl. 4 persons	€ 15.00 - € 28.50
extra person	€ 4.00 - € 5.00
dog	€ 4.00

FREE Alan Rogers Travel Card
Extra benefits and savings - see page 12

Limburg

Limburg has a range of attractive landscapes: the green hills in the south, a large area of waterland at its heart, the scenic countryside of Peel and Maas, and the marshes and dunes in the north.

CAPITAL: MAASTRICHT

Limburg's multi-faceted landscape – woodland, peat moorland, sand dunes and marl plateaux – offers endless opportunites for the active holidaymaker. The extensive cycle network, ferries across the River Maas and delightful mountain bike trails are all waiting to be enjoyed. The numerous marked trails passing by nature reserves and areas of outstanding natural beauty are a gift for hikers and cyclists alike who can pause to admire some of the most beautiful areas of Limburg.

Limburg offers a taste of the good life – its shopping, fine dining, and wealth of tourist attractions, coupled with the locals' warm hospitality will make your visit an experience to remember. Maastricht is believed to be the oldest city in the Netherlands. It has grown from a Roman settlement on the banks of the Meuse to a thriving city with a large student population and a reputation for cordiality – the number of beautiful cafés that line its streets may have something to do with that. With its wealth of romantic streets, picturesque squares and historical architecture, there are plenty of opportunities for sightseeing.

Places of interest

Maastricht: Bonnefanten Museum, classic paintings in a spectacular building by Aldo Rossi; Thiessen Wijnkoopers is the oldest wine house in the country.

Baarlo: typical village along the Maas with four castles, and the former home of the CoBrA artist, Tajiri.

Thorn: known as the white town, because many buildings are white limed, it has intimate courtyards, streets cobbled with Maas stone, mosaic floors and a beautiful abbey church.

Valkenburg: tourist town in the middle of the hills with various attractions including marl caves.

Attractions

Old mill: the Friedesse mill in Neer is mentioned in a document dating from 1343. Open Sundays from May to September.

Montfort Castle: dating from 1260 and for centuries one of the largest castles in the Netherlands, impressive ruins with visitors' centre in a restored tower.

Wijlre: the oldest brewery in the Netherlands in a beautiful location. Discover the ancient history of Brand beer, one of Limburg's treasures.

Stef's house, Brunssum: recreates life in a mining village using film footage and photographs, historical artifacts and props from a television series.

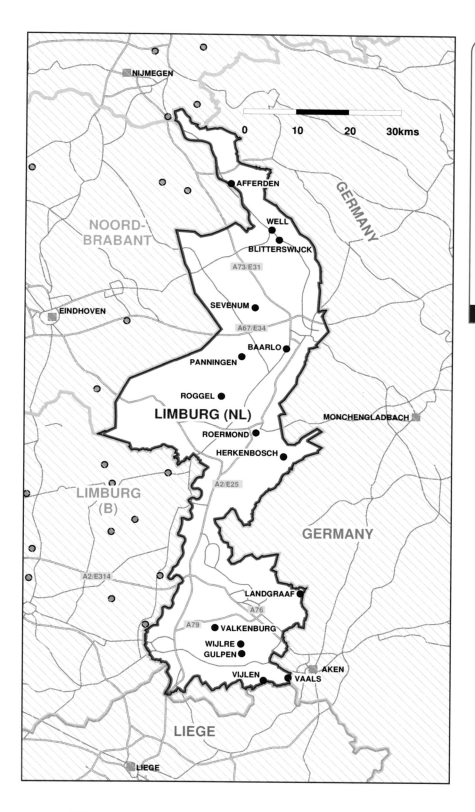

NIJMEGEN

AFFERDEN

GERMANY

WELL
BLITTERSWIJCK

NOORD-
BRABANT

A73/E31

EINDHOVEN

SEVENUM

A67/E34

BAARLO
PANNINGEN

ROGGEL

LIMBURG (NL)

MONCHENGLADBACH

ROERMOND
HERKENBOSCH

LIMBURG
(B)

A2/E25

GERMANY

A2/E314

LANDGRAAF

A76

A79   VALKENBURG

WIJLRE
GULPEN

VIJLEN   AKEN
           VAALS

LIEGE

LIEGE

0   10   20   30kms

Afferden

Camping Roland

Rimpelt 33, NL-5851 EK Afferden (Limburg) T: 0485 531 431. E: info@campingroland.nl

alanrogers.com/NL5892

Family run Camping Roland is a quiet site in an attractive region between the River Maas and the German border. The surroundings are made up of dunes, woods, moorland and lakes. Pitches here are divided into two groups, each with its own charm. All 90 spacious, grassy pitches have 6A electricity, water, drainage and cable TV connections. Swimming, sailing, fishing, mountain biking and hiking are amongst the activities on offer here. The swimming pool has a 40 m. water slide and a large sun terrace. This region has signed cycle routes both around the site and on the far side of The Maas, reached by ferry.

Facilities

Two well maintained, attractive sanitary blocks with showers (token), hot water, dishwashing facilities and laundry with washing machines and dryers. No facilities for disabled visitors. Shop (1/4-12/9). Cafeteria, restaurant and bar with billiards and large screen TV (15/3-20/9). Swimming pool with water slide and sun terrace. Fishing pond. Large playground. Sports field. Entertainment and activity programme. Tennis. WiFi over site (charged). Off site: Golf courses at Bleijenbeek (discounted fees).

Open: All year.

Directions

From A73 Nijmegen-Venlo motorway, take exit 2 (Rijkevoort) and follow A77. Then, join N271 towards Bergen. After a further 5 km. (at Afferden) site is signed to left. Continue for 1.5 km. and site is on left just past windmill. GPS: 51.635117, 6.034203

Charges guide

Per unit incl. 2 persons and electricity	€ 19.00 - € 27.00
extra person (over 3 yrs)	€ 4.00
dog (max. 2)	€ 2.50

Baarlo

Oostappen Vakantiepark De Berckt

Napoleonsbaan Noord 4, NL-5991 NV Baarlo (Limburg) T: 077 477 7222. E: info@deberckt.nl

alanrogers.com/NL6545

De Berckt is a friendly, family site in the southeast of the Netherlands. Much of the development of the site has been inspired by the medieval history of the region. Pitches here are grassy and of a good size. All have electrical connections, water and drainage. Accommodation to rent here includes chalets and mobile homes, such as the Knight's chalet and the Castle chalet. On-site amenities include a tropical swimming pool complex with a Water Dragon slide and a lazy river. There is plenty of entertainment in peak season including children's clubs and live music.

Facilities

Bar/restaurant. Shop. Takeaway. Tropical swimming pool complex. Children's pool. Minigolf. Sports field. Balloon rides. Tennis. Bicycle and go-kart hire. Playground. Activity and entertainment programme. Tourist information. Mobile homes and chalets for rent. Off site: Shops and restaurants in Baarlo. Walking and cycle tracks. Fishing.

Open: 22 April - 31 October.

Directions

Approaching from the east (Venlo) use N273 and pass Hout-Blerick. Continue to Baarlo and then follow signs to the site. GPS: 51.345562, 6.105319

Charges guide

Per unit incl. 2 persons and electricity	€ 15.00 - € 29.00

Blitterswijck

Camping 't Veerhuys

Veerweg 7, NL-5863 AR Blitterswijck (Limburg) T: 0478 531 283. E: info@campingveerhuys.nl

alanrogers.com/NL6532

Camping 't Veerhuys is a quiet site extending along the Maas river, opposite the Maasduinen National Park in northern Limburg. The 80 touring pitches are grassy and equipped with 6/10A electricity and water. All have panoramic views over the Maas. The site features a cosy bar and a restaurant, Tanty Jet (discount for campers), with a terrace with views over the river, where you can enjoy a quiet drink and a meal. The MaasHopper, a boat that takes passengers and bicycles, calls in three times a week, stopping at several locations from where you can return on foot or by bike. There are various watersports available including water skiing (lessons available), banana rides, wake boarding, swimming and fishing. A recreational park and indoor pool are 500 m. This is a good base for cyclists and wanderers.

Facilities

One basic, but clean and heated, sanitary block is located behind the restaurant. It has all necessary facilities including those for children and disabled visitors. Showers are on payment (SEP key) and washbasins are open style. Laundry with washing machine and dryer. Traditional bar and restaurant with terrace and snacks. Paddling pool. Children's playgrounds. Trampoline. Bicycle hire. WiFi over site (charged). No charcoal barbecues.

Open: 1 April - 31 October.

Directions

Site is 18 km. northwest of Venlo. From A73 take exit 9 towards Wanssum. Turn right at roundabout and then left in Wanssum. Follow signs to Blitterswijck. The site is signed from there. GPS: 51.5309, 6.11805

Charges guide

Per unit incl. 2 persons and electricty	€ 18.80 - € 21.60
extra person	€ 3.10

Beside the many historical cities and densely populated, modern residential areas, there is plenty of space for unique landscapes such as Waterland (near Amsterdam) and the Kennemer Dunes (near Haarlem).

CAPITAL: HAARLEM

Noord-Holland is a broad peninsula lying between the North Sea and the IJsselmeer. With more than 2.5 million people sharing an area of 2,670 sq.km, it is the country's second most populated province. In 1600, half of its surface was covered by water, then began the reclamation of land, and the construction of giant polders such as Beemster, Purmer and Schermer, a testament to the relationship between man and the sea. But there is much more to this province: forests, moors, dunes, beaches and meadows form a diverse landscape embroidered with quaint towns and charming, sleepy villages, rich in folklore and legend.

Almost the entire west coast of the province is made up of dunes and beaches. You have a choice of secluded bays or lively seaside resorts, simple pavilions or trendy beach restaurants. The east coast is bordered by the fresh water of the IJsselmeer, which offers numerous activities on its many ponds, lakes and canals. Noord-Holland's rich trading history is reflected in the elegant and vibrant cities, where there are ample opportunities to shop, visit museums and galleries, or just sit at a terrace café and watch the world go by.

Places of interest

Amsterdam: picturesque canals, 'brown cafés', restaurants, theatres and many museums make this city the cultural and artistic hub of the country.

Hoorn, Enkhuizen, Medemblik: historical cities at the IJsselmeer, formerly important sea ports, with beautiful 17th-century city centres.

Stelling van Amsterdam: a 135 km. defensive ring encircling Amsterdam, with 36 fortifications, set among beautiful landscapes and nature reserves.

Zaanstreek: the oldest industrial area of Europe with a unique heritage.

Texel: much of this island is given over to nature reserves; home to rare plants, animals and birds.

Attractions

Zuiderzeemuseum: reconstruction of an early modern Dutch fishing village in an open-air setting at Enkhuizen.

Zaansche Schans: open-air museum with working mills, old handicrafts, special features and characteristic green wooden houses.

Sprookjeswonderland: fairytale theme park for youngsters in Enkhuizen.

Naarden: fortified city with interesting walks, shopping and adventure playground at Oud Valkeveen.

Beemster: famous polder and UNESCO World Heritage Site. Visit the very interesting arboretum (free).

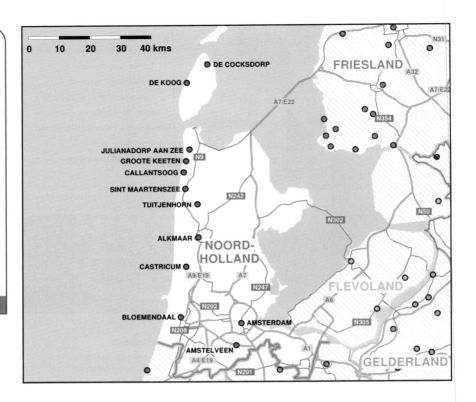

Alkmaar
Camping Alkmaar

Bergerweg 201, NL-1817 ML Alkmaar (Noord-Holland) T: 0725 116 924. E: info@campingalkmaar.nl

alanrogers.com/NL6705

Camping Alkmaar is a friendly, family run campsite on the outskirts of the charming town of Alkmaar and near to the artisan village of Bergen. A short cycle ride will take you to the peaceful countryside of Noord-Holland with its dunes, wide sandy beaches, woods and unique polder landscape. Alternatively, a stroll along the canals in the picturesque heart of Alkmaar with its architecture, culture and cheese market may appeal. This is a tranquil site - there is no bar or restaurant and radios are not permitted. All 120 touring pitches have 6/10A electricity; 46 have hardstanding, and 21 are comfort pitches with water and drainage. A regular bus service runs to the town centre and the train station for connections to Amsterdam. A boat tour around the canals is also recommended.

Facilities

New sanitary block in the touring area is clean and well maintained and has coin-operated showers and open style washbasins. Facilities for disabled visitors. Washing machine and dryer. Two motorcaravan service points. Play area. Fishing. Bicycle hire. Tourist information. WiFi over part of site (charged). Off site: Shops and restaurants in Alkmaar. Golf and riding 3 km. Beach 8 km. Walking and cycle trails. Batavier children's park.

Open: All year.

Directions

From the western ring road of Alkmaar (N9), turn left towards Bergen (N510). After 300 m. turn left to the site. GPS: 52.6421, 4.72329

Charges guide

Per unit incl. 2 persons and electricity (5 kWh)	€ 21.00 - € 29.00
electricity per kWh	€ 0.35
extra person	€ 4.00
dog	€ 3.00

For latest campsite news, availability and prices visit

alanrogers.com

Amstelveen

Camping Het Amsterdamse Bos

Kleine Noorddijk 1, NL-1187 NZ Amstelveen (Noord-Holland) T: 0206 416 868.
E: info@campingamsterdam.com **alanrogers.com/NL5660**

Het Amsterdamse Bos is a large park to the southwest of Amsterdam, one corner of which has been specifically laid out as the city's municipal campsite and is now under family ownership. Close to Schiphol Airport (expect some noise), it is a walk/bus and a metro ride into central Amsterdam. The site is well laid out alongside a canal, with unmarked pitches on separate flat lawns mostly backing onto pleasant hedges and trees, with several areas of paved hardstandings. It takes 400 touring units, with 100 electrical connections (10A) and some with cable TV. An additional area is available for tents and groups. Some pitches can become very wet in the rain.

Facilities

Three new sanitary blocks are light and airy with showers (on payment). Facilities for babies and disabled visitors. Laundry facilities. Motorcaravan services. Gas supplies. Small shop with basics. Fresh bread from reception. Cooking and dining area. Play area. Bicycle hire. Internet and free WiFi over site. Twin-axle caravans not accepted. Off site: Fishing, boating, pancake restaurant in the park. Riding 5 km.

Open: 15 March - 15 December.

Directions

Amsterdamse Bos and site are west of Amstelveen. From the A9 motorway take exit 6 and follow N231 to site (2nd traffic light). GPS: 52.29357, 4.82297

Charges guide

Per unit incl. 2 persons and electricity	€ 23.50 - € 25.50
extra person	€ 5.00
child (4-12 yrs)	€ 2.50
Group reductions.	

Amsterdam

Camping Vliegenbos

Meeuwenlaan 138, NL-1022 AM Amsterdam (Noord-Holland) T: 0206 368 855
alanrogers.com/NL5675

Vliegenbos enjoys the best of both worlds with an appealing location in a large wood, ten minutes from the lively centre of Amsterdam and five minutes by bike from the countryside of the Waterland region, best known for its open expanses and picturesque towns such as Marken, Edam and Volendam. It extends over an 8.5-acre site and has a good range of amenities including a restaurant, shop and recently renovated toilet blocks. Most pitches are for tents, but there are 19 hardstandings (10A electricity) and a further 40 smaller hardstandings (no electricity). Several hikers' cabins can be reserved in advance. The site reception is open from 09.00 until 21.00 throughout the season and is able to offer advice on sightseeing options, as well as the exploration of the Waterland by bicycle. There is a bus stop 200 m. from the campsite with a good service to the city centre. Alternatively, a ferry operates from Centraal Station to a terminal 15 minutes walk from the site.

Facilities

Renovated toilet blocks with facilities for disabled campers. Motorcaravan services. Bar/restaurant and takeaway. Shop (fresh bread daily). Free WiFi over part of site. Cabins for rent. Reservations are not accepted for touring pitches. Dogs are not accepted. Off site: Bus stop 200 m. Cycle tracks in the surrounding Waterland. Ferry terminal 15 minutes walk with regular free service to Amsterdam.

Open: 1 April - 30 September.

Directions

Leave the A10 Amsterdam ring road at exit S116 and follow signs to Camping Vliegenbos. GPS: 52.39055, 4.928083

Charges guide

Per unit incl. 2 persons and electricity	€ 28.50 - € 30.00
extra person	€ 7.70 - € 8.70
child (2-14 yrs)	€ 5.40

Receptie geopend van 09.00 tot 21.00 uur
Reception open from 09:00 until 21:00

Camping Vliegenbos
Amsterdam-Noord

Meeuwenlaan 138 · 1022 AM Amsterdam
tel. +31 (0)20 - 636 88 55
www.vliegenbos.com

Amsterdam
Camping Zeeburg

Zuider IJdijk 20, NL-1095 KN Amsterdam (Noord-Holland) T: 0206 944 430. E: info@campingzeeburg.nl
alanrogers.com/NL5665

Camping Zeeburg is a welcoming site attractively located to the east of Amsterdam on an island in the IJmeer and, unusually, combines a sense of nature with the advantage of being just 20 minutes from the city centre. In a sense, Zeeburg reflects the spirit of Amsterdam, claiming to be open, friendly and tolerant. The site offers 400 pitches, mostly for tents, with 75 on hardstandings with 10A electricity, for larger caravans and motorcaravans. Many pitches have views over the IJmeer. Tent pitches cannot be booked in advance and the maximum duration allowed on site is 14 days. Zeeburg also offers a number of low cost wooden cabins and wagonettes. The city centre is 5 km. distant and can be easily accessed by bicycle (hire available on site). Alternatively, a regular bus service runs close to the site. On-site amenities include a busy bar/restaurant, a shop including a bakery (which claims to bake Amsterdam's best croissants), a children's farm and a canoe rental service. The wetlands of the IJmeer are well worth exploration, extending to the Diemerpark and new city of IJburg.

Facilities

Three toilet blocks are generally basic and well used, but clean. Although adequate, facilities may be stretched at peak times. Facilities for disabled visitors (key access). Small laundry. Shop (all year), bar/restaurant (1/4-11/11). Very small playground. Games room. Bicycle hire. Motorcaravan services. Children's farm. Canoe hire. Cabins and wagonettes to rent. Free WiFi over site. Off site: Swimming pool. Buses and trains to city centre.

Open: All year.

Directions

Site is on the eastern side of Amsterdam. From the A10 (Amsterdam ring road) take exit S114 to Zeeburg. Then follow signs to the city centre and, before reaching the Piet Hein tunnel turn left and then right into the campsite. The site is well signed from the A10. GPS: 52.36532, 4.95871

Charges guide

Per unit incl. 2 persons and electricity	€ 15.00 - € 31.00
extra person	€ 3.50 - € 5.50
child (2-12 yrs)	€ 2.50 - € 3.50
dog	€ 2.00 - € 3.00
Reduced rates for tents.	

Amsterdam
Gaasper Camping Amsterdam

Loosdrechtdreef 7, NL-1108 AZ Amsterdam (Noord-Holland) T: 0206 967 326
alanrogers.com/NL5670

Amsterdam is probably the most popular destination for visits in the Netherlands, and Gaasper Camping is on the southeast side, a short walk from a Metro station with a direct 20 minute service to the centre. The site is well kept and neatly laid out on flat grass with attractive trees and shrubs. There are 350 touring pitches in two main areas – one more open and grassy, mainly kept for tents (30 pitches with 10A connections), the other more formal with numbered pitches mainly divided by shallow ditches or good hedges. Areas of hardstanding are available and all caravan pitches have electrical connections.

Facilities

Three modern, clean toilet blocks (one unisex) for the tourist sections are an adequate provision. Nine new cabins with basin and shower. Hot water for showers and some dishwashing sinks on payment. Facilities for babies. Washing machine and dryer. Motorcaravan services. Gas supplies. Supermarket (1/4-1/11), café/bar/restaurant plus takeaway (1/6-1/9). Play area on grass. Off site: Riding 200 m. Fishing 1 km. Golf 4 km.

Open: 15 March - 1 November.

Directions

Take exit 1 for Gaasperplas-Weesp (S113) from the section of A9 motorway which is on the east side of the A2. Note: do not take the Gaasperdam exit (S112) which comes first if approaching from the west. GPS: 52.312222, 4.991389

Charges guide

Per unit incl. 2 persons and electricity	€ 23.50 - € 27.50
extra person	€ 4.75 - € 5.50
child (4-11 yrs)	€ 2.25 - € 2.75
dog	€ 2.50 - € 3.00

Bloemendaal

Kennemer Duincamping De Lakens

Zeeweg 60, NL-2051 EC Bloemendaal aan Zee (Noord-Holland) T: 0235 411 570.
E: delakens@kennemerduincampings.nl **alanrogers.com/NL6870**

De Lakens is beautifully located in the dunes at Bloemendaal aan Zee. This site has 900 reasonably large, flat pitches of varying sizes, whose layout makes them feel quite private - some come with a ready erected hammock! There are 410 pitches for tourers (255 with 16A electricity) separated by low hedging. This site is a true oasis of peace in a part of the Netherlands usually bustling with activity. From this site it is possible to walk straight through the dunes to the North Sea. Although there is no pool, there is the sea. The reception and management are very friendly and welcoming.

Facilities

The five new toilet blocks for tourers include controllable showers, washbasins (open style and in cabins), facilities for disabled visitors and a baby room. Launderette. Two motorcaravan service points. Bar/restaurant with terrace, pizzeria and snack bar. Supermarket. Adventure playgrounds. Basketball. Bicycle hire. Entertainment (high season). WiFi over most of site (charged). Glamping-style accommodation for rent. No twin-axle caravans or large motorcaravans. Dogs are not accepted.

Open: 28 March - 28 October.

Directions

From Amsterdam go west to Haarlem and follow the N200 from Haarlem towards Bloemendaal aan Zee. Site is on the N200, on the right hand side. GPS: 52.40563, 4.58652

Charges guide

Per unit incl. 4 persons	€ 25.60 - € 55.00
extra person	€ 5.35

Callantsoog

Camping Tempelhof

Westerweg 2, NL-1759 JD Callantsoog (Noord-Holland) T: 0224 581 522. E: info@tempelhof.nl
alanrogers.com/NL5735

This first class site on the Dutch coast has 470 pitches with 220 for touring units, the remainder used by seasonal campers and a number of static units (mostly privately owned). All touring pitches have electricity (10/16A), water, drain and TV aerial point (40-110 sq.m. but car free). Two pitches have private sanitary facilities. The grass pitches are arranged in long rows which are separated by hedges and shrubs, with access from hardcore roads. There is hardly any shade. There are facilities for many activities, including a heated indoor pool, a fitness room and tennis courts. Tempelhof is close to the North Sea beaches (1 km). Member of Leading Campings group.

Facilities

Two modern toilet blocks include washbasins (some in cabins) and controllable hot showers (SEP key). Children's area. Baby room. Private bathroom (€ 50 p/w). Facilities for disabled visitors. Fully equipped laundry. Motorcaravan services. Shop, restaurant, takeaway, bar, indoor heated swimming pool with paddling pool (all 22/3-3/11). Fitness room (€ 2,50). Recreation hall. Climbing wall. Tennis. Trim court. Play area. Extensive animation programme in high season. WiFi over site (charged). Bicycle hire. Max. 2 dogs.

Open: All year.

Directions

From Alkmaar take N9 road towards Den Helder. Turn left towards Callantsoog on the N503 road and follow site signs. GPS: 52.846644, 4.715506

Charges 2013

Per unit incl. 2 persons and electricity (plus meter)	€ 17.00 - € 39.00
extra person	€ 4.50
electricity per kWh	€ 0.35

Castricum

Kennemer Duincamping Bakkum

Zeeweg 31, NL-1901 NZ Castricum aan Zee (Noord-Holland) T: 0251 661 091.
E: bakkum@kennemerduincampings.nl **alanrogers.com/NL6872**

Kennemer Duincamping Bakkum lies in a wooded area in the centre of a protected dune reserve. There are 1,800 pitches of which 400 are used for touring units. These pitches are spacious and 300 are equipped with electricity (10A Europlug). Mobile homes and seasonal units use the remaining pitches in separate areas of the site. For safety and tranquillity the majority of the site is kept free of cars. Family activities and special entertainment for children are arranged in high season. The dunes are accessible from the site and offer opportunities for walking and cycling, with the beach a walk of only 25 minutes.

Facilities

Three toilet blocks for tourers with toilets, washbasins in cabins, free, controllable showers and family rooms. Facilities for disabled visitors. Laundry area. Excellent supermarket, baker, fish shop and chicken shop. Snack bar and restaurant. Gas supplies. Play area. Sports pitch. Tennis. Bicycle hire. Activities for children and teens. WiFi (charged). Motorbikes and dogs are not accepted.

Open: 28 March - 27 October.

Directions

On the A9 between Alkmaar and Amsterdam take exit west onto the N203. Turn left onto the Zeeweg (N513) and after a few kilometres the site is on the right. GPS: 52.5614, 4.6331

Charges guide

Per unit incl. 4 persons and electricity	€ 31.70 - € 52.90
extra person (over 2 yrs)	€ 4.85

FREE Alan Rogers Travel Card
Extra benefits and savings - see page 12

Castricum

Kennemer Duincamping Geversduin

Beverwijkerstraatweg 205, NL-1901 NH Castricum (Noord-Holland) T: 0251 661 095.
E: geversduin@kennemerduincampings.nl **alanrogers.com/NL6862**

The comfortable, family site of Gerversduin lies in an area of forests and sand dunes. The site offers 614 pitches of which 221 are for touring units and 14 for accommodation to rent. With good shade and privacy, most of the pitches have 4/16A electricity connections. The pitches without electricity have a unique location and cars must be parked elsewhere. In high season, many activities are organised for youngsters including the unusual opportunity to join a forestry worker for the day. The beach is only 4 km. away and is easily accessible by bike or on foot.

Facilities

Four sanitary blocks with WCs, open style basins, preset hot showers and family shower rooms including baby room. Facilities for disabled visitors. Laundry with washing machines and dryers. Supermarket. Snack bar and café for meals with large terrace. Recreation area. Sports pitch. Play area. Bicycle hire. WiFi over part of site (charged). Safes. Only gas barbecues are permitted. Dogs only accepted in designated areas. Off site: Riding 0.5 km. Beach and fishing 4 km. Golf 9 km. Sailing 6 km.

Open: 27 March - 31 October.

Directions

On the A9 (Amsterdam-Alkmaar) take exit for the N203 and continue north towards Castricum. In Castricum follow signs to the station and from there drive south towards Heemskerk via the Beverwijkse straatweg. Site is south of Castricum and signed on the Beverwijkse straatweg. GPS: 52.53038, 4.64839

Charges guide

Per unit incl. 4 persons and electricity	€ 26.50 - € 38.95
extra person (over 2 yrs)	€ 4.00

De Cocksdorp

Camping De Krim Texel

Roggeslootweg 6, NL-1795 JV De Cocksdorp (Noord-Holland) T: 0222 390 111. E: info@krim.nl
alanrogers.com/NL6860

Camping De Krim Texel is an attractive, well maintained campsite which is open all year round. There are 650 pitches which include 400 for touring units and tents. All have electricity and 175 have electricity, water and drainage; there are 100 pitches with private sanitary facilities. There are separate areas for bungalows and mobile homes. The manager tells us that Texel records the lowest rainfall and the most hours of sunshine than any other part of the Netherlands. The site is 400 m. from the northern point of Texel, De Cocksdorp.

Facilities

Five excellent toilet blocks, all heated, include baby rooms, washbasins in cabins, showers (free), family showers and facilities for disabled visitors. Free dishwasher. Microwave. Motorcaravan service point. Gas supplies. Laundry. Three restaurants and snack bar. Large supermarket. Outdoor and indoor pools with slides. Sauna, massage, sunbeds. Riding. Minigolf. Bowling. Internet café. Indoor play paradise and play station. Tennis. Multisports court. Bicycle hire. Skelter track. Entertainment programme.

Open: All year.

Directions

From Amsterdam drive towards Den Helder on A9/N9 and take ferry to Texel. From the boat take N501 to north of island towards De Cocksdorp. Site is 500 m. from De Cocksdorp, signed on the left hand side. GPS: 53.15163, 4.85855

Charges guide

Per unit incl. 4 persons and electricity	€ 37.00 - € 41.00
extra person	€ 3.50

De Koog

Texelcamping De Shelter

Boodtlaan 43, NL-1796 BD De Koog (Noord-Holland) T: 0222 317 208. E: info@texelcampings.nl
alanrogers.com/NL6877

Camping De Shelter, on the island of Texel, is an all year site. There are just 70 pitches here, set out on small fields, surrounded by clusters of trees. Pitches are large (min. 100 sq.m) and equipped with electricity (16A), water and drainage, with little shade. The emphasis here is on peace and quiet, so there are no organised activities, except for children's entertainment in high season, shared with the sister site, Om de Noord, and relatively few amenities. Under 25s are not admitted unless accompanied by adults. The village of De Koog is within walking distance for shops and restaurants.

Facilities

One clean, modern toilet block has controllable, hot showers and some sinks in cubicles, two family shower rooms with baby bath, but no facilities for disabled visitors (these can be found at Om de Noord). Bread to order. Small playground. Boules. Football field. Children's entertainment (high season). High speed WiFi (charged). Tourist information. Cycling paths from site.

Open: All year.

Directions

Drive to Den Helder on A7 motorway. Directions to ferry are clearly signed. On Texel, follow signs to De Koog. In De Koog, continue until you see FC De Koog's football field with a road to the left, which leads to the site. GPS: 53.104202, 4.769547

Charges guide

Per unit incl. 2 persons and electricity (plus meter)	€ 17.00 - € 39.00

For latest campsite news, availability and prices visit

alanrogers.com

De Koog
Texelcamping Kogerstrand

Badweg 33, NL-1796 AA De Koog (Noord-Holland) T: 0222 317 208. E: info@texelcampings.nl

alanrogers.com/NL6850

A large, well managed site (divided into northern and southern areas), it is uniquely situated in the dunes and shrubs on the island of Texel. The unlevelled and numbered pitches are within five minutes walking distance of both the beach and the village. Cars are parked away from the pitches. A total of 1,200 pitches includes 1000 for tourers and 150 for seasonal caravans and tents. All caravan pitches have electricity and cable TV connections. Motorcaravans are only accepted outside July and August when they are placed in the parking area facing the dunes (with electricity). The large restaurant has an adjoining games and entertainment area, and prices are reasonable with families in mind.

Facilities

Seven clean, modern and heated buildings include washbasins in cabins, family bathrooms and showers on payment. Laundries with spin dryer and ironing board. Access to building by electronic card only. Restaurant/bar with takeaway, games and pool tables. Play area. Entertainment for children is organised during May holiday and high season. WiFi over site (charged). Raised barbecues allowed except in very hot weather. Parking in Texel: annual € 15 vignette or € 2.50/hour.

Open: 24 March - 27 October.

Directions

Take A9 from Amsterdam to Alkmaar, N9 to Den Helder and ferry signs to Texel, follow signs to De Koog, then site signs. GPS: 53.100934, 4.758464

Charges guide

Per unit incl. 2 persons and electricity	€ 10.00 - € 32.50
extra person (over 4 yrs)	€ 1.75 - € 3.10
dog	€ 4.00

Credit cards accepted up to € 50.

De Koog
Texelcamping Om de Noord

Boodtlaan 80, NL-1796 BG De Koog (Noord-Holland) T: 0222 317 208. E: info@texelcampings.nl

alanrogers.com/NL6879

Camping Om de Noord is located on the island of Texel, 900 m. from a sandy dune beach and is a friendly, family site within walking distance of the lively village of De Koog. There are 147 level, grassy touring pitches (average 100 sq.m) all equipped with electricity, water and drainage. Thirty-six comfort plus pitches have their own private sanitation facilities. This is a lively site for children in peak season with many games and activities organised for them.

Facilities

Modern and clean toilet block with family rooms. Facilities for disabled campers. Dishwasher. Launderette. Play area (up to 12 yrs). Activity and entertainment programme for children (high season). WiFi (charged). Texel parking scheme: annual vignette € 15 or € 2.50/h. Off site: Shops and restaurants in De Koog. Beach 900 m. Fishing and riding 2 km. Sailing 5 km. Golf 10 km. Walking and cycle tracks across Texel. Boat trips for seal spotting and shrimping. Guided sand walking (low tide).

Open: 22 March - 27 October.

Directions

Drive to Den Helder on A7 motorway. Directions to the ferry are clearly indicated. On Texel, follow signs towards De Koog. In De Koog, continue until you see FC De Koog's football field with a road to the left, which leads to the site. Check in at sister site (signed). GPS: 53.10317, 4.771076

Charges guide

Per unit incl. 2 persons and electricity (plus meter)	€ 17.00 - € 39.00

No credit cards.

Groote Keeten
Camping Callassande

Voorweg 5A, NL-1759 NX Groote Keeten (Noord-Holland) T: 0224 581 663. E: info@callassande.nl

alanrogers.com/NL6876

Callassande is a popular family run site 900 metres from a sandy beach and welcomes families with teenagers. The 500 grassy pitches include 340 for tourers; half are 89 sq.m. with electricity (10A) and TV point, the other half are slightly larger and also have water and drainage. The indoor heated pool (charged) is fun for everyone with a large chute, a jacuzzi, a special paddling area and an opening roof for sunny days. There is a children's play area adjacent to the pool with a pirate ship, a climbing dome and trampolines. Parents of young children should be aware of the canals around the edge of the site.

Facilities

Three, clean, modern toilet blocks have some washbasins in cubicles, family showers, baby rooms and facilities for disabled visitors. Launderette. Shop (mornings and w/ends in low season). Bar/restaurant. Covered swimming pool with water slides. Play area. Internet café. Tennis. Bicycle hire. Sports field. Skateboard park. Tourist information. Activity programme. WiFi over site (charged). Accommodation for rent. Off site: Sandy beach 900 m.

Open: 1 April - 28 October.

Directions

Head north from Alkmaar on N9 (towards Den Helder) as far as Zand. Here, follow signs to Groote Keeten and the site. GPS: 52.856165, 4.71719

Charges guide

Per unit incl. 2 persons and electricity	€ 24.00 - € 39.50
extra person	€ 4.40
dog	€ 3.00

FREE Alan Rogers Travel Card
Extra benefits and savings - see page 12

Julianadorp aan Zee

Camping 't Noorder Sandt

Noorder Sandt 2, NL-1787 CX Julianadorp aan Zee (Noord-Holland) T: 0223 641 266.

E: noordersandt@ardoer.com **alanrogers.com/NL6866**

Close to the marine city of Den Helder and about 600 m. from a wide, sandy beach is Camping 't Noorder Sandt. Adjacent to the site is the Duinvliet, a route for hikers, cyclists and horse riders – you can even do the route in a canoe! Both open and shady pitches are available here. They are comfortable and are all equipped with 10A electricity, water, drainage and cable connections. Also worth noting is the friendly atmosphere here and also the well maintained sanitary facilities. For many, the site's main attraction is its sub-tropical paradise pool complex. In the early mornings, it is only open for older people to start the day, and after 10am it is open to all. Clean air, space and relaxation are only a few of the site's advantages. You could go for a walk on the Wad, try a spot of sea fishing, or take an excursion to one of the Dutch islands. The site is not far from the famous city of Alkmaar with its cheese market, and the Dutch capital of Amsterdam. Member of the Ardoer group.

Facilities

Two good toilet blocks with controllable hot showers and open style washbasins. Facilities for disabled campers. Laundry with washing machines and dryers. Kiosk for basics. Café/bar for small meals. Indoor pool with fun pool and slide. Fishing. Riding. Bicycle hire. Canoes for hire. Entertainment team in high season. Off site: Boat launching, beach and sailing 600 m. Alkmaar and Amsterdam are close.

Open: 26 March - 26 October.

Directions

From the N9 take exit for Julianadorp and Julianadorp aan Zee. From Julianadorp follow the site signs. Site is to the north of Julianadorp aan Zee. GPS: 52.90667, 4.72499

Charges guide

Per unit incl. 2 persons	
and electricity	€ 28.08 - € 34.78
extra person (over 2 yrs)	€ 5.26
pet	€ 3.25

ADRESS Noordersandt 2
1787 CX Julianadorp aan Zee
The Netherlands
TEL +31 223 641 266
www.ardoer.com/noordersandt

't Noorder Sandt
CAMPING FUN FOR FAMILY AND PETS

Sint-Maartenszee

Camping Sint-Maartenszee

Westerduinweg 30, NL-1753 BA Sint-Maartenszee (Noord-Holland) T: 0224 561 401.

E: info@campingsintmaartenszee.nl **alanrogers.com/NL5740**

Situated within easy travelling distance of the attractive and interesting towns of North Holland, especially Alkmaar, this excellent family site is separated from the sea by 900 m. of grassy dunes. With the dune environment, the ground is basically sandy but grass has grown well and hedges are now established. Specialising in family holidays, unusually for the Netherlands only touring units are taken (with a bungalow park adjacent). The 300 pitches are arranged in lines backed by high hedging. All have 6A electricity and 110 are fully serviced with water, drainage and cable TV connections. A good restaurant/bar has an attractive terrace.

Facilities

Two modern toilet blocks are in neat, low buildings. Hot water for showers is free (with a fascinating panel demonstrating how solar power helps to heat the water). Private washing cabins, family shower rooms, baby bathrooms and raised level showers for children. Three private bathrooms to rent. Kitchen room with hot water on payment and microwave. Laundry room with washing machines and dryer on payment. Motorcaravan services. Gas supplies. Shop. Restaurant/bar, takeaway (all season). Bicycle hire. Play areas. Minigolf. Recreation room. WiFi (charged). Off site: Fishing 1 km. Bus service from village to Alkmaar (cheese market Fridays April-Sept).

Open: 22 March - 29 September.

Directions

From Alkmaar, take N9 northwards towards Den Helder. Site is signed after 18 km. towards the sea at St Maartensvlotbrug. GPS: 52.79428, 4.68835

Charges guide

Per unit incl. 2 persons	
and electricity	€ 22.20 - € 40.40
extra person (over 2 yrs)	€ 4.00

No credit cards.

For latest campsite news, availability and prices visit

alanrogers.com

Tuitjenhorn

Campingpark De Bongerd

Bongerdlaan 3, NL-1747 CA Tuitjenhorn (Noord-Holland) T: 0226 391 481. E: info@bongerd.nl

alanrogers.com/NL5705

Campingpark De Bongerd is an attractive, child friendly site with 550 pitches. Of these, 159 are for touring units arranged separately from static units and seasonal pitches in a former orchard. The grass touring areas are immaculately kept with 10A electricity, drainage and cable TV connections. Some of the pitches are smaller than others. The main attraction at this site is a large indoor play hall, De Holle Bolle Boom, which is where the enthusiastic entertainment team is based. There are ponds for adventure play with floating games and small beaches, and an open-air pool (10x15 m) with paddling pool. In high season and school holidays the site organises an extensive activity programme.

Facilities

Modern toilet block with preset, hot showers (free), washbasins (open and in cabins) and toilets. Toilets and basins for children. Fully equipped baby room. Laundry with washing machines and dryers. Shop, restaurants and bar (April-Sept). Swimming and paddling pools. Indoor play hall and several outdoor play areas. Playing field. Tennis. Boules. Bicycle hire. Fishing. Entertainment programme. Internet and WiFi over site (charged). Off site: Beach, golf and riding 10 km.

Open: 5 April - 30 September.

Directions

Site is north of Tuitjenhorn, which is some 15 km. north of Alkmaar. It is well signed on the N245 road to Schagen. GPS: 52.735064, 4.774407

Charges guide

Per unit incl. 2-5 persons and all services	€ 28.90 - € 46.50
extra person	€ 3.50 - € 5.40
dog	€ 2.35

Camping Cheques accepted.

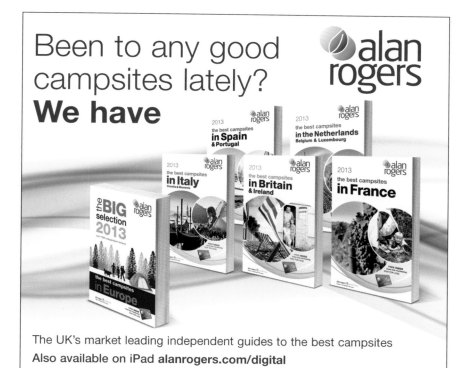

FREE Alan Rogers Travel Card
Extra benefits and savings - see page 12

Overijssel sits on sandy soil dissected by rivers and streams, except in the northwest, where polders and lakes dominate. It has three regions: Kop van Overijssel, Twente and Salland.

CAPITAL: ZWOLLE

The meandering IJssel river carves a route through the classic landscape of Holland; past beaches, ports and the unswerving lines of the Mastenbroek polder, one of the oldest in the Netherlands. The flood plains stand in sharp contrast to the Hanseatic towns of Kampen, Zwolle, Deventer and Hasselt; beautiful towns on shimmering water, where monuments from the past stand proudly in a contemporary setting. Salland, a lesser known part of eastern Holland, is a paradise for cyclists with romantic castles, tree-lined roads and traditional farms.

Weerribben-Wieden National Park is the principal low-lying marshland of Northwest Europe – an endless maze of narrow strips of water, mysterious forests and swampy reed beds. Twente is the country seat of the Netherlands, where historic towns and villages, and impressive estates such as Twickel and Weldam now stand alongside the newer wellness resorts. In the peaceful Vechtdal, with its Saxon farmhouses and ancient forests, nature imposes her own unique atmosphere of verdant tranquillity.

Places of interest

Giethoorn: 'Green Venice' where electric boats glide silently through the water and under the characteristic high bridges.

Kampen: city of monuments with no less than 500 examples including old and new town halls, the new tower and three city gates.

Zwolle: founded in the 9th century, with many historic buildings dating from the 15th century - the golden age of Zwolle.

Hattem: old town with historic buildings, the Anton Pieck Museum and the National Bakery Museum.

Industrial heritage in Twente: cycling and walking trails taking in buildings used in the textile and metal industries.

Delden: Salt Museum – all you need to know about salt, including that it is extracted at the nearby Twickel estate.

Attractions

Slagharen: discover and enjoy over 40 attractions including shows and parades in this family adventure park.

Estate Anningahof: sculpture park on the edge of Zwolle with new exhibitions annually.

Hellendoorn: adventure park with more than 30 attractions, including a new show based on the Excalibur legend.

De Holterberg: part of the Sallandse Ridge National Park with nature diorama, museum, Canadian war cemetery, minigolf and five restaurants.

De Scheg sports complex: superb swimming facility with adventure river, bubbles, 80 m. water slide, etc.

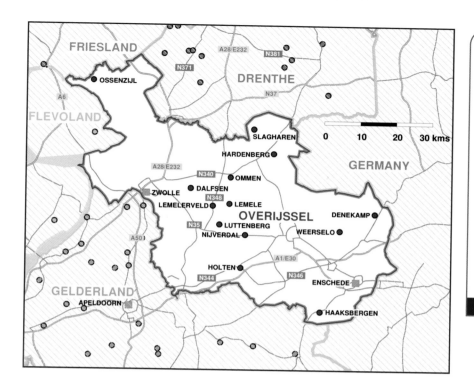

Dalfsen

Vechtdalcamping Het Tolhuis

Het Lageveld 8, NL-7722 HV Dalfsen (Overijssel) T: 0529 458 383. E: info@tolhuis.com

alanrogers.com/NL6000

Vechtdalcamping Het Tolhuis is a pleasant, well established site with 195 pitches. Of these, 70 are for tourers, arranged on well kept, grassy lawns off paved and gravel access roads. All touring pitches have 4-10A electricity, water, waste water, cable and WiFi. Some are shaded by mature trees and bushes. The touring pitches are located apart from static units. To the rear of the site is an open-air pool (25x8 m; heated by solar power) with a small paddling pool for toddlers and new attractive terracing.

Facilities

Two heated toilet blocks, an immaculate new one to the front and an older one to the back, with toilets, washbasins (open style and in cabins) and controllable hot showers (key). Some rain and body showers. Special, attractive children's section. Family shower rooms. Baby room. Laundry. Small shop (bread daily). Restaurant/bar also serves snacks and drinks. Open-air pool with paddling pool. Playing field. Playground and trampoline. Entertainment team for children (high season). ATM point. WiFi over site (charged). Gas barbecues only. Dogs are not accepted in high season. Off site: Riding 3 km. Fishing 5 km. Golf 7 km.

Open: 1 April - 1 October.

Directions

From the A28 take exit 21 and continue east towards Dalfsen. Site is signed in Dalfsen. GPS: 52.50228, 6.3224

Charges guide

Per unit incl. 2 persons and electricity	€ 20.75 - € 32.50
extra person	€ 3.50
dog (not high season)	€ 4.00

No credit cards.

alan rogers
Winner 2012 Awards

Denekamp
Camping De Papillon

Kanaalweg 30, NL-7591 NH Denekamp (Overijssel) T: 0541 351 670. E: info@depapillon.nl

alanrogers.com/NL6470

De Papillon is perhaps one of the best and most enjoyable campsites in the Netherlands. All 245 touring pitches are spacious (120-160 sq.m), all have electricity (4/10/16A), and 220 have water and drainage. An impressive, new sanitary block has state-of-the-art equipment and uses green technology. There is a new entertainment centre with outdoor auditorium for children, and the water play area by the adventure playground and covered, heated pool is among the most imaginative and exciting we have seen. The restored heathland area offers opportunities for nature lovers; there is also a large fishing lake and a swimming lake with beach area and activities. A member of Leading Campings group.

Facilities
Two large sanitary buildings (one new for 2012) with showers, toilets, washbasins in cabins, facilities for babies and disabled visitors. Laundry room. Spacious reception area with supermarket, restaurant, bar and takeaway. Heated pool with children's pool and sliding roof. Lake swimming with sandy beach. Play areas. Pétanque. Bicycle hire. Fishing pond. Tennis. Max. 1 dog. Bungalows to rent. Water spray park (up to 13 yrs). Free WiFi over site.

Open: 1 April - 1 October.

Directions
From the A1 take exit 32 (Oldenzaal-Denekamp) and continue to Denekamp. Pass Denekamp and turn right at village of Noord-Deurningen and follow signs to site. GPS: 52.39200, 7.04900

Charges guide
Per unit incl. 2 persons and 4A electricity	€ 27.00
incl. full services	€ 30.25
extra person	€ 4.25

Haaksbergen
Vakantiepark 't Stien'n Boer

Scholtenhagenweg 42, NL-7481 VP Haaksbergen (Overijssel) T: 0535 722 610. E: info@stien-nboer.nl

alanrogers.com/NL6010

Deep in the Twente countryside, this is a pleasant site with 125 grass pitches. Some are in secluded settings, others in open fields, all numbered and with 6A electricity. Much emphasis is put on facilities for children with several play areas situated throughout the site. A large indoor play area on sand is ideally located next to the restaurant/bar. A small heated swimming pool has a separate area for children. The comfortable bar and restaurant opens according to visitor numbers. It is also possible to find a quiet corner and just enjoy the beautiful surroundings.

Facilities
One older and three newer, well located toilet blocks. All were clean when visited. Large controllable hot showers (on payment). Good room containing baths and showers for children. Washing machine and dryers. Shop (all season). Restaurant, bar and takeaway. Outdoor heated pool. Entertainment programme in season. Multi-purpose all weather sports pitch. Indoor pool complex (all year). Minigolf. Boules. Pedal go-karts. WiFi over site (charged).

Open: 1 April - 25 October.

Directions
From the A1 take exit 28 (Goor). Follow the N347 to Haaksbergen and site is signed from the village. GPS: 52.140067, 6.724405

Charges guide
Per unit incl. 2 persons and electricity	€ 19.50 - € 27.50
extra person	€ 3.25
dog (max. 2)	€ 2.50
No credit cards.	

Hardenberg
Camping De Zandstuve

Grose Beltenweg 3, NL-7794 RA Rheeze-Hardenberg (Overijssel) T: 0523 262 027. E: info@zandstuve.nl

alanrogers.com/NL5995

De Zandstuve rightly promotes itself as a holiday village for children. Amenities include an attractively decorated indoor pool with two fun pools (one in forest style, the other as a shipwreck), an outdoor pool, little play areas on most fields and a giant indoor play castle. Large, grassy, circular meadows surrounded by mature trees (which provide some shade in summer) provide 400 pitches with 380 used for touring units. All have 4/10A electricity, most have a water tap and 120 full service pitches include electricity, water, drain and TV aerial point. There is also a full entertainment programme in high season with theatre and musical nights.

Facilities
Three modern toilet blocks with toilets, washbasins (open and in cabins) and controllable hot showers. Family rooms with basin and 3 showers. Baby room. Washing machines and dryers. Motorcaravan services. Shop. Bar/restaurant and takeaway. Heated indoor and outdoor pools. Play areas and indoor play castle (€ 5). Entertainment in high season for children. Internet access (free). Dogs only accepted in some areas. No single sex groups.

Open: 1 April - 1 October.

Directions
From Zwolle follow N340 road east towards Ommen and from there the N34 east towards Hardenberg. Site is signed 2 km. from Hardenberg. GPS: 52.55862, 6.58761

Charges guide
Per unit incl. 2 persons and electricity	€ 22.75 - € 40.50
extra person	€ 4.00 - € 5.00

For latest campsite news, availability and prices visit
alanrogers.com

Ommen

Camping De Roos

Beerzerweg 10, NL-7736 PJ Beerze-Ommen (Overijssel) T: 0523 251 234. E: info@campingderoos.nl

alanrogers.com/NL5980

De Roos is a family run site in an Area of Outstanding Natural Beauty, truly a nature lovers' campsite, immersed in an atmosphere of tranquillity. It is situated in Overijssel's Vecht Valley, a unique region set in a river dune landscape on the River Vecht. The river and its tributary wind their way unhurriedly around and through this spacious campsite. It is a natural setting that the owners of De Roos have carefully preserved. The 285 pitches and necessary amenities have been blended into the landscape with great care. Pitches, most with electricity hook-up (6A Europlug), are naturally sited, some behind blackthorn thickets, in the shadow of an old oak, or in a clearing scattered with wild flowers. For some there are lovely views over the Vecht river. De Roos is a car-free campsite during peak periods – vehicles must be parked at the car park, except on arrival and departure. Motorcaravan owners can drive to their pitch then cycle or walk for the duration of their holiday. Vehicles are allowed on site in low season at extra cost. Swimming, fishing and boating are possible in the river, or from an inlet that runs up into the site where there is a small beach with a protected area for swimming and landing stages with steps.

Facilities

Four well maintained sanitary blocks are kept fresh and clean. The two larger blocks are heated and include baby bath/shower and wash cabins. Launderette. Motorcaravan services. Gas supplies. Health food shop and tea room serving snacks (1/5-1/9). Bicycle hire. Boules. Several small playgrounds and field for kite flying. Sports field. Football. Volleyball. River swimming. Fishing. Internet access (charged). Dogs are not accepted. Torch useful.

Open: 12 April - 30 September.

Directions

Leave A28 at Ommen exit 21, join N340 for 19 km. to Ommen. Turn right at traffic lights over bridge and immediately left on local road towards Beerze. Site on left after 7 km. GPS: 52.51075, 6.515059

Charges 2013

Per unit incl. 2 persons and electricity	€ 18.50 - € 21.50
extra person	€ 3.10 - € 3.80

www.campingderoos.nl
Beerzerweg 10 • 7736 PJ Beerze-Ommen • Overijssel • Netherlands

Ommen

Vrijetijdspark Beerze Bulten

Kampweg 1, NL-7736 PK Beerze-Ommen (Overijssel) T: 0523 251 398. E: info@beerzebulten.nl

alanrogers.com/NL5985

Beerze Bulten is a large leisure park which is open all year and has superb indoor and outdoor amenities, so you can enjoy yourself whatever the weather. A large, partly underground 'rabbit hole' provides a big indoor playground for children, a theatre for both indoor and outdoor shows, a buffet, a superb full wellness spa and a very large, specially designed indoor pool. Beerze Bulten has 550 pitches, mainly for touring units, but also accommodation for hire (all year). In the shade of mature woodland, all the pitches are level and numbered, and all have 10A Europlug electricity, water, drainage and TV connections. To the rear of the site is a large lake area with a sandy beach and new, exciting adventure play equipment.

Facilities

Several toilet blocks, well placed around the site, with toilets, washbasins in cabins and hot showers. Laundry. Shop. Bar and snack bar/restaurant with open-air terrace. Heated indoor and outdoor pool complex and spa centre. Multisports court. Bicycle hire. Indoor playground and theatre. Playgrounds. WiFi over site (charged). Full entertainment team in season and school holidays. Dogs only allowed on some fields.

Open: April - November.

Directions

From A28, take exit 21 (Ommen) and continue east towards Ommen. From Ommen, follow N34 northeast and turn south on N36 at crossing. Site is signed from there. GPS: 52.51139, 6.54618

Charges guide

Per unit incl. 2 persons and full service pitch	€ 23.00 - € 45.30
extra person	€ 4.00 - € 5.20
dog	€ 3.50

FREE Alan Rogers Travel Card
Extra benefits and savings - see page 12

Ossenzijl

Recreatiecentrum De Kluft

Hoogeweg 26, NL-8376 EM Ossenzijl (Overijssel) T: 0561 477 370. E: info@dekluft.nl

alanrogers.com/NL6230

De Kluft is located on the border of the two Dutch provinces of Friesland and Overijssel at the heart of the Weerribben-Wieden National Park. It is attractively situated with most of the pitches being along open waterways. The site has a very impressive range of amenities including a marina, hotel, restaurant, lodges. One area of the site is close to the marina and canoes, electric boats, rowing boats and bicycles can all be hired. Most of the 180 touring pitches have a view across the water (drainage variable) and all have electrical connections (6A). Children will be entertained by a very well designed play area, and at the small beach by a natural lake that is suitable for swimming.

Facilities

Five toilet blocks, four modern and one older one, are spread over the site. They are clean and well maintained with showers (on payment) and facilities for children and disabled visitors. Indoor dishwashing and laundry sinks. Motorcaravan service point. Shop (May-Aug). Restaurant and snack bar. Swimming in river and lake. Canoe school. Fishing. Bicycles, canoes, kayaks and sloops for hire. Eight-room hotel. Lodges to rent. WiFi (charged).

Open: 1 April - 30 October.

Directions

From A6 motorway take exit 15 (De Munt) and follow N331 and N352 towards Wolvega. Turn right in Kuinre and after 1.5 km. left to Ossenzijl (5 km). Site is clearly signed. GPS: 52.80785, 5.93188

Charges guide

Per unit incl. 2 persons and electricity	€ 21.55
extra person	€ 4.20
child (3-11 yrs)	€ 2.30
dog	€ 3.35

Slagharen

Camping Attractiepark Slagharen

Knappersveldweg 3, NL-7776 PA Slagharen (Overijssel) T: 0523 683 000. E: info@attractiepark-slagharen.nl

alanrogers.com/NL6450

The main attraction of Camping Attractiepark Slagharen is its location beside a theme park, where visitors staying on the site have free access to the attractions. Here you will also find a large supermarket, clothes shops and the Crazy Horse Saloon, as well as American and Chinese restaurants. The site itself only has a snack bar and the Sitting Bull Saloon where discos and country evenings are organised. All 260 reasonably spacious touring pitches are level and on grass with 10A electricity. They are partly separated by hedges, though generally with an open aspect.

Facilities

One modern toilet building with toilets, washbasins (open and in cabins) and spacious showers. Family showers and baby room. Facilities for disabled visitors. Launderette. Motorcaravan service point. Bar and snack bar (many snack and restaurant amenities at the theme park). Adventure playground. Limited entertainment. Free entrance to theme park. Max. 1 dog per pitch.
Off site: Bicycle hire 500 m. Riding 5 km.

Open: 29 March - 25 October.

Directions

From A28 between Zwolle and Meppel take exit 22 Nieuwleusen/Dedemsvaart and follow signs to Slagharen. The site is just past the entrance to the Attraction Park on the other side of the road. Look for Wigwam Wereld sign. GPS: 52.63100, 6.54000

Charges guide

Per 8 days, 4 persons incl. tent or caravan	€ 145.00 - € 329.00
Min. 2 nights.	

Weerselo

Camping De Molenhof

Kleijsenweg 7, NL-7667 RS Reutum/Weerselo (Overijssel) T: 0541 661 165. E: info@demolenhof.nl

alanrogers.com/NL6480

De Molenhof is a pleasant family site which generally caters for children under 12 rather than teenagers. It has 450 well laid out pitches of which 430 are for touring units, all with water, drainage, electricity (10A) and cable connections. Children will enjoy themselves in the covered, adventure playground or the two heated swimming pools (one outdoor, one covered) with a large slide on the outside. The entertainment team provides a full daily programme in high season, including theatre nights in De Hooischuur, a specially designed entertainment hall.

Facilities

Four toilet blocks, three fairytale themed for children, provide washbasins (open style and in cabins), controllable showers, bathrooms and a baby room. Facilities for disabled visitors. Launderette. Motorcaravan service. Well stocked shop. Bar/restaurant. Pancake restaurant. Swimming pools (outdoor, 26/4-1/9: indoor all season). Playgrounds (1 covered). Sports court. All-weather sports area. Fishing. Bicycle and go-kart hire. Boules. Extensive entertainment programme in high season. WiFi over site.

Open: 29 March - 29 September.

Directions

Follow A1 from Amsterdam east to Hengelo and take exit 31, Hengelo Noord. Go through Deurningen to Weerselo and from there the N343 towards Tubbergen and site signs. GPS: 52.36200, 6.81400

Charges 2013

Per unit incl. 2 persons and electricity	€ 18.50 - € 39.00
extra person	€ 5.00
Camping Cheques accepted.	

For latest campsite news, availability and prices visit

alanrogers.com

Utrecht, the smallest province of the Netherlands, has plenty to offer the visitor in regions such as the Utrecht Hill Ridge, its very own Lake District, the Vecht and the rural Green Heart. Notable cities are Utrecht and Amersfoort.

CAPITAL: UTRECHT

The suburbs of Utrecht merge with commuter towns such as Nieuwegein and Houten in the south and Maarssen in the north. Southwest of this urban area is rural Lopikerwaard and northwest, the peat-rich lands of Vinkeveen and Mijdrecht. North of the city of Utrecht are the River Vecht and the Loosdrecht Lakes, two of the region's most popular recreational areas.

The eastern part of the province is bisected by the Utrecht Hill Ridge. Along the southern flank of the old glacial moraine are leafy oases like Zeist and Doorn. Between the hills and the Rhine lies the rural district of Kromme-Rijn, centre of fruit cultivation with Wijk bij Duurstede at its heart. On the other side of the hills lies the Gelderland Valley with the town of Veenendaal. The northeast corner of the province is occupied by the city of Amersfoort and the Eemland polder. At the former Zuiderzee you'll find the archetypal town of Bunschoten-Spakenburg.

Places of interest

Utrecht: city with narrow streets, interesting shops, lively squares and canals and the imposing Dom Tower; Central Museum with a wide variety of exhibitions.

Amersfoort: Museum Flehite, Armando Museum, Mondriaan House, Eem harbour, a brewery and a children's farm.

Langbroek: rural village and site of the first 'donjons' built in the 12th century; several castles.

Oudewater: charming historic town featuring witches scales, a rope factory and museum.

Wijk bij Duurstede: located on the shores of the River Lek with many attractions, including Duurstede Castle, a church with flat-roofed tower, and the world's only drive-through windmill.

Attractions

Boat Cruises: shipping company Schuttevaer provides year-round tourist and party cruises, in and around the city of Utrecht.

Makeblijde Gardens: landscape design park featuring 16 modern gardens, including a jungle and a Zen garden.

Dick Bruna House: displays of work by Bruna, Dutch author, illustrator and creator of the internationally famous Miffy, the little rabbit.

Amersfoort Zoo: home to over 1,000 animals and 130 species.

Kasteel Huis Doorn: late 18th-century renovated castle, located in a beautiful wooded park, best known as the home of Germany's ex-emperor William II.

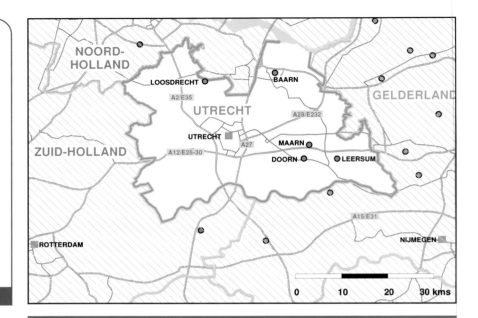

Baarn
Allurepark Zeven Linden
Zevenlindenweg 4, NL-3744 BC Baarn (Utrecht) T: 0356 668 330. E: info@dezevenlinden.nl
alanrogers.com/NL6824

Zeven Linden was created in 1938 and since then has been a popular site for those seeking a peaceful holiday in a natural setting. There are 261 spacious touring pitches (6-10A electricity), some shaded by trees, and spread over 13 separate fields. They are large and grassy, mostly with electrical connections. Unusually, the whole area is car free, which goes a long way to ensuring peace and quiet, as well as improving safety for children around the site. Within walking distance are Drakensteyn castle, Soestdijk palace and the beautiful village of Lage Vuursche.

Facilities

Modern, child friendly and spacious toilet blocks (two heated in low season). Two blocks have special family rooms with family showers and a separate children's area. Special facilities for disabled visitors. Washing machine and dryer. Small shop (bread daily). Snack bar/takeaway (weekends in low season). Small field with animals. Football pitch. WiFi over site (charged). Hut forest.

Open: 31 March - 17 October.

Directions

Approaching from the west, site is well signed from the N415 Hilversum-Baarn road shortly before reaching the intersection with the N221.
GPS: 52.19652, 5.24747

Charges guide

Per unit incl. 2 persons, water and electricity € 24.15
extra person € 3.00

Doorn
RCN Het Grote Bos
Hydeparklaan 24, NL-3941 ZK Doorn (Utrecht) T: 0343 513 644. E: hetgrotebos@rcn.nl
alanrogers.com/NL6828

Het Grote Bos (the large forest) is ideally located for a tranquil woodland holiday, but is also an ideal base to explore the western part of the Netherlands, or for visits to Amsterdam, Utrecht and Amersfoort. The site is located in the grounds of a former estate called Hydepark, and the prevailing atmosphere still reflects this parkland setting. Touring fields with 270 pitches are surrounded by high trees and are marked out by shrubs and hedges. Amenities include a heated outdoor pool complex with slides.

Facilities

There are six toilet blocks around the site. Launderette. Restaurant, café/bar, takeaway. Bakery and supermarket. Motorcaravan services. Heated outdoor pool with lazy river, water slides, children's pool and sunbathing area. Sports hall. Picnic area. Various themed play areas (such as a butterfly garden). Fitness trail. Tennis courts. Minigolf. Basketball. Bicycle and go-kart hire. Mobile homes and chalets to rent. WiFi throughout (charged). Torches useful.

Open: April - October.

Directions

From A12 take Driebergen/Rijsenburg exit and turn right on N225 towards Driebergen/Rijsenburg. Turn left after 200 m. (Loolaan), then (600 m) take second exit on the roundabout. Turn left in 2.5 km. on Hydeparklaan to site. GPS: 52.056117, 5.313716

Charges guide

Per unit incl. 2 persons
and electricity € 22.80 - € 34.05

For latest campsite news, availability and prices visit
alanrogers.com

Leersum

Molecaten Park Landgoed Ginkelduin

Scherpenzeelseweg 53, NL-3956 KD Leersum (Utrecht) T: 0343 489 999.
E: landgoedginkelduin@molecaten.nl **alanrogers.com/NL6827**

The Ginkelduin estate is located within the woods of the Utrechtse Heuvelrug National Park. The park extends over 95 ha. and is an Area of Outstanding Natural Beauty consisting of woodland, moors and drifting sands. The car-free estate includes this high quality campsite, a member of the Molecaten group, with generously sized pitches (225 for touring with 10A electricity) fringed with mature trees. There is plenty here for children, including indoor and outdoor swimming pools, a large football pitch and a special ten-pin bowling area. A number of fully equipped tents and bungalows are for rent.

Facilities

Two large, centrally located toilet blocks with open style washbasins and some in cabins. Controllable showers and family shower room. Baby bathroom. Good facilities for disabled visitors. Restaurant. Bamboo garden with brasserie, snack bar and supermarket. Indoor swimming pool with whirlpool and Turkish bath, solarium. Heated outdoor swimming pool (8/5-2/9) with slide, paddling pool and sunbathing area. Tennis. Sports field. Playgrounds. Minigolf. Bowling alleys. Bicycle hire. Information kiosk. WiFi over site (charged). Children's entertainment. No dogs.

Open: 29 March - 1 November.

Directions

From A12 motorway exit 22 follow signs to Woudenberg, Leersum and Maarsbergen. Continue on N225 as far as Leersum. After 1 km. turn left on Bentincklaan. Site is well signed from here. GPS: 52.028336, 5.457705

Charges 2013

Per unit incl. 2 persons, water and electricity	€ 22.50 - € 42.00
extra person	€ 3.90

No credit cards.

Loosdrecht

Recreatiecentrum Mijnden

Bloklaan 22A, NL-1231 AZ Loosdrecht (Utrecht) T: 0294 233 165. E: info@mijnden.nl
alanrogers.com/NL6830

Mijnden is in a central position in the Vechtstreek, one of the most beautiful parts of the Netherlands. The Recreatiecentrum is located amidst typically Dutch countryside alongside the River Drecht and close to cities such as Amsterdam, Utrecht and Hilversum. The site has 120 level pitches for tourers, some on hardstanding, all with 10A electricity and 20 with water and drainage. The pitches are on grassy fields and almost all provide lovely views over the lake. There are also 80 seasonal pitches. The site has its own boat slipway so you could bring your own boat and navigate the Loosdrechtse Plassen. The waterfront is not fenced or gated.

Facilities

Three modern, heated sanitary blocks with showers on payment, washbasins, toilets and facilities for disabled visitors. Launderette. Motorcaravan service point. Gas. Supermarket (1/4-15/9). Restaurant and snack bar (1/4-1/10). A natural paddling pond, fed by spring water, with a beach area. New play area. Sports field. Boat slipway. Children's entertainment in high season. Fishing. Bicycle hire. Caravan storage. WiFi throughout (charged).

Open: 7 April - 30 September.

Directions

Take A2 from Utrecht towards Amsterdam. Exit for Hilversum and after bridge turn right. Drive through village of Loenen and turn left to site. GPS: 52.20260, 5.03013

Charges guide

Per unit incl. 2 persons and electricity	€ 21.00 - € 26.00
extra person	€ 5.00

Maarn

Allurepark Laag Kanje

Laan V Laagkanje 1, NL-3951 KD Maarn (Utrecht) T: 0343 441 348. E: allurepark@laagkanje.nl
alanrogers.com/NL6832

This is a perfect region for a hospitable stay in a wooded and hilly environment, still dominated by peace and quiet, space and style. Originally part of a great estate, Allurecamping Laag Kanje has been developed into a top quality campsite over the last 40 years with the unusual, but attractive feature that cars are not allowed in the camping area. This is a spacious site with a relaxed and tranquil atmosphere. There are 800 pitches in total, mainly for privately owned mobile homes, 150 are available for touring with 5A electricity. The park is at the heart of the forest, so sandy beaches may be the last thing you would expect. However, there is a fine sandy beach nearby, which surrounds a beautiful swimming lake.

Facilities

Modern toilet blocks with special facilities for children and disabled visitors. Laundry facilities. Motorcaravan services. Small restaurant and snack bar. Well stocked shop with fresh produce daily. Entertainment and activity programme. Bicycle hire. WiFi throughout (charged). No dogs.

Open: 1 April - 1 October.

Directions

Heading south from Amersfoort on N227 towards Doorn, site is well signed shortly before arrival at the village of Maarn. GPS: 52.07724, 5.37932

Charges guide

Per unit incl. 2 persons and electricity	€ 22.50
extra person	€ 2.50

No credit cards.

FREE Alan Rogers Travel Card
Extra benefits and savings - see page 12

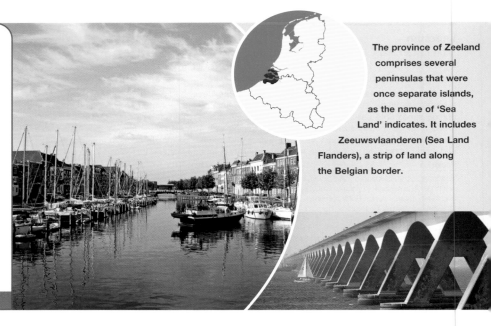

Zeeland

The province of Zeeland comprises several peninsulas that were once separate islands, as the name of 'Sea Land' indicates. It includes Zeeuwsvlaanderen (Sea Land Flanders), a strip of land along the Belgian border.

CAPITAL: MIDDELBURG

Zeeland sits mainly on clay intersected with canals and former creeks, while the south of the region is sandy. Outside the dykes, the land is mainly salt marshes and mud flats, while along the coast there are dunes; the largest can be seen on Schouwen-Duiveland, the north coast of Walcheren, and in the south. Despite the impact of the war and the demolition of many old buildings in the 'fifties and 'sixties, the capital Middelburg still has over 1,200 communal and national monuments, most notably the gothic Town Hall, the abbey with its 'Long John' tower, and the Arsenal.

Zeeland has the cleanest beaches in the Netherlands as well as the most sunshine. The vast polders etch straight lines into the landscape, but also visible are the outlines of ancient, jagged polders nestling between small dykes. Reminders of Zeeland's fascinating history are everywhere: fossilised sharks' teeth on the beach, magnificent merchants' houses from the Golden Age, and echoes of the dramatic floods of 1953. It's a wonderful region for hiking, cycling, skating and riding along the dunes, beaches and flower-clad dykes, but also for exploring the mudflats and salt marshes.

Places of interest

Veere: one of Zeeland's most beautiful old cities with historic church, 15th-century town hall, Campveerse tower; cafés and restaurants.

Goeree-Overflakkee: the Grevelingen Dam and the Brouwersdam are wonderful for swimming, (kite) surfing, diving, fishing and sailing; Ouddorp and Middelharnis have a good selection of shops.

Colijnsplaat: a paradise for fish lovers; modern fishing port and fascinating fish auction every Thursday; fishermen's festivals in August are an absolute must!

Borssele: attractive, symmetrical village of tree-lined streets, lawns and beautiful old houses; the 'Mountain of Troy' mound – a remnant of the castle of the once powerful lords of Borssele (c.1243); early 18th-century working corn mill, open Saturdays.

Attractions

Delta Park Neeltje Jans: centre for nature, culture and technology with films and exhibitions showing the catastrophic floods of 1953 and the world famous Delta Works sea defences.

Vuurtorens: Breskens, Westkapelle and Haamstede have beautiful old lighthouses, some open to the public.

Shipping Company Verhoef: runs cruises on the Westerschelde, where you can see seals, and on the busy Gent to Terneuzen canal.

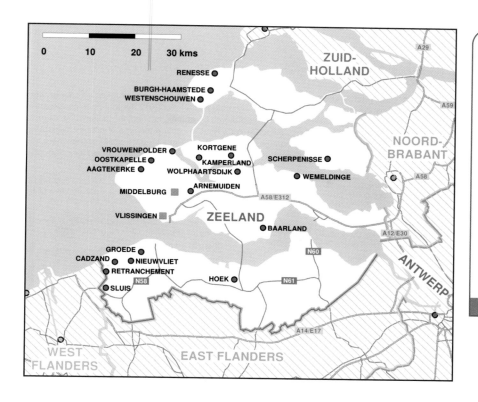

Aagtekerke
Camping Westhove

Zuiverseweg 2, NL-4363 RJ Aagtekerke (Zeeland) T: 0118 581 809. E: westhove@ardoer.com
alanrogers.com/NL6990

Camping Westhove is an ideal site for all ages and has some high quality play facilities for children. It is situated on the island Walcheren (the garden of Zeeland). There are 366 spacious pitches of which 275 are for touring with 6A electricity. The possibilities are endless – whether you wish to enjoy the beach, nature or the towns. There are marked tracks through the woods and dunes, and historical villages and towns with opportunities for cycling, walking and riding. The site's sanitary facilities are of a high standard, and there is an excellent new wellness and fitness centre. Even in wet weather there is plenty to do as the huge adventure play area is indoors and the swimming pool with separate children's section is covered. There is a ball pool, a lookout tower, a climbing frame and a toddler corner.

Facilities

Three heated sanitary units with washbasins in cabins, showers and WCs and en-suite facilities. Baby room. Free hot water. Launderette with ironing facilities. Well stocked supermarket. Bar. Good restaurant. Snack bar. Fresh bread is available daily. Heated indoor swimming pool. Paddling pool. Excellent wellness and fitness centre. Indoor and outdoor play areas. Sports field. Boules. Bicycle and tricycle hire. Entertainment team in high season. Miniclub. Recreation area. TV. Electronic games. WiFi (charged). Dogs are not accepted in high season. Off site: Golf and beach 1.5 km. Domburg 2 km.

Open: 30 March - 28 October.

Directions

From A58 take exit for Domburg and Oostkapelle (N57 and N287). Just before entering Domburg site is signed and is a left turn (Zuiverseweg) and on left after 900 m. GPS: 51.55578, 3.51516

Charges guide

Per unit incl. 2 persons	
and electricity	€ 20.00 - € 44.00
extra person	€ 5.00
dog	€ 2.50

FREE Alan Rogers Travel Card
Extra benefits and savings - see page 12

Arnemuiden

Camping De Witte Raaf

Muidenweg 3, NL-4341 PX Arnemuiden (Zeeland) T: 0118 601 212. E: witteraaf@ardoer.com

alanrogers.com/NL6934

Camping De Witte Raaf is undergoing extensive restructuring including construction of new sanitary units and additional permanent buildings offering accommodation. For 2012 the touring pitches were in the original circular area, surrounded by hedges and served by a clean, but ageing, sanitary unit. It would be prudent to contact reception before visiting De Witte Raaf to confirm the type of pitches available in 2013. This site is popular with those who enjoy watersports as it has its own small marina where you can moor your own boat. You can also windsurf and sail on the lakes. A small lake is ideal for introducing children to watersports.

Facilities

Heated sanitary building with toilets, showers and washbasins in cabins. Family cabins and baby room. Free warm water. Laundry facilities. Shop, bar, restaurant and takeaway (high season). Bicycle hire. Play area. WiFi over site (charged). Dogs are not accepted. Off site: Watersports and places of interest nearby.

Open: 21 March - 1 October.

Directions

Follow the A58 from Bergen op Zoom to Vlissingen. Take exit for Arnemuiden. Follow the main road through the village (site is well signed). Out of the village take first right (Oranjepolderseweg) and site is on the left after 3 km. GPS: 51.51051, 3.70909

Charges guide

Per unit incl. 2 persons and electricity	€ 16.00 - € 41.00
extra person	€ 4.25

Baarland

Comfortcamping Scheldeoord

Landingsweg 1, NL-4435 NR Baarland (Zeeland) T: 0113 639 900. E: scheldeoord@ardoer.com

alanrogers.com/NL5575

The site is situated behind the Westerschelde dyke, from where you can watch the passing sea-going ships and below the dyke one can fish from the beach. It is a good quality family site with 514 pitches including 214 for touring units. The touring pitches are pleasantly arranged in small fields and all have electricity (6-16A), water, drainage and TV aerial connection. One area is reserved for those travelling with disabilities and this is located near one of the very well equipped toilet blocks. There are heated indoor and outdoor pools with a slide (unsupervised), both with excellent separate areas for young children. Member of the Ardoer group.

Facilities

Three excellent, modern toilet blocks include washbasins (open style and in cabins) and en-suite shower rooms with controllable showers (card operated). Attractive children's section. Bathrooms for rent. Facilities for disabled visitors. Laundry. Motorcaravan service point. Supermarket. Bar/restaurant and snack bar with takeaway. Indoor and outdoor pools with paddling pools. Several play areas. TV room. Tennis. Bicycle hire. Fishing. Entertainment in high season. WiFi (charged). Off site: Riding 2 km.

Open: 1 April - 30 October.

Directions

From the A58 take exit 35 to 's Gravenpolder. Then follow signs to Hoedekenskerke and then south for Scheldeoord and the campsite. GPS: 51.39675, 3.89825

Charges guide

Per unit incl. 2 persons and electricity	€ 21.00 - € 49.00
extra person	€ 5.00
dog (max. 2)	€ 5.00

Burgh-Haamstede

Camping Ginsterveld

Maireweg 10, NL-4328 GR Burgh-Haamstede (Zeeland) T: 0111 651 590. E: info@ginsterveld.nl

alanrogers.com/NL6936

This is a fantastic family site for both parents and children. Not only is the nearby wide sandy beach popular, but there is also a swimming paradise with different water levels, a lazy river, water slides (one 40 m. long), pools for toddlers and children, a whirlpool and a steam cabin. With other amenities including several play fields, bicycle hire and spacious play areas, this site is ideal for children. When the weather is poor there is an indoor play area. This site provides excellent sanitary facilities which of course include special facilities for babies and children. Member of the Ardoer group.

Facilities

Two excellent heated toilet blocks. Washbasins in cabins and large controllable showers. Motorcaravan service point. Shop. Restaurant. Bar. Takeaway. Good heated indoor pool. Tennis. Sports field. Good playgrounds. Pets are not accepted. WiFi throughout (free). Off site: Beach and fishing 2 km. Riding 4 km. Golf 10 km.

Open: 22 March - 27 October.

Directions

From the A15 take exit 17 towards Middelburg. Follow the N57 towards Burgh-Haamstede and site is well signed from centre. GPS: 51.71617, 3.729

Charges guide

Per unit incl. 2 persons and electricity	€ 19.00 - € 36.00
extra person	€ 5.00

For latest campsite news, availability and prices visit

alanrogers.com

Cadzand

Camping Wulpen

Vierhonderdpolderdijk 1, NL-4506 HK Cadzand (Zeeland) T: 0117 391 226. E: info@campingwulpen.nl

alanrogers.com/NL5535

Camping Wulpen is located in the southernmost resort in the Netherlands, with a wide, clean beach nearby. This is a quiet, sheltered, well maintained site with excellent sanitary facilities. Most of the 100 spacious touring pitches (80-130 sq.m) have electricity (6/10A), water and drainage. There is a recreation room with table tennis, several playgrounds and a room dedicated to children's activities in high season. Other leisure activities include boules, football and volleyball. Throughout the site there is an emphasis on attention to detail and those interested in the environment will appreciate the diversity in plant life in specially created and tended gardens.

Facilities

Two heated toilet blocks are clean and well maintained, and two additional units are used in peak season. Laundry facilities. Shop with newspapers, fresh bread, ice creams and gas. Games room. Playgrounds. Outdoor fitness equipment. Spacious sports area. WiFi over part of site (charged). Tourist information. Off site: The Zwin nature reserve. Cycling and walking. The historic villages of Retranchement, Aardenburg and IJzendijke. The town of Sluis for shopping or walking on the ramparts. Belgium.

Open: 1 April - 15 October.

Directions

From Breda/Eindhoven on A58 take the exit Terneuzen to the Westerschelde Tunnel. After the tunnel, turn right at roundabout towards Oostburg and then Cadzand. Upon entering Cadzand go right at the mill and then take first right. The site is on your left. GPS: 51.3699, 3.41670

Charges guide

Per unit incl. 2 persons and electricity	€ 18.40 - € 23.10
extra person	€ 3.50

Cadzand

Molecaten Park Hoogduin

Zwartepolderweg 1, NL-4506 HT Cadzand (Zeeland) T: 0117 391 235. E: hoogduin@molecaten.nl

alanrogers.com/NL6937

Molecaten Park Hoogduin can be reached in less than two hours' drive from Calais. The location of this site is imposing, and, as its name Hoogduin suggests, it can be found within high dunes. Just over the dunes, there is a broad sandy beach with a panoramic view over the site and the surrounding area. This beach is well known as one of the cleanest in the Netherlands, and slopes gently into the sea. Pitches are large and grassy, and are equipped with electricity (6-10A). They are divided by trees and shrubs.

Facilities

Four clean, well maintained sanitary units housed in variety of buildings. Facilities for disabled campers (key access). Very well stocked supermarket. Restaurant with pub and terrace, takeaway food. Sports pitches. Large trampoline. Several play areas throughout the site. Volleyball. Games room. Activity and entertainment programme (4-10 yrs; high season). Bicycle hire. WiFi (charged). Chalets for rent. Off site: Sandy beach (adjacent). Cadzand-Bad 2 km. Sluis 6 km. Knokke 7 km.

Open: All year.

Directions

From the south take the E40 motorway (in Belgium) to Oostkamp take E403 to Brugge (Bruges) and Knokke-Heist. Follow this road into the Netherlands following directions to Cadzand. Continue on N674. At the T-junction (at the coast) turn right and you will find the site after 1 km. GPS: 51.38453, 3.41397

Charges 2013

Per unit incl. 2 persons, water and electricity	€ 14.00 - € 32.50
extra person	€ 3.90

Groede

Strandcamping Groede

Zeeweg 1, NL-4503 PA Groede (Zeeland) T: 0117 371 384. E: info@strandcampinggroede.nl

alanrogers.com/NL5510

A warm welcome awaits you at Strandcamping Groede, which has all you need for the perfect family seaside holiday. Family run and located close to one of the cleanest sandy beaches in the Netherlands, it aims to cater for the individual needs of visitors with pitches available for all tastes. There are 870 pitches in total, 500 for tourers, the majority of these with electrical connections (4-10A). Sympathetic landscaping has taken the natural surroundings of the dunes and sand to create areas for larger groups, families, and for those who prefer peace and quiet. The seaside feel continues in the layout of the comprehensive sports and play aeas and in the brasserie and other main buildings.

Facilities

Excellent toilet facilities include some wash cabins, baby baths, a family room and a unit for disabled visitors. Motorcaravan services. Gas. Shop, restaurant and snack bar (all weekends only in low seasons). Recreation room. Trampoline. Bouncy castle. Sports area. Several play areas (bark base). Plenty of activities for children in peak season. Bicycle hire. Fishing. WiFi over site (charged).

Open: 22 March - 1 November.

Directions

From Breskens take the coast road for 5 km. to site. Alternatively, the site is signed from Groede village on the more inland Breskens-Sluis road. GPS: 51.39582, 3.48772

Charges 2013

Per unit incl. 2 persons and electricity	€ 19.70 - € 46.00

No credit cards.

Hoek

Vakantie-Eiland Braakman

Middenweg 1, NL-4542 PN Hoek (Zeeland) T: 0115 481 730. E: info@braakman.nl

alanrogers.com/NL5520

Situated on the shores of the Braakmanmeer (a slightly brackish lake) this holiday park provides fun for the whole family. The comprehensive recreation areas are also open to day visitors. The 210-hectare site is divided by tall trees into several touring areas of varied sizes, both open and shaded. A wide range of pitches are available, from the most simple without a power supply, to luxury camping beside the water with full services including 6A electricity, TV, water and sewerage connections. In addition, there is a range of luxury bungalows, mobile homes and seasonal caravan pitches.

Facilities

Six fully equipped toilet blocks have facilities for disabled visitors. Laundry facilities in most blocks. Supermarket. Bar. Restaurant. Lake swimming with slides, diving board, beach and waterplay equipment. Play area with pool for small children. Sports field. Tennis (tuition). Amusement hall (games). Minigolf. Basketball. Fitness trail. Activity and entertainment team. Watersports and sailing on the lake. Fishing (with disabled access). Minifarm and aviary. WiFi over part of site (charged). Off site: Scheldorado pool complex (free transport). Nature reserve.

Open: All year.

Directions

From A58 (Bergen op Zoom-Middelburg/Vlissingen) take exit for Terneuzen to Westerscheldetunnel. At roundabout turn right to Hoek, Breskens and Oostburg. From Belgium: N49 (Antwerp-Zelzate) take N252 to Terneuzen and N61 to Hoek. Do not turn off to Hoek but proceed to Braakman-Noord. GPS: 51.314635, 3.725972

Charges guide

Per unit incl. 2 persons	
and electricity	€ 13.50 - € 33.00
extra person	€ 3.50

Kamperland

Camping De Molenhoek

Molenweg 69a, NL-4493 NC Kamperland (Zeeland) T: 0113 371 202. E: info@demolenhoek.com

alanrogers.com/NL5570

This rural, family run site makes a pleasant contrast to the livelier coastal sites in this popular holiday area. There is an emphasis on catering for the users of the 300 permanent or seasonal holiday caravans and 100 tourers. Eighty of these have 6A electricity, water and drainage. The site is neat and tidy with surrounding hedges and trees giving privacy and some shade, and electrical connections are available. A large outdoor pool area has ample space for swimming, children's play and sun loungers. Entertainment, including dance evenings and bingo, is organised in season.

Facilities

Two very clean and well appointed sanitary blocks include some washbasins in cabins and children's facilities. Toilet and shower facilities for disabled visitors and for babies. Laundry facilities. Motorcaravan services. Bar/restaurant with terrace and large TVs and LCD projection. Snack bar. Swimming pool (15/5-15/9). Playground. Bicycle hire. Pool tables. Sports field. Entertainment for children. WiFi (charged). Off site: Tennis and watersports nearby.

Open: 1 April - 27 October.

Directions

Site is west of the village of Kamperland on the island of Noord Beveland. From the N256 Goes-Zierikzee road, exit west onto the N255 Kamperland road. Site is signed south of this road. GPS: 51.57840, 3.69642

Charges guide

Per unit incl. 2 persons	
and electricity	€ 23.00 - € 36.00
extra person	€ 2.00 - € 3.50

Kamperland

RCN de Schotsman

Schotsmanweg 1, NL-4493 ZG Kamperland (Zeeland) T: 0113 371 751. E: schotsman@rcn.nl

alanrogers.com/NL6924

De Schotsman is located on the island of Noord-Beveland, on the shores of Veerse Meer. It has its own marina with a slipway and a good selection of boats for hire for all abilities. In the high season, there is a full programme of windsurfing and sailing lessons. There is also a large, heated, outdoor pool with a separate children's pool, and an inviting restaurant with a terrace overlooking the lake. It is within reach of the ports of Hook of Holland, Zeebrugge, Dunkerque, and two and a half hours from Calais, so may also be ideal for a short break in the low season.

Facilities

Four spacious sanitary units are clean and well equipped and have facilities for disabled visitors. Launderette. Bakery and well stocked supermarket. Bar, restaurant and takeaway. Heated outdoor pool with separate children's pool, slides and water chute and paddling pool. Sports hall. Play area. Bicycle and go-kart hire. Windsurf, pedalo and canoe hire. Lake beach. Marina with slipway. WiFi (charged). Accommodation to rent.

Open: 30 March - 29 October.

Directions

From autoroute A58 Bergen op Zoom-Vlissingen, take exit Zierikzee (N256). Then go left to join N255 to Kamperland. From here the site is clearly indicated (to the left). GPS: 51.568527, 3.662787

Charges guide

Per unit incl. 2 persons	
and electricity	€ 22.00 - € 39.50
dog	€ 4.95 - € 7.50

For latest campsite news, availability and prices visit

alanrogers.com

Kortgene
Camping en Villapark De Paardekreek
Havenweg 1, NL-4484 NT Kortgene (Zeeland) T: 0113 302 051. E: paardekreek@ardoer.com
alanrogers.com/NL5585

Located directly on the Veerse Meer, with access to the vast lake, this superb family site has additional but not sole, appeal for watersports enthusiasts. There are both seasonal pitches and 120 pitches for touring units, all fully serviced including 10A electricity, television and WiFi. The pitches are pleasant and some are directly by the water's edge and with boat launching facilities, water and a sailing school on site, many units have a boat of some sort. There is an exciting indoor water adventure play park with a long water chute and a small beach also allows swimming and zip wire fun over the water.

Facilities

Three very good toilet blocks and one smaller unit include en-suite shower rooms. Excellent facilities for disabled visitors, babies and children. Motorcaravan services. Pleasant bar with terrace. Restaurant. Snack bar with takeaway. Indoor heated water adventure area and water chute. Lake swimming. Adventure play areas. Indoor play area. Mooring facilities. Bicycle hire. Pedal kart and dune buggy hire. Entertainment for children (high season). WiFi.

Open: 27 March - 1 November.

Directions

From the A256 take exit signed Goes, Zierikzee. Follow N256 through Oost Westweg and Oudedijk. In the village of Kortgene the site is well signed. GPS: 51.5511, 3.80834

Charges guide

Per serviced pitch incl. 2 persons	€ 25.00 - € 45.00
extra person	€ 5.00
dog	€ 5.00

Nieuwvliet
Camping International
Sint Bavodijk 2D, NL-4504 AA Nieuwvliet (Zeeland) T: 0117 371 233. E: international@ardoer.com
alanrogers.com/NL5525

This is a large, well managed site sheltered partly by trees and shrubbery, which also separate the various camping areas and the extensive activity area for children of all ages. It is ideal for family holidays, offering a wide range of entertainment opportunities on the site, whatever the weather, as well as access to the nearby beaches. Different types of touring pitch are available, all with electricity (6A) and most with water, drainage and cable TV. Thirty-three pitches have individual sanitary units. A modern, clean and well maintained sanitary block serves the remaining touring pitches. A member of the Ardoer group.

Facilities

One major sanitary building has free showers, dishwashing sinks. Microwave. Bar and lounge with library, boardgames, LCD Projector TV screen. Small shop for basics and bakery (high season and weekends). Snack bar/takeaway. Water play area with slides, water features and paddling pool for under 10s. Indoor and outdoor play areas. Football. Tennis. Boules. Volleyball. Chess. Bicycle hire. WiFi over site (charged). Mobile homes to rent. Off site: Riding and fishing 1 km. Beach 1.8 km. Golf 7 km.

Open: 1 April - 31 October.

Directions

From Belgium: take N49 to Kaprijke/Breskens, enter the Netherlands at IJzendijke and follow signs to Breskens and Schoondijke. At roundabout in Breskens turn left to Groede and Cadzand, following site signs. GPS: 51.37468, 3.46944

Charges guide

Per unit incl. 2 persons and electricity	€ 17.00 - € 37.00
extra person	€ 4.50

Nieuwvliet
Camping Zonneweelde
Baanstpoldersedijk 1, NL-4504 PS Nieuwvliet (Zeeland) T: 0117 371 910. E: info@campingzonneweelde.nl
alanrogers.com/NL5530

This family run site, only 600 m. from kilometres of wide, sandy beaches, is ideal for family holidays. Children will enjoy a walkway and a large slide through the dunes to the beach. There are 70 touring pitches, a wide choice of luxury holiday cottages and log cabins, plus places for 50 seasonal caravans. Electricity (10A) is available throughout. The Natural Reserve of Het Zwin is nearby (ideal for birdwatching) and many interesting villages are in the area. The landscape is perfect for exploring on bicycles along the safe, well signed routes.

Facilities

Two modern, heated, well maintained sanitary buildings provide roomy adjustable showers and some washbasins in cabins. Family shower room. Children's bathroom. Laundry facilities. Supermarket. Restaurant, bar and terrace. Separate takeaway. Swimming pool (unheated) and separate pool for children with slides. Play areas and sports field. Boules. Volleyball. Children's entertainment (in holiday periods). Excursions (low season). Bicycle hire.

Open: 1 April - 31 October.

Directions

From Westerscheldetunnel, turn right at roundabout to Breskens-Hoek-Oostburg. At Schoondijke roundabout follow Breskens/Groede, turn left at first lights to Groede/Nieuwvliet then right at first roundabout in Nieuwvliet. Site is signed. GPS: 51.382207, 3.458188

Charges guide

Per unit incl. 2 persons and electricity	€ 20.00 - € 40.00

FREE Alan Rogers Travel Card
Extra benefits and savings - see page 12

Oostkapelle
Camping De Pekelinge

Landmetersweg 1, NL-4356 RE Oostkapelle (Zeeland) T: 0118 582 820. E: pekelinge@ardoer.com

alanrogers.com/NL6926

Camping De Pekelinge is a good quality, family site only 3 km. from the beach. There are 320 spacious touring pitches, all with electricity (10A). These include special pitches for motorcaravans and four pitches with private bathrooms and car parking, designed for visitors with disabilities. The site is of a high standard and its imaginative facilities are designed for both good and bad weather. Good sports facilities include an all-weather swimming pool with a slide (65 m), a children's pool and water play areas, plus an indoor play area. Food and drink can be enjoyed at the Grand Café complex.

Facilities

Sanitary facilities include family bathrooms and facilities for disabled visitors. Private sanitary units on many pitches. Launderette. Well stocked supermarket. Café. Snack bar. All-weather swimming pool with water chute and paddling pool. Water play areas. Indoor and outdoor play areas. Football pitch. Tennis. Volleyball. Beach volleyball. Basketball. Air trampolines. Climbing wall. 2 PlayStations. Small animal farm. Bicycle hire. Dogs are not accepted in July/Aug. Free WiFi over site. Off site: Riding 1 km. Beach and golf 3 km. Sailing and boat launching 6 km.

Open: 22 March - 3 November.

Directions

From A58 take Domburg exit. Continue on N57 towards Domburg and Oostkapelle. Take the N287 towards Oostkapelle. Site is well signed from the town. GPS: 51.55715, 3.55161

Charges 2013

Per unit incl. 2 persons and electricity	€ 20.00 - € 55.00
extra person	€ 4.50
dog (excl. July/Aug)	€ 2.50

Only Maestro debit cards accepted.

Oostkapelle
Camping Park & Wellness Ons Buiten

Aagtekerkseweg 2a, NL-4356 RJ Oostkapelle (Zeeland) T: 0118 581 813. E: onsbuiten@ardoer.com

alanrogers.com/NL6928

Camping Ons Buiten is a high quality site set amongst the landscapes of the Zeeuws, just 2.5 km. from the sea. The pitches are a minimum of 100 sq.m. and are serviced with electricity, cable TV, water and drainage. The pitch areas are kept free of cars with parking adjacent. Ons Buiten is a destination for the whole family and many activities are organised in high season for all ages. Children can play in the imaginative pool area and adults can spoil themselves at the site's excellent wellness centre. The three sanitary units have delightful themed facilities for children.

Facilities

Toilet block including special facilities for children and disabled visitors. Private sanitary units on comfort pitches. Launderette. Motorcaravan service point. Shared kitchen with fridge, microwave and hob. Supermarket. Bakery. Café/restaurant. Takeaway. Heated covered swimming pool. Play area. Sports pitch. Minigolf. Tennis. Wellness centre with sauna, salt cave and infrared cabin. WiFi over site (charged). Dogs are not accepted. Off site: Beach 2.5 km. Golf 4 km.

Open: 31 March - 3 November.

Directions

From the A15 take exit 12 towards Middleburg and then the N57 for 50 km. and join the N287 (Waterstraat) towards Oostkapelle. Site is well signed. GPS: 51.56253, 3.54627

Charges guide

Per unit incl. 2 persons and electricity	€ 24.00 - € 67.00
extra person	€ 5.50

Renesse
Camping de Oase

Roelandseweg 8, NL-4325 CS Renesse (Zeeland) T: 0111 461 358. E: info@campingdeoase.nl

alanrogers.com/NL5555

De Oase is situated on the outskirts of Renesse, a lively, North Sea holiday resort with long, sandy beaches. Campers will have free transport to the beach, around Schouwen-Duiveland, one of the islands in Zeeland, and further afield to Goes and Middleburg. It is ideal for those who enjoy an active holiday, being connected to the many cycle and walking tracks that are laid out in this typically flat Dutch landscape. There are 450 pitches, including 146 for touring units. They are grassy and spacious and all have electricity (6/10A), water, drainage and WiFi; 90 are also equipped with TV connections.

Facilities

Modern, clean and spacious sanitary facilities include rooms for babies, children and disabled visitors. Family showers. Launderette. Supermarket with fresh bread. Recreation areas and sports fields. Entertainment for children in high season. Free local transport. Dogs are not accepted. Off site: Renesse centre 300 m. Riding 500 m. Fishing 1 km. Beach 1.5 km. Town of Zierikzee 15 km.

Open: 15 March - 1 November.

Directions

Site is just south of Renesse. Follow signs for Renesse Transferium and site is opposite. GPS: 51.72838, 3.77179

Charges guide

Per unit incl. 2 persons and electricity	€ 22.50 - € 32.50
extra person (over 3 yrs)	€ 5.00

For latest campsite news, availability and prices visit

alanrogers.com

Renesse

Camping De Wijde Blick

Lagezoom 23, NL-4325 CP Renesse (Zeeland) T: 0111 468 888. E: wijdeblick@ardoer.com

alanrogers.com/NL5560

The Van Oost family run this neat campsite in a pleasant and personal way. It is located on the outskirts of the village of Renesse in a quiet rural spot. From May to September a free bus runs to Renesse and the beach, just 2 km. away. De Wijde Blick has 328 pitches with 218 for touring units, all with 6/10A electricity and TV connections, and 90-120 sq.m. in area. Of these, 16 have private sanitary facilities and 202 are fully serviced. There are 20 attractively arranged motorcaravan pitches with hardstanding, and ten special 'bike and hike' pitches for those touring without a car. Cars are parked away from pitches.

Facilities	Directions
Three first class, modern toilet blocks are heated, with clean facilities including washbasins in cabins, controllable showers and facilities for disabled campers. Microwave and fridge. Bath (on payment). Laundry (with pleasant waiting area). Gas supplies. Motorcaravan services. Shop. Restaurant/bar (15/3-31/10). Swimming pool (1/5-15/9; can be covered). Free WiFi over site. Good playgrounds. Air trampoline. Volleyball area. Open-air theatre. Bicycle hire. Activities for children. Hotel chalets for rent. Breakfast service available. Off site: Tennis and minigolf. Riding and golf 1.5 km. Beach and fishing 2 km.	Renesse is on the island of Schouwen (connected to the mainland by a bridge and three dams). On the N57 from Middelburg take the Renesse exit. After 2 km. follow road 106 to the left and then site signs. Site is on the east side of the village. GPS: 51.71843, 3.76713

Open: All year.

Charges guide

Per unit incl. 2 persons	€ 18.00 - € 51.00
extra person	€ 4.75
dog	€ 2.00

Renesse

Camping Duinhoeve

Scholderlaan 8, NL-4325 EP Renesse (Zeeland) T: 0111 461 309. E: post@campingduinhoeve.nl

alanrogers.com/NL6946

Camping Duinhoeve is located within a nature reserve, close to the important resort of Renesse, and is just five minutes from the beach, across the sand dunes. Various grades of pitch are available – standard (75-90 sq.m. with electricity); pitch plus (as standard but with water and drainage); and comfort pitches (95-120 sq.m. with electricity, water and drainage). The latter also have cable TV connections. A number of chalets and mobile homes are available for rent. On-site amenities include a well stocked shop, and a swimming pool that can be covered in cooler weather.

Facilities	Directions
Shop. Bar/restaurant/snack bar. Swimming pool. Playground. Volleyball. Activity and entertainment programme. Tourist information. Mobile homes and chalets for rent. Direct beach access. Off site: Shops, restaurants and cafés in Renesse. Walking and cycling routes. Riding. Watersports. Nature reserve.	Approaching from Zierikzee, follow signs to Renesse on N59 and N653. At Renesse, turn right at roundabout and follow signs to site. GPS: 51.739377, 3.777682

Open: 17 February - 28 October.

Charges guide

Per unit incl. 2 persons and electricity (plus meter)	€ 18.00 - € 28.00
dog	€ 3.50

Renesse

Camping International Renesse

Scharendijkseweg 8, NL-4325 LD Renesse (Zeeland) T: 0111 461 391. E: info@camping-international.net

alanrogers.com/NL6950

Situated 300 m. from the beach at Renesse in Zeeland, this is a friendly, family run site. Its owners have set a high standard, which is demonstrated by the immaculate and tastefully decorated sanitary facilities. There are 200 pitches, all for touring units and with electricity connections (16A). These are a generous size and laid out in bays and avenues surrounded by hedging. Around a courtyard area beyond reception is a supermarket and a bar which is attractively decorated with novel figures and the owner's personal memorabilia. Outside bench seating and umbrellas turns this corner of the site into a popular meeting place.

Facilities	Directions
Two luxury sanitary blocks provide showers, washbasins (some in cabins) and a baby room. Laundry room. Motorcaravan service point. Supermarket. Bar. Games room. TV. Play area. Bicycle hire. Entertainment in high season for all. Max. 1 dog.	From Zierikzee follow N59 to Renesse for 15 km. and turn right at roundabout (before town) onto local road signed R101. Continue for 1 km. and turn left, then first right to site. GPS: 51.73981, 3.78912

Open: 1 March - 31 October.

Charges guide

Per unit incl. 2 persons	€ 26.40 - € 38.10
extra person	€ 4.85

FREE Alan Rogers Travel Card
Extra benefits and savings - see page 12

Renesse

Camping Strandpark De Zeeuwse Kust

Helleweg 8, NL-4326 LJ Noordwelle/Renesse (Zeeland) T: 0111 468 282.
E: info@strandparkdezeeuwsekust.nl **alanrogers.com/NL6948**

Whether you want relaxation, something for the children, the seaside or activities, you will find all of these at De Zeeuwse Kust located just 250 m. from the sea with its beautiful sandy beach. The outstanding, hotel standard facilities contained within the centrally located building are in a class of their own, offering a haven whatever the weather. From the open plan kitchen, the oversized wooden stools, to the open fireplace, they are all first class. This site has 168 spacious and comfortable pitches, some with private sanitary provision. The modern sanitary unit is heated and includes facilities for children and disabled visitors.

Facilities

Modern, first class sanitary building has showers, washbasins, private cabins, family shower rooms and facilities for children and disabled visitors. Launderette. Motorcaravan service point. Shop/mini market. Fresh bread. Heated swimming pool. Play areas. Sports field. Outdoor table football. Games room with Xbox. Small film theatre. Recreation room. Entertainment team (special holidays, weekends and July-Aug). Sauna. Whirlpool. First aid post. Free WiFi. Dogs welcome all year – showers near sanitary block. Off site: Riding 500 m. Golf 7 km.

Open: All year (with most facilities).

Directions

From the A15 take exit 12 towards Middelburg. Follow the N57 through Ouddorp and then turn right on the N652. Immediately turn left for the N651 and follow to Noordwelle. Site is well signed. GPS: 51.739062, 3.802369

Charges guide

Per unit incl. 2 persons, electricity, water and drainage	€ 19.50 - € 59.50
extra person (over 2 yrs)	€ 5.75

No credit cards.

Renesse

Camping Julianahoeve

Hoogenboomlaan 42, NL-4325 DM Renesse (Zeeland) T: 0111 461 414. E: julianahoeve@ardoer.com
alanrogers.com/NL6952

A very large site with 1,400 pitches, mainly for mobile homes and chalets, Camping Julianahoeve still retains a few pitches for touring units and tents. You cannot get much closer to the sea, and a path leads through the dunes to the beach. All the main touring pitches are large and fully serviced. Some have individual sanitary units, and others have hardstandings. Located in what is said to be the sunniest area of the Netherlands, this is an ideal site for a family holiday by the beach. A member of the Ardoer group.

Facilities

Several well appointed toilet blocks serve the site with facilities for younger children, babies and disabled visitors. Individual sanitary units. Launderette. Supermarket. Bar. Brasserie. Café with terrace. Snack bar. Indoor pool complex with 60 m. water slide. Play areas. Sports pitches. Theatre with entertainment for all ages. WiFi. Dogs are not accepted. Off site: Fishing 500 m. Golf and riding 1 km. Boat launching 5 km.

Open: 1 April - 6 November.

Directions

From the A5 take exit 12 and follow the N57 through Ouddorp, then follow signs to Renesse. Site is well signed from the town. GPS: 51.72738, 3.75897

Charges guide

Per unit incl. 2 persons and electricity	€ 20.00 - € 58.00
extra person (over 2 yrs)	€ 5.25
child (2-4 yrs)	€ 3.50

Retranchement

Camping De Zwinhoeve

Duinweg 1, NL-4225 LX Retranchement (Zeeland) T: 0117 392 120. E: zwinhoeve@ardoer.com
alanrogers.com/NL6944

Camping De Zwinhoeve is a family campsite that lies directly on the dunes and borders of Belgium and Holland. Within minutes you can either be on the beach of the North Sea or in the nature reserve, Het Zwin. The site has 411 spacious pitches, of which 120 are for touring and all with 10A electricity. The comfort pitches also have water, drainage and cable TV, while super comfort pitches have private sanitary units. Facilities include a supermarket, a restaurant and a bar where you can relax and enjoy a drink. The wellness area has a sauna, massage and a jacuzzi. In high season, an entertainment programme is arranged for children.

Facilities

Heated toilet block including a baby room and facilities for disabled visitors. Launderette. Well stocked shop. Bar. Restaurant. Snack bar with takeaway. Play area. Entertainment and miniclub (high season). Recreation and sports areas. WiFi. TV. Sauna. Cycle routes. WiFi on part of site (charged). Off site: Golf 9 km. Fishing. Swimming in the sea. Various watersports.

Open: 14 March - 26 October.

Directions

The site is on the coastal border with Belgium, 10 km. from Knokke-Heist. From Sluis-Breskens N675, exit towards Retranchement N674 and follow site signs. GPS: 51.36621, 3.3739

Charges guide

Per unit incl. 2 persons, water and electricity	€ 20.00 - € 49.00
extra person (over 2 yrs)	€ 5.00

For latest campsite news, availability and prices visit

alanrogers.com

Retranchement
Camping Cassandria Bad

Strengweg 4, NL-4525 LW Retranchement (Zeeland) T: 0117 392 300. E: info@cassandriabad.nl
alanrogers.com/NL5502

Cassandria Bad was established in 1992, lying very close to the Belgian border and the resort of Cadzand Bad, just under 2 km. from the nearest North Sea beach. Pitches are grassy and spacious; some are privately let for the full season. All pitches are equipped with 10A electricity and free cable TV connections. Except for loading and unloading, cars are not allowed in the camping area, but a large parking area is provided. On-site amenities include a bar, snack bar, shop services and games room. During the peak season, a variety of activities are organised, including bingo, sports tournaments and karaoke. This part of the Netherlands, south of the Schelde, has strong contacts with Belgium and trips to Bruges and Gent are popular. Retranchement translates as bulwarks and there are still remains of vast earthen sea walls, although now this area is best known as a paradise for nature lovers and walkers. It is also the area for cycling with excellent trails from town to town along the dykes that protect the coast.

Facilities

Two clean and well maintained sanitary units with free showers, and two family bathrooms in the main block. Good laundry facilities. Small shop (fresh bread daily). Bar with LCD projector and screen. Snack bar. Sports fields with volleyball, and 2 football pitches. Games room with table football, air hockey and electronic games. Trampoline. Several well appointed and interesting play areas. Bicycle hire. WiFi over site (charged). 1 dog allowed per pitch. Off site: Nearest beach 1.7 km. Walking and cycle routes. Fishing 5 km.

Open: 23 March - 31 October.

Directions

Approaching from the west and Bruges, use the Belgian N31 and then N376 towards Knokke-Heist and then across the Dutch border to Sluis. Here take the road to Groede and turn left towards Cadzand Bad at the second crossroads. Site is well signed from here. GPS: 51.36613, 3.38583

Charges guide

Per unit incl. up to 4 persons and electricity	€ 25.00 - € 33.00
extra person	€ 4.50
dog	€ 2.50

Discounts available in low season.

Camping Cassandria-Bad
Strengweg 4, NL-4525 LW Retranchement
Tel.+31-117-392300, Fax 392425, www.cassandriabad.nl, info@cassandriabad.nl
✓open from 23.3-31.10 ✓1700m from the northseaborder (Cadzand-Bad)
✓fishing directly next to the campsite ✓canteen ✓fries stand ✓launderette
✓sport-and playgrounds ✓heated sanitary block ✓Kabeltelevision
✓ permanent internet-connection on all the pitches (on payment)

Scherpenisse
Vakantiepark De Pluimpot

Geertruidaweg 3, NL-4694 PH Scherpenisse (Zeeland) T: 0166 662 727. E: pluimpot@ardoer.com
alanrogers.com/NL7086

De Pluimpot is located on the island of Tholen, in the east of Zeeland, and lies adjacent to a beach and also to the Oosterschelde National Park. Around 300 pitches are occupied by mobile homes but there are a further 50 touring pitches. These are all equipped with cable TV connections and 6A electricity. Pitches are large (100 sq.m) and well shaded. On-site leisure amenities include bicycle and go-kart hire, an 18-hole minigolf course and two children's playgrounds; guests have free admission to a local swimming pool. There is good road access to a slipway for boat launching, with ample parking. A member of the Ardoer group.

Facilities

Three heated sanitary units, two for the touring pitches, have controllable showers, one with disability access. Private cabins available. Baby bath and changing facilities. Bath with jacuzzi (charged). Laundry. Bar/brasserie. Small shop. Play area. Minigolf. Sports competitions. Sports field. Fishing. Activity and entertainment programme. Boat launching 750 m. Free WiFi over part of site. Mobile homes and chalets for rent. Off site: Watersports. Cycle trips. Riding. Oosterschelde National Park.

Open: 1 April - 31 October.

Directions

Approaching from Bergen op Zoom, head west on N286, passing Tholen. Continue to Sint Maartensdijk and then follow signs to the site. GPS: 51.533259, 4.074536

Charges guide

Per unit incl. 2 persons and electricity	€ 20.00 - € 28.00
extra person	€ 4.50
child (2-12 yrs)	€ 3.00
dog	€ 3.00

Sluis

Camping De Meidoorn

Hoogstraat 68, NL-4524 LA Sluis (Zeeland) T: 0117 461 662. E: info@camping-meidoorn.eu

alanrogers.com/NL5505

This is a friendly, family run site within 400 m. of the historic city of Sluis on the Belgian border, yet bounded by mature trees, open countryside and a small lake. Laid out in groups divided by hedges and small trees, there are 250 pitches including about 100 for touring units and six cabins. Public transport operates in July and August between Breskens, Sluis and Knokke, which is free to guests and can take you to the coast. The bus stop is 100 m. away and buses run every hour.

Facilities

One large sanitary building provides modern showers, washbasins with cold water, 2 private cabins, facilities for disabled visitors. All hot water is charged. Launderette (coins). Recreation room (with toys). Bar and restaurant with simple menu. Takeaway. Playground and sports field. Boules. Air hockey. Pool table. Fishing (licence from reception). Children's art and craft sessions (Mon, Wed, Fri). WiFi (charged). Off site: Tennis 500 m. (charged). Bicycle hire 1 km. Beach 7 km. Golf 8 km. Brugge 16 km.

Open: 1 April - 1 November.

Directions

From Calais, Dunkerque, Ostend or Brugge take N374 to Sluis. Entering Sluis from N58 turn right and first right again. GPS: 51.313372, 3.391305

Charges guide

Per unit incl. 2 persons	
and electricity	€ 20.00 - € 23.35
extra person	€ 4.40

Vrouwenpolder

Camping Oranjezon

Koningin Emmaweg 16a, NL-4354 KD Vrouwenpolder (Zeeland) T: 0118 591 549. E: info@oranjezon.nl

alanrogers.com/NL7066

Oranjezon (orange sun) is an environmentally conscious, family run site located close to the sand dunes of the Schouwen-Duiveland peninsula. It is a pleasant fifteen minute stroll to the beach following a path across a nature reserve and through the dunes to the sea. There are 400 pitches here varying in size and price but all have 6/10A electricity. On-site amenities include a swimming pool with separate shallow area for young children, two children's playgrounds and an area with chickens, ducks and goats. The campsite store stocks basics, newspapers and household items; fresh bread is available every morning.

Facilities

Two main sanitary units are modern and have free showers, colourful children's areas, a family room and facilities for disabled visitors. There are four smaller units around the site. Additional private sanitary units on 18 pitches. Motorcaravan service point. Shop. Café/restaurant. Snack bar. Swimming pool. Paddling pool. Wellness area with sauna, cold tub and solarium. Children's playgrounds. Small animal area for children. Activity team (high season; under 13s). WiFi over site (charged). Tourist information. Off site: Vrouwenpolder 3 km. Old fishing village of Veere 8 km. Golf 13 km.

Open: 31 March - 21 October.

Directions

From A58 motorway, take exit for Domburg (N57) and follow signs for Oostkapelle. After St. Laurens. At Serooskerke go towards Oostkapelle/Domburg (N287). After 3 km. (immediately after green/white hotel) turn right into Munnikweg. Continue for 2.5 km. turn left campsite access road. Entrance is 200 m. on right. GPS: 51.58402, 3.58479

Charges guide

Per unit incl. 4 persons	
and electricity	€ 23.50 - € 43.50
extra person	€ 4.00
dog	€ 3.50

Wemeldinge

Camping Linda

Oostelijke kanaalweg 4, NL-4424 NC Wemeldinge (Zeeland) T: 0113 621 259. E: info@campinglinda.nl

alanrogers.com/NL6915

Camping Linda is a welcoming, family run site, situated behind the dyke on the shores of the Oosterschelde, with direct access to a small beach. The area is ideal for watersports enthusiasts and particularly popular with divers. Pitches are a good size, level and grassy, with 70 out of 350 places reserved for touring. Most of these are situated in the quieter part of the site, across a narrow lane close to the beach access and fishing. Other pitches are closer to the reception area. All have electricity (6/10A), water and TV connection. In high season there is a comprehensive entertainment programme.

Facilities

Two modern, clean sanitary buildings with showers (coin operated) and washbasins (some in cabins). Well equipped children's shower and baby room. No facilities for disabled visitors. Motorcaravan service point. Laundry facilities. Small shop (w/ends only). Bar and large function room. Snack bar/takeaway. Play areas. Games room. Bicycle hire. Max. 2 dogs. WiFi over site (charged).

Open: 1 April - 1 November.

Directions

From the south, take A58 towards Vlissingen. Leave at exit 35 and head north towards Kapelle. Continue on N670 to Wemeldinge. Site is next to Yacht Haven and is well signed. GPS: 51.516122, 4.007424

Charges guide

Per unit incl. 2 persons	
and electricity	€ 15.50 - € 21.50
extra person	€ 6.50

For latest campsite news, availability and prices visit

alanrogers.com

Westenschouwen
Camping Duinoord

Steenweg 16, Duinoord aan Zee, NL-4328 RM Westenschouwen (Zeeland) T: 0111 658 888.
E: duinoord@ardoer.com **alanrogers.com/NL6942**

Camping Duinoord lies directly beside a wide sandy North Sea beach and a large forest. The site itself is divided between two locations: Duinoord aan Zee and Landgoed Duinoord. The main site and reception are beside the sea and forest. There are 100 serviced touring pitches with 4/6A electricity, water, drainage and cable TV. Camping Landgoed Duinoord is five minutes away and is set peacefully in the polders. The pitches here are larger and less enclosed. Both sites have a similar ambience of space and tranquillity and the proximity of the beach and the forest make them special.

Facilities

Good, clean sanitary provision on both sites, incorporating a full range of facilities. Laundry facilities. Bakery. Small paddling pool with water jets. Recreation room with weekly theatrical productions. Outdoor football table. Play areas for under 12s. Off site: Bars and restaurants close to beach access. Shop 300 m. Bicycle hire 500 m. Golf and riding 2 km.

Open: All year.

Directions

From Rotterdam follow the A15 to the west and take exit 12, signed Brielle and Middelburg onto the N57. Follow for 42 km. until Westenschouwen. From here site is 1.5 km. GPS: 51.67228, 3.70629

Charges guide

Per unit incl. 2 persons and electricity	€ 17.00 - € 41.00
extra person (over 2 yrs)	€ 4.50 - € 5.00

Wolphaartsdijk
Camping 't Veerse Meer

Veerweg 71, NL-4471 NB Wolphaartsdijk (Zeeland) T: 0113 581 423. E: info@campingveersemeer.nl
alanrogers.com/NL6920

This well cared for, family run site is situated beside the Veerse Meer, on the island of Zuid-Beveland, in Zeeland. Emphasis at this site is on a neat and tidy appearance, quality facilities and a friendly reception. The site occupies both sides of Veerweg with one side providing seven touring pitches with individual sanitary facilities and fully serviced hardstanding pitches for motorcaravans. On the other side are the main buildings and 40 generous touring pitches, many fully serviced and separated by hedging, and a tent field. Further seasonal and static places are kept apart. A feature of this campsite is a narrow canal crossed by a bridge, leading to an area of seasonal units. Some attractive chalets are for rent.

Facilities

The single, modern toilet block is clean and has showers (token operated), open style wash areas, two wash cabins, facilities for children, and a baby bath. Laundry with book/magazine exchange. Motorcaravan service point. Bar. Play area. Trampoline. Boules. Organised events for all in high season. Bicycle hire. Fishing. Free WiFi over site. Off site: Supermarket 500 m. Bars, restaurants and minigolf at the watersports marina complex 900 m. Riding 1.5 km. Golf 6 km.

Open: 1 April - 31 October.

Directions

From N256 Goes-Zierikzee road take Wolphaartsdijk exit heading west. Turn right after 1 km. and follow signs to Veerse Meer (the lake) along Kwistenburg, bearing left on to Aardebolle–weg, right turn onto Veerweg at mini roundabout and site reception is to left in 500 m. GPS: 51.54436, 3.81242

Charges guide

Per unit incl. 2 persons and electricity	€ 15.00 - € 22.50
extra person	€ 2.50 - € 3.00
No credit cards.	

Wolphaartsdijk
Camping De Veerhoeve

Veerweg 48, NL-4471 NC Wolphaartsdijk (Zeeland) T: 0113 581 155. E: info@deveerhoeve.nl
alanrogers.com/NL5580

This is a family run site near the shores of the Veerse Meer, which is ideal for family holidays. It is situated in a popular area for watersports and is well suited for sailing, windsurfing and fishing enthusiasts, with boat launching 100 m. away. A sandy beach and recreation area, ideal for children, is only a five minute walk. As with most sites in this area there are many mature static and seasonal pitches. However, part of the friendly, relaxed site is reserved for touring units with 90 marked pitches on grassy ground, all with electrical connections. A member of the Holland Tulip Parcs group.

Facilities

Sanitary facilities in three blocks have been well modernised with full tiling. Hot showers are on payment. Laundry facilities. Motorcaravan services. Supermarket (all season). Restaurant and snack bar. TV room. Tennis. Playground and playing field. Games room. Bicycle hire. Fishing. Accommodation for groups. Max. 1 dog. WiFi (charged). Off site: Slipway for launching boats 100 m.

Open: 1 April - 30 October.

Directions

From N256 Goes-Zierikzee road take Wolphaartsdijk exit. Follow through village and signs to site (one of the site signs is obscured by other road signs and could be missed). GPS: 51.54678, 3.81345

Charges guide

Per unit incl. up to 4 persons and electricity	€ 20.00 - € 27.00
Camping Cheques accepted.	

Been to any good campsites lately?
We have

You'll find them here...

The UK's market leading independent
guides to the best campsites

Also available on iPad alanrogers.com/digital

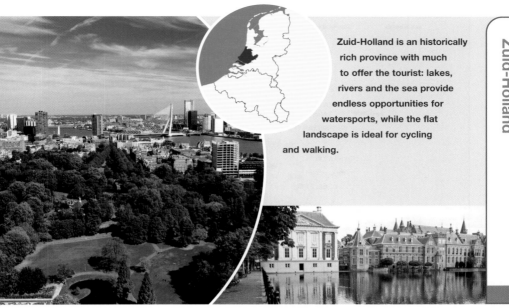

Zuid-Holland is an historically rich province with much to offer the tourist: lakes, rivers and the sea provide endless opportunities for watersports, while the flat landscape is ideal for cycling and walking.

CAPITAL: DEN HAAG (THE HAGUE)

Together with Nord-Holland, Zuid-Holland is one of the most prosperous areas of the lowlands. Most industry these days is confined to the middle sized Dutch towns and cities, but everywhere you will see evidence of the country's more extensive commercial past, particularly in the cities of Rotterdam and The Hague.

The modern port of Rotterdam is a vibrant city packed with art and cultural activities – galleries, concert halls, theatres and museums abound. In The Hague, the seat of government, royal palaces, stately embassies and town houses give the city a regal atmosphere; a stone's throw from the city are the resorts of Scheveningen and Kijkduin and the theme parks of Duinrell and Drievliet.

In the north of Zuid-Holland is the landscape of the Holland Lakes, an area dotted with lakes, rivers and drainage canals, all interspersed with wide, open polders. The Green Heart, hidden between the big cities of the Randstad, is a vast oasis of peace and tranquillity that lends itself to a variety of open-air activities. With its coastline and pleasant resorts, the bulb region also has much to offer visitors who want a summer beach holiday.

Places of interest

The Hague (Den Haag): important museums such as the Mauritshuis, The Hague Municipal Museum and Panorama Mesdag.

Rotterdam: Museum Boymans van Beuningen, contemporary architecture and culture, port area.

Leiden: large student population brings this historical city to life, with many bars, restaurants and good museums.

Gouda: famous for its cheese, 'stroopwafels' and beautiful 15th-century town hall.

Delft: medieval centre with canals, bridges, squares and historic façades - a charming backdrop whether shopping or just taking a relaxing stroll.

Attractions

Bulb Region: its extensive and colourful tulip fields make a truly unique sight in spring.

Duinrell: large theme park for the whole family.

Madurodam: famous miniature city where you can enjoy the highlights of the Netherlands on a scale of 1:25.

Animal parks: Avifauna, bird park in Alphen aan den Rijn, Blijdorp Zoo in Rotterdam

Vlaggetjesdag Scheveningen: famous festival in mid June celebrating the arrival of the first herring; Scheveningen resort with a casino, large hotels, discos and theatres.

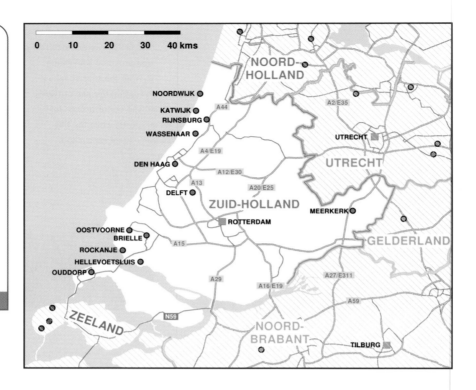

Brielle

Camping De Krabbeplaat

Oude Veerdam 4, NL-3231 NC Brielle (Zuid-Holland) T: 0181 412 363. E: info@krabbeplaat.nl

alanrogers.com/NL6980

Camping De Krabbeplaat is a family run site situated near the ferry port in a wooded, recreation area next to the Brielse Meer lake. There are 448 spacious pitches, with 68 for touring units, all with electricity (10A), cable connections and a water supply nearby. A nature conservation plan exists to ensure the site fits into its natural environment. The lake and its beaches provide the perfect spot for watersports and relaxation and the site has its own harbour where you can moor your own boat. This excellent site is very convenient for the Europort ferry terminal.

Facilities

One large and two smaller heated toilet blocks in traditional style provide separate toilets, showers and washing cabins. High standards of cleanliness, a dedicated unit for disabled campers and provision for babies. Warm water is free of charge. Dishwasher. Launderette. Motorcaravan services. Supermarket, snack bar, restaurant and takeaway (all season). Recreation room. Youth centre. Tennis. Playground and play field. Animal farm. Bicycle and children's pedal hire. Canoe, surf, pedal boat and boat hire. Fishing. WiFi over site (charged). Two cottages for hikers. No dogs allowed. Off site: Golf 3 km. Riding 6 km. Beach 7 km.

Open: 31 March - 30 September.

Directions

From the Amsterdam direction take the A4 (Europoort), then the A15 (Europoort). Take exit for Brielle on N57 and, just before Brielle, site is signed. GPS: 51.9097, 4.18536

Charges guide

Per unit incl. 2 persons	
and electricity	€ 18.00 - € 25.00
extra person	€ 3.30
child (under 12 yrs)	€ 2.80

For latest campsite news, availability and prices visit

alanrogers.com

Delft

Recreatiecentrum Delftse Hout

Korftlaan 5, NL-2616 LJ Delft (Zuid-Holland) T: 0152 130 040. E: info@delftsehout.nl
alanrogers.com/NL5600

Pleasantly situated in Delft's park and forest area on the eastern edge of the city, this well run, modern site is part of the Koningshof group. It has 160 tourist pitches quite formally arranged in groups of four to six and surrounded by attractive trees and hedges. All have sufficient space and electrical connections (10A). Modern buildings near the entrance house the site amenities. A good sized first floor restaurant serves snacks and full meals and has an outdoor terrace overlooking the swimming pool and pitches. Walking and cycling tours are organised and there is a recreation programme in high season. A special package deal can be arranged including tickets to local Royal attractions and a visit to the Royal Delftware factory. Delftse Hout is also conveniently located for a visit to Madurodam (the smallest city in the Netherlands), the North Sea beaches at Scheveningen and the Keukenhof in Lisse. The site attracts many British visitors, many coming for the cycling tours.

Facilities

Modern, heated toilet facilities include a spacious family room and children's section. Facilities for disabled visitors. Laundry. Motorcaravan services. Shop for basic food and camping items (22/3-1/11). Restaurant and bar (22/3-1/10). Small outdoor swimming pool (15/5-15/9). Adventure playground. Recreation room. Internet access. Bicycle hire. Gas . Max. 1 dog. Off site: Fishing 1 km. Riding and golf 5 km. Regular bus service to Delft centre.

Open: 22 March - 1 November.

Directions

Site is 1 km. east of Delft. From A13 motorway take Delft (exit 9), turn towards Delft Centre and then right at first traffic lights, following camping signs through suburbs and park to site. GPS: 52.01767, 4.37908

Charges guide

Per unit incl. 2 persons	
and electricity	€ 15.00 - € 36.00
extra person (3 yrs and older)	€ 3.25
dog (max. 1)	€ 3.00

Low season discounts and for senior citizens (over 55). Special packages.

Camping Cheques accepted.

culture, beach, nature and comfortable camping
VERSATILE AND SURPRISING
www.delftsehout.nl

Den Haag

Vakantiecentrum Kijkduinpark

Machiel Vrijenhoeklaan 450, NL-2555 NW Den Haag (Zuid-Holland) T: 0704 482 100. E: info@kijkduinpark.nl
alanrogers.com/NL5640

This is an ultra-modern, all-year-round centre and family park with many chalets, villas and bungalows for rent and a large indoor swimming pool complex. The wooded touring area is immediately to the left of the entrance, with 330 pitches in shady glades of bark-covered sand. All pitches have electricity (10A), water, waste water and cable TV connections. In a paved central area are a supermarket, a snack bar and a restaurant. The main attraction here is the Meeresstrand, 500 m. from the site entrance. This is a long, wide sandy beach with flags to denote suitability for swimming. Windsurfing is popular.

Facilities

There are five modern sanitary blocks. Four private cabins for rent. Launderette. Snack bar. Shop. Restaurant. Supermarket. Indoor pool. Sunbeds. Tennis. Bicycle hire. Special golfing breaks. Entertainment and activities organised in summer. WiFi over site (free in restaurant). Off site: Beach, golf and fishing 500 m. Riding 5 km.

Open: All year.

Directions

Site is southwest of Den Haag on the coast and Kijkduin is well signed as an area from all round Den Haag. GPS: 52.05968, 4.21118

Charges guide

Per unit incl. 5 persons	
and electricity	€ 19.00 - € 37.00
incl. electricity, water and drainage	€ 20.00 - € 48.25
extra person	€ 4.00

Hellevoetsluis
Camping Caravaning 't Weergors

Zuiddijk 2, NL-3221 LJ Hellevoetsluis (Zuid-Holland) T: 0181 312 430. E: weergors@pn.nl
alanrogers.com/NL6970

A rustic-style site built around old farm buildings, 't Weergors has a comfortable mature feel. At the front of the site is a well presented farmhouse which houses reception and includes the main site services. The sanitary blocks have been renewed recently, as has the farm accommodating an attractive à la carte restaurant and pancake outlet. The reception has also been renewed including a new minimarket from where you can order fresh bread. There are currently 100 touring pitches (plus seasonal and static places), with another field at the back of the site under development to provide a further 70 or 80 touring places. Some of the touring pitches are exceptionally large, divided by hedging with a 'drive in, drive out' system (cars charged if kept on pitch). Each pitch has a cable TV connection and the site now has WiFi Internet access. An appealing feature of this site is the lake which lies to the rear, offering a quiet corner where you might head for an evening stroll. The old centre of Hellevoetsluis is worthy of a visit and the bustling city of Rotterdam is not far.

Facilities

Three sanitary blocks have showers (by key), washbasins, some in cabins, children's showers and toilets plus baby baths. Laundry facilities. Motorcaravan service point. Small shop (1/4-31/10). Restaurant and bar (snacks) and pancakes. Tennis. Internet access. Play area. Paddling pool. Organised entertainment in high season. Fishing pond. Bicycle hire. Rally field.

Open: 1 April - 31 October.

Directions

From Rotterdam join A15 west to Rozenburg exit 12 and join N57 south for 11 km. Turn left on N497 signed Hellevoetsluis and follow site signs for 4.5 km. to roundabout. Turn right at roundabout to site 1.5 km. on right. GPS: 51.82943, 4.11618

Charges 2013

Per unit incl. 2 persons and electricity	€ 20.30
extra person	€ 3.50
child (3-12 yrs)	€ 2.00
dog	€ 1.75

Camping Cheques accepted.

Hellevoetsluis
Camping De Quack

Duinweg 14, NL-3221 LC Hellevoetsluis (Zuid-Holland) T: 0181 312 646. E: info@dequack.nl
alanrogers.com/NL6965

Camping De Quack is situated on the former island of Voorne with direct access to the long sandy beaches along the Haringvliet and the North Sea. Two nature reserves on the other side offer a completely different landscape where you can see, for example, orchids, spoonbills and small deer. The spacious site provides 130 grass touring pitches (100 sq.m), all with electricity (10A). Visitors with dogs are restricted to a separate area of 35 pitches. You may choose where to park your car, either beside your pitch or in a separate parking area. The nearby sea, rivers and lake are ideal for those who like watersports.

Facilities

Modern, clean sanitary facilities with free showers. Facilities for disabled visitors. Laundry. Motorcaravan service point. Supermarket. Snack bar. Games room. Sea canoe hire. Bicycle hire. Boat launching. Recreation and sporting field. Playgrounds. Pets' corner. Minigolf. Tennis. Recreation team for children in high season. Free WiFi over part of site. Hikers' cabins for rent. Off site: Restaurant at the adjacent bungalow park. The fortified village of Hellevoetsluis with a wide range of shops and a historic dry dock dating from 1802, 3 km. Tropical swimming pool in Stellendam 8 km. Brielle 10 km. Delta works (30 min). Rotterdam (30 min).

Open: 1 April - 31 October.

Directions

Camping De Quack is 3 km. west of Hellevoetsluis near the N57, the main link from the north to Zeeland and to the A15, which connects to the main motorways near Rotterdam. GPS: 51.83794, 4.09021

Charges guide

Per unit incl. 2 persons and electricity	€ 17.60
extra person (over 3 yrs)	€ 3.70
dog	€ 1.60

For latest campsite news, availability and prices visit
alanrogers.com

Katwijk

Recreatiecentrum De Noordduinen

Campingweg 1, NL-2221 EW Katwijk aan Zee (Zuid-Holland) T: 0714 025 295. E: info@noordduinen.nl
alanrogers.com/NL5680

This is a large, well managed site surrounded by dunes and sheltered partly by trees and shrubbery, which also separate the various camping areas. The 200 touring pitches are marked and numbered but not divided. All have electricity (10A) and 75 are fully serviced with electricity, water, drainage and TV connection. There are also seasonal pitches and mobile homes for rent. Entertainment is organised in high season for various age groups. A new complex with indoor and outdoor pools, restaurant, small theatre and recreation hall provides a good addition to the site's facilities. Seasonal pitches and mobile homes are placed mostly away from the touring areas and are unobtrusive.

Facilities

The three sanitary blocks are modern and clean, with washbasins in cabins, a baby room and provision for visitors with disabilities. Laundry. Motorcaravan services. Supermarket with fresh bread daily, bar, restaurant, takeaway (all 1/4-31/10). Recreation room. Swimming pool complex. Play area. Only gas barbecues are permitted. Dogs are not accepted. Off site: Riding 150 m. Beach and fishing 300 m. Golf 6 km.

Open: All year.

Directions

Leave A44 at exit 8 (Leiden-Katwijk) to join N206 to Katwijk. Take Katwijk Noord exit and follow signs to site. GPS: 52.21103, 4.40978

Charges guide

Per unit incl. 2 persons and electricity	€ 23.50 - € 31.50
extra person	€ 4.00

Camping Cheques accepted.

Katwijk

Recreatiecentrum De Zuidduinen

Zuidduinseweg 1, NL-2225 JS Katwijk aan Zee (Zuid-Holland) T: 0714 014 750. E: info@zuidduinen.nl
alanrogers.com/NL6982

De Zuidduinen is a pleasant, family site of 5 ha. in a protected nature reserve beside the sea. The site is only 200 m. from the beach and the seaside town of Katwijk is within walking distance. There are around 200 touring pitches (70 sq.m) of which 15 are larger, serviced pitches (90 sq.m). All have 4A electricity and cable connections for TV and radio. Camping bungalows and dune houses are available for rent. A programme of entertainment and activities for all ages is provided by an enthusiastic team in high season. The dunes are an ideal setting for families with children and people looking for a relaxing holiday. There are several walking and cycling tracks in and around the dunes.

Facilities

The heated toilet block is clean and well equipped. Facilities for babies and disabled visitors. Laundry. Motorcaravan service point. Shop, restaurant and takeaway (all 20/3-10/9). Playground. TV room. Boules. Free WiFi over site. Off site: Beach 200 m. Tennis 250 m. Bicycle hire 1 km. Riding 2 km. Golf 5 km.

Open: 1 April or 1 week before Easter - 30 September.

Directions

The site is just southwest of Katwijk. From A44 take exit 8 onto the N206 (Katwijk aan Zee) and then follow the signs to Zuid-Boulevard and the site. GPS: 52.19319, 4.38986

Charges guide

Per unit incl. 4 persons and electricity	€ 24.50 - € 32.50
extra person	€ 2.50

Meerkerk

Camping De Victorie

Broekseweg 75-77, NL-4231 VD Meerkerk (Zuid-Holland) T: 0183 352 741. E: info@campingdevictorie.nl
alanrogers.com/NL5690

Within an hour's drive of the port of Rotterdam you can be pitched on this delightful, spacious site in the green heart of the Netherlands. De Victorie, a working farm and a member of an organisation of farm sites, offers an alternative to the bustling seaside sites. A modern building houses reception, an open plan office and a space with tables and chairs, where the friendly owners may well invite you to have a cup of coffee. The 100 grass pitches (100-200 sq.m) are level and have 6A electricity supply. Everything about the site is surprising and contrary to any preconceived ideas.

Facilities

The main sanitary block is kept spotlessly clean, tastefully decorated and fully equipped. Showers are on payment. Laundry room. Additional sanitary facilities are around the site. Farm shop and small bar (once a week). Play area. Trampoline, and play field. Fishing. Riding. WiFi throughout (charged). Off site: Bicycle hire 2 km.

Open: 15 March - 31 October.

Directions

From Rotterdam follow A15 to junction with A27. Proceed 6 km. north on A27 to Noordeloos exit (no. 25) and join N214. Site is signed 200 m. after roundabout at Noordeloos. GPS: 51.93623, 4.95748

Charges guide

Per unit incl. 2 persons and electricity	€ 12.50
extra person	€ 3.00

No credit cards. Large units may be charged extra.

FREE Alan Rogers Travel Card
Extra benefits and savings - see page 12

Noordwijk

Camping le Parage

Langevelderlaan 43, NL-2204 BC Noordwijk (Zuid-Holland) T: 0252 375 671. E: info@leparage.nl

alanrogers.com/NL6992

Camping Le Parage is set in an area of woodland and dunes and its French name can be translated as 'the area behind the dunes'. The site borders a nature area where you can enjoy plenty of cycling and walking tracks. There are 150 pitches of which 34 are for touring units, all with 4A electricity. Arranged over several fields, they are surrounded by hedges. A riding school is next door (50 m) and you can even bring your own horse. The surrounding area offers plenty of things to do. There are opportunities for swimming and watersports either in the sea or the lake. In spring you can enjoy the lovely blossoming bulb fields.

Facilities

Two heated sanitary blocks for tourers are very clean and include free preset showers and open style washbasins. Baby room. Laundry facilities. Bar. Restaurant. Snack bar with takeaway. Well stocked shop. Play area. Sports area. Riding. Games room. TV. WiFi over part of site (charged). Off site: Beach 1.5 km. Shops. Restaurants. De Keukenhof. Pretpark Duinrell. Linnaeushof.

Open: 15 March - 1 October.

Directions

From the N206 take exit for, and turn towards, Langevelderslag. Take second turn to the left and at the end turn right. The site is well signed. GPS: 52.282454, 4.486778

Charges guide

Per unit incl.4 persons, water and electricity	€ 21.00
extra person (over 2 yrs)	€ 2.50

Oostvoorne

Molecaten Park Kruininger Gors

Gorsplein 2, NL-3233 XC Oostvoorne (Zuid-Holland) T: 0181 482 711. E: kruiningergors@molecaten.nl

alanrogers.com/NL6978

Kruininger Gors can be found just 30 minutes from the busy port of the Hook of Holland. This is a very green campsite located close to the banks of Lake Brielle (Brielse Meer). The site is made up of pitches (80 for tourers, most with electricity, 6A Europlug) on fields which are divided by high trees and shrubs. This is a spacious site with plenty of space for children to safely play. The site is within walking distance of a sandy lake beach (good for younger children). For older children and all those who love the outdoors, it is an ideal place to go surfing, sailing and water skiing. The lake and neighbouring Lake Oostvoorne are also very popular with anglers.

Facilities

One main toilet block has some washbasins in cabins, baby room and facilities for disabled visitors. Restaurant with pub and terrace. Various shops including supermarket and baker. Takeaway. Sandy lake beach. Play area. Small deer park. Tennis. Bicycle hire. Activity and entertainment programme. Dogs are not accepted. WiFi over site (charged). Off site: Lake beach. Oostvoorne 2 km. Sea beach 5 km. Rotterdam 30 km.

Open: 31 March - 1 October.

Directions

From Hook of Holland, follow signs to Rotterdam on A20. At exit 13 follow signs to Rotterdam-Zuid, Hoogvliet. After 7 km. take A15 towards Hellevoetsluis, Europoort. Follow the A15 (becomes N15) for 25 km. to exit 8 (Oostvoorne). Follow this road for 1.5 km. and turn left. Site is signed. GPS: 51.922583, 4.105344

Charges guide

Per unit incl. 2 persons and electricity	€ 15.00 - € 18.00

Ouddorp

RCN Toppershoedje

Strandweg 2-4, NL-3253 LR Ouddorp (Zuid-Holland) T: 0187 682 600. E: toppershoedje@rcn.nl

alanrogers.com/NL6988

Toppershoedje is a great choice for a seaside holiday. A large, sandy beach is easily reachable on the other side of the dunes (five minutes on foot). This beautiful beach is probably the main appeal of this site, particularly as it gently slopes into the sea and is therefore ideal for children. Even in high season the beach is never crowded. Toppershoedje has spacious, grassy pitches with 10A electricity, but shade is limited. It is located at the western end of the island of Goerre-Overvalkkee, and close to Lake Grevelingen. This lake is very popular with watersports enthusiasts.

Facilities

Three heated sanitary blocks with showers, washbasins in cubicles and facilities for babies and disabled campers. Launderette. Restaurant, bar, takeaway, bakery. Sports hall. Play area. Multisports terrain. Bicycle and go-kart hire. WiFi over site (charged). Mobile homes and chalets to rent. Off site: Supermarket 300 m. Sandy beach 5 minutes walk. Ouddorp 3 km.

Open: 20 March - 27 October.

Directions

Head towards the centre of Ouddorp on N57 signed Oosterweg. Follow this road for 1.5 km. and turn left at the last T-junction onto Vrijheidsweg. Turn left at the next roundabout 600 m. and then turn right after 200 m. GPS: 51.823484, 3.916803

Charges guide

Per unit incl. 2 persons and electricity	€ 19.50 - € 35.00

Ouddorp

Recreatiepark De Klepperstee

Vrijheidsweg 1, NL-3253 ZG Ouddorp (Zuid-Holland) T: 0187 681 511. E: info@klepperstee.com
alanrogers.com/NL6960

De Klepperstee is a good quality, family site. The site itself is peacefully located in tranquil countryside amid renowned nature reserves and just outside the village of Ouddorp in Zuid-Holland. It offers excellent recreation areas that are spread over the centre of the site giving it an attractive open parkland appearance which is enhanced by many shrubs, trees and grass areas. The 338 spacious touring pitches are in named avenues, mostly separated by hedging and spread around the perimeter, together with the seasonal and static caravans. There is a new 24-hour, drive-in motorcaravan park with 16A electricity, sanitary facilities and a service point.

Facilities

One main sanitary block and a number of WC/shower units around the touring area provide free hot showers, washbasins, some in cabins (hot water only), baby bath and shower, child size toilets and a unit for campers with disabilities. Laundry. Motorcaravan service point. Supermarket. Restaurant, bar and takeaway. Play areas. Tennis. TV, pool and electronic games. Entertainment. No animals are accepted and no single sex groups.
Off site: Fishing 500 m. Beach 600 m. Riding, bicycle hire 4 km. Golf 10 km.

Open: Easter - 31 October.

Directions

From Rotterdam follow A15 west to Rozenburg exit 12 and join N57 south for 22 km. Take exit for Ouddorp and follow signs for Stranden. Site is on the left after 3 km. GPS: 51.8161, 3.89958

Charges guide

Per unit incl. up to 4 persons	€ 14.50 - € 18.00
incl. 16A electricity	€ 18.50 - € 22.50
extra person	€ 2.50
dog (max. 2)	€ 3.50

Rijnsburg

Recreatiecentrum Koningshof

Elsgeesterweg 8, NL-2231 NW Rijnsburg (Zuid-Holland) T: 0714 026 051. E: info@koningshofholland.nl
alanrogers.com/NL5630

This popular site is run in a personal and friendly way. The 200 pitches for touring units (some with hardstandings for larger units) are laid out in small groups, divided by hedges and trees and all with 10A electrical connections. Cars are mostly parked in areas around the perimeter and 100 static caravans, confined to one section of the site, are entirely unobtrusive. Reception, a pleasant good quality restaurant, bar and a snack bar are grouped around a courtyard-style entrance which is decorated with seasonal flowers. The site has a small outdoor, heated pool (13.5x7 m) with a separate paddling pool and imaginative children's play equipment. A member of the Holland Tulip Parcs group.

Facilities

Three good toilet blocks, two with underfloor heating, with washbasins in cabins and provision for disabled visitors. Laundry facilities. Motorcaravan services. Gas supplies. Shop (1/4-15/10). Bar, snacks and takeaway (1/4-1/11). Restaurant (1/4-10/9). Small outdoor pool (unsupervised; 15/5-15/9). Indoor pool (1/4-1/11). Adventure playground and sports area. Tennis. Fishing pond (free). Bicycle hire. Entertainment in high season. Room for shows. Max. 1 dog, accepted in a limited area of the site. WiFi.
Off site: Sandy beach 5 km. Riding and golf 5 km. Den Haag 15 km. and Amsterdam 30 km.

Open: 16 March - 16 November.

Directions

From N44/A44 Den Haag-Amsterdam motorway, take exit 7 for Oegstgeest and Rijnsburg. Turn towards Rijnsburg and follow site signs. GPS: 52.20012, 4.45623

Charges guide

Per unit incl. 2 persons and electricity	€ 24.50 - € 29.50
extra person	€ 3.75
dog (max. 1)	€ 3.00
Senior citizen discounts, group rates and special packages.	

Camping Cheques accepted.

FREE Alan Rogers Travel Card
Extra benefits and savings - see page 12

Rockanje
Molecaten Park Rondeweibos

Schapengorsedijk 19, NL-3235 LA Rockanje (Zuid-Holland) T: 0181 401 944. E: info@molecaten.nl
alanrogers.com/NL5590

Rondeweibos is a pleasant family site within walking distance of a sandy North Sea beach. The flora and fauna in this beautiful dune area is unusual, and, adjacent to the site, there is a pretty lake, Het Quakjeswater, home to various birds including spoonbills and silver herons. The sea here is calm and excellent for younger children to swim, play or paddle. All pitches at Rondeweibos are comfort pitches, and there is also the option of renting a private sanitary unit (with shower, toilet and wash basin). A number of mobile homes (beach home caravans) are available for rent.

Facilities

Sanitary facilities in two blocks (one new) provide neat, clean, acceptable facilities with hot showers on payment. One block can be heated. Supermarket. Restaurant and bar with terrace, takeaway food. Heated outdoor pool with children's pool and slides. Tennis. Sports field. Play areas. Bicycle hire. Activity programme. WiFi over site (charged). Off site: Bus service 100 m. Beach (10-minute walk). Fishing 2 km. Riding 6 km. Golf and bicycle hire 10 km. Rotterdam.

Open: 1 April - late October.

Directions

Approaching on A15 follow directions towards Hellevoetsluis and N57. Join N57 and drive towards Brielle/Hellevoetsluis/Middelburg. After 7 km, at the roundabout, head towards Rockanje. The site is well signed. GPS: 51.856222, 4.082483

Charges guide

Per unit incl. 2 persons and electricity	€ 20.00 - € 27.50

Rockanje
Molecaten Park Waterbos

Duinrand 11, NL-3235 CC Rockanje (Zuid-Holland) T: 0181 401 900. E: waterbos@molecaten.nl
alanrogers.com/NL6975

Molecaten Park Waterbos is a small, friendly campsite located behind sand dunes on the island of Voorne. The site is within easy walking distance of the broad sandy beach at Rockanje. This beach slopes gradually and is ideal for young children. There are 340 pitches here, of which 140 are for touring units, shaded by large trees and located on a number of grassy fields, often with play areas at the centre. There is a choice of basic, comfort and comfort-plus pitches, all with electricity (6/10A). The latter group are deluxe pitches, each equipped with an individual shower, toilet and washbasin. There are also mobile homes, luxury accommodation and fully equipped tents for hire.

Facilities

Restaurant with bar and terrace, takeaway food. Small shop for bread and basics. Heated outdoor swimming pool (29/4-1/9). Fishing pond. Play area. Bicycle and go-kart hire. Entertainment and activity programme. WiFi throughout (charged). Dogs are not accepted. Off site: Beach adjacent. Rockanje, Brielle, Hellevoetsluis, Voornes Duin and Rotterdam port. Sub-tropical swimming pool 10 km.

Open: 1 April - 28 October.

Directions

From Hook of Holland, follow signs to Rotterdam on A20. At exit 13 follow Rotterdam-Zuid/Hoogvliet. After 7 km. join A15 (Hellevoetsluis/Europoort). Continue to Rozenburg (now N15) then take N57 to Hellevoetsluis. After 8 km. take third junction to right (Rockanje) and proceed to town. Go through town centre and site is signed.
GPS: 51.879991, 4.053982

Charges 2013

Per unit incl. 2 persons and electricity	€ 19.25 - € 33.50
extra person	€ 3.90
child (2-10 yrs)	€ 2.90

For latest campsite news, availability and prices visit
alanrogers.com

Wassenaar
Camping Duinhorst

Buurtweg 135, NL-2244 BH Wassenaar (Zuid-Holland) T: 0703 242 270. E: info@duinhorst.nl
alanrogers.com/NL5625

Camping Duinhorst is set in the centre of a richly wooded area just north of The Hague (Den Haag). The site is close to the rolling dunes that run between the lively sea resort of Scheveningen and the quieter beaches of the Wassenaarse Slag. There are around 500 pitches, including 160 for touring units. All are equipped with electricity (6/10A), cable TV, waste water hook-ups and mains water points. A variety of small and large, open and shaded pitches are available for tents with a limited number of electricity hook-ups. The Paviljoen Duinhorst restaurant is located above the sanitary building near the tennis court and swimming pool. This building accommodates the restaurant, bar, a snack bar and an auditorium. A small shop for your daily needs is next to this building.

Facilities

Heated toilet blocks include facilities for babies and disabled visitors. Launderette with dishwasher, washing machines, dryers and ironing facilities. Shop. Cafeteria with takeaway meals. Restaurant. Snack bar. Bar. Outdoor wading and swimming pools. Recreation team during holidays and peak season. Recreation hall. TV. Amusement arcade. Tennis. Bicycle hire. Free WiFi in restaurant area. Dogs are not accepted.

Open: 1 April - 30 September.

Directions

From north take A44, later N44, passing Wassenaar to Den Haag. After viaduct turn right at second lights (van Alkemadelaan) towards Scheveningen. Turn right at third lights (Wassenaar). Immediately left and right again. At roundabout first exit (Wassenaar). Take first exit signed Duindigt and small sign Duinhorst. GPS: 52.11149, 4.34364

Charges guide

Per unit incl. 2 persons and electricity	€ 22.20
extra person	€ 5.50
child (under 10 yrs)	€ 3.40

Wassenaar
Vakantiepark Duinrell

Duinrell 1, NL-2242 JP Wassenaar (Zuid-Holland) T: 0705 155 255. E: info@duinrell.nl
alanrogers.com/NL5620

A very large site, Duinrell's name means 'well in the dunes' and the water theme is continued in the adjoining amusement park and in the extensive indoor pool complex. The campsite itself is very large with 750 tourist places on several flat, grassy areas (60-140 sq.m) and it can become very busy in high season. As part of a continuing improvement programme, the marked pitches have electricity, water and drainage connections and some have cable TV. Amenities shared with the park include restaurants, takeaways and pancake house, supermarket and a theatre. Entry to the popular pleasure park is free for campers – indeed the camping areas surround and open out from the park.

Facilities

Six heated toilet blocks serve the touring areas. Laundry facilities. Amusement park and Tiki tropical pool complex. Restaurant, cafés, pizzeria and takeaways (weekends only in winter). Supermarket. Entertainment and theatre with shows in high season. Rope Challenge trail and training circuit. Bicycle hire. Mini-bowling. All activities have extra charges. WiFi over site (charged). Off site: Beach 4 km. Golf 12 km.

Open: All year.

Directions

Site is signed from the N44/A44 (Den Haag-Amsterdam), but from the south the turning is 5 km. after passing sign for start of Wassenaar town – then follow site signs. GPS: 52.14642, 4.38737

Charges guide

Per unit incl. 2 persons and electricity	€ 30.00 - € 36.50
extra person	€ 10.25
dog	€ 6.00

Accommodation

Over recent years many of the campsites featured in this guide have added large numbers of high quality mobile homes and chalets. Many site owners believe that some former caravanners and motorcaravanners have been enticed by the extra comfort they can now provide, and that maybe this is the ideal solution to combine the freedom of camping with all the comforts of home.

Quality is consistently high and, although the exact size and inventory may vary from site to site, if you choose any of the sites detailed here, you can be sure that you're staying in some of the best quality and best value mobile homes available.

Home comforts are provided and typically these include a fridge with freezer compartment, gas hob, proper shower – often a microwave and radio/cassette hi-fi too, but do check for details. All mobile homes and chalets come fully equipped with a good range of kitchen utensils, pots and pans, crockery, cutlery and outdoor furniture. Some even have an attractive wooden sundeck or paved terrace – a perfect spot for outdoors eating or relaxing with a book and watching the world go by.

Regardless of model, colourful soft furnishings are the norm and a generally breezy décor helps to provide a real holiday feel.

Although some sites may have a large number of different accommodation types, we have restricted our choice to one or two of the most popular accommodation units (either mobile homes or chalets) for each of the sites listed.

The mobile homes here will be of modern design, and recent innovations, for example, often include pitched roofs which substantially improve their appearance.

Design will invariably include clever use of space and fittings/furniture to provide for comfortable holidays – usually light and airy, with big windows and patio-style doors, fully equipped kitchen areas, a shower room with shower, washbasin and WC, cleverly designed bedrooms and a comfortable lounge/dining area (often incorporating a sofa bed).

In general, modern campsite chalets incorporate all the best features of mobile homes in a more traditional structure, sometimes with the advantage of an upper mezzanine floor for an additional bedroom.

Our selected campsites offer a massive range of different types of mobile home and chalet, and it would be impractical to inspect every single accommodation unit. Our selection criteria, therefore, primarily takes account of the quality standards of the campsite itself.

However, there are a couple of important ground rules:

* Featured mobile homes must be no more than 5 years old

* chalets no more than 10 years old

* All listed accommodation must, of course, fully conform with all applicable local, national and European safety legislation.

For each campsite we have given details of the type, or types, of accommodation available to rent, but these details are necessarily quite brief. Sometimes internal layouts can differ quite substantially, particularly with regard to sleeping arrangements, where these include the flexible provision for 'extra persons' on sofa beds located in the living area. These arrangements may vary from accommodation to accommodation, and if you're planning a holiday which includes more people than are catered for by the main bedrooms you should check exactly how the extra sleeping arrangements are to be provided!

Charges

An indication of the tariff for each type of accommodation featured is also included, indicating the variance between the low and high season tariffs. However, given that many campsites have a large and often complex range of pricing options, incorporating special deals and various discounts, the charges we mention should be taken to be just an indication. We strongly recommend therefore that you confirm the actual cost when making a booking.

We also strongly recommend that you check with the campsite, when booking, what (if anything) will be provided by way of bed linen, blankets, pillows etc. Again, in our experience, this can vary widely from site to site.

On every campsite a fully refundable deposit (usually between 150 and 300 euros) is payable on arrival. There may also be an optional cleaning service for which a further charge is made. Other options may include sheet hire (typically 30 euros per unit) or baby pack hire (cot and high chair).

BE0732 Camping Floréal La Roche

▶ see report page 48

Route de Houffalize 18, B-6980 La Roche-en-Ardenne, Belgium

AR1 – LUXE CARAVAN – Mobile Home

Sleeping: 2 bedrooms, sleeps 4: 1 double, 2 singles, sofa bed, pillows and blankets provided

Living: living/kitchen area, heating, TV, shower, seperate WC

Eating: fitted kitchen with hobs, microwave, coffee maker, fridge, freezer

Outside: table & chairs, parasol, barbecue

Pets: not accepted

Other (AR1 and AR2): bed linen, cot, highchair to hire

Open: All year	
Weekly Charge	**AR1**
Low Season **(from)**	€ 135
High Season **(from)**	€ 460

Low Cost Flights

An Inexpensive Way To Arrive At Your Campsite

Many campsites are conveniently served by a wide choice of low cost airlines. Cheap flights can be very easy to find and travellers increasingly find the regional airports often used to be smaller, quieter and generally a calmer, more pleasurable experience.

Low cost flights can make campsites in more distant regions a much more attractive option: quicker to reach, inexpensive flights, and simply more convenient.

Many campsites are seeing increased visitors using the low cost flights and are adapting their services to suit this clientele. An airport shuttle service is not uncommon, meaning you can take advantage of that cheap flight knowing you will be met at the other end and whisked to your campsite. No taxi queues or multiple drop-offs.

Obviously, these low cost flights are impractical when taking all your own camping gear but they do make a holiday in campsite owned accommodation much more straightforward. The low cost airline option makes mobile home holidays especially attractive: pack a suitcase and use bed linen and towels provided (which you will generally need to pre-book).

Travelling - in Europe

When taking your car (and caravan, tent or trailer tent) or motorcaravan to the continent you do need to plan in advance and to find out as much as possible about driving in the countries you plan to visit. Whilst European harmonisation has eliminated many of the differences between one country and another, it is well worth reading the short notes we provide in the introduction to each country in this guide in addition to this more general summary.

Of course, the main difference from driving in the UK is that in mainland Europe you will need to drive on the right. Without taking extra time and care, especially at busy junctions and conversely when roads are empty, it is easy to forget to drive on the right. Remember that traffic approaching from the right usually has priority unless otherwise indicated by road markings and signs. Harmonisation also means that most (but not all) common road signs are the same in all countries.

Your vehicle

Book your vehicle in for a good service well before your intended departure date. This will lessen the chance of an expensive breakdown. Make sure your brakes are working efficiently and that your tyres have plenty of tread (3 mm. is recommended, particularly if you are undertaking a long journey).

Also make sure that your caravan or trailer is roadworthy and that its tyres are in good order and correctly inflated. Plan your packing and be careful not to overload your vehicle, caravan or trailer – this is unsafe and may well invalidate your insurance cover (it must not be more fully loaded than the kerb weight of the insured vehicle).

CHECK ALL THE FOLLOWING:

- GB sticker. If you do not display a sticker, you may risk an on-the-spot fine as this identifier is compulsory in all countries. Euro-plates are an acceptable alternative within the EU (but not outside). Remember to attach another sticker (or Euro-plate) to caravans and trailers. Only GB stickers (not England, Scotland, Wales or N. Ireland) stickers are valid in the EU.

- Headlights. As you will be driving on the right you must adjust your headlights so that the dipped beam does not dazzle oncoming drivers. Converter kits are readily available for most vehicles, although if your car is fitted with high intensity headlights, you should check with your motor dealer. Check that any planned extra loading does not affect the beam height.

- Seatbelts. Rules for the fitting and wearing of seatbelts throughout Europe are similar to those in the UK, but it is worth checking before you go. Rules for carrying children in the front of vehicles vary from country to country. It is best to plan not to do this if possible.

- Door/wing mirrors. To help with driving on the right, if your vehicle is not fitted with a mirror on the left hand side, we recommend you have one fitted.

- Fuel. Leaded and Lead Replacement petrol is increasingly difficult to find in Northern Europe.

Compulsory additional equipment

The driving laws of the countries of Europe still vary in what you are required to carry in your vehicle, although the consequences of not carrying a required piece of equipment are almost always an on-the-spot fine.

To meet these requirements you should make sure that you carry the following:

- FIRE EXTINGUISHER
- BASIC TOOL KIT
- FIRST AID KIT
- SPARE BULBS

- TWO WARNING TRIANGLES – two are required in some countries at all times, and are compulsory in most countries when towing.

- HIGH VISIBILITY VEST – now compulsory in France, Spain, Italy and Austria (and likely to become compulsory throughout the EU) in case you need to walk on a motorway.

- BREATHALYSERS – now compulsory in France. Only breathalysers that are NF-approved will meet the legal requirement. French law states that one breathalyser must be produced, but it is recommended you carry two in case you use or break one.

Insurance and Motoring Documents

Vehicle insurance

Contact your insurer well before you depart to check that your car insurance policy covers driving outside the UK. Most do, but many policies only provide minimum cover (so if you have an accident your insurance may only cover the cost of damage to the other person's property, with no cover for fire and theft).

To maintain the same level of cover abroad as you enjoy at home you need to tell your vehicle insurer. Some will automatically cover you abroad with no extra cost and no extra paperwork. Some will say you need a Green Card (which is neither green nor on card) but won't charge for it. Some will charge extra for the Green Card. Ideally you should contact your vehicle insurer 3-4 weeks before you set off, and confirm your conversation with them in writing.

Breakdown insurance

Arrange breakdown cover for your trip in good time so that if your vehicle breaks down or is involved in an accident it (and your caravan or trailer) can be repaired or returned to this country. This cover can usually be arranged as part of your travel insurance policy (see below).

Documents you must take with you

You may be asked to show your documents at any time so make sure that they are in order, up-to-date and easily accessible while you travel.

These are what you need to take:

- Passports (you may also need a visa in some countries if you hold either a UK passport not issued in the UK or a passport that was issued outside the EU).

- Motor Insurance Certificate, including Green Card (or Continental Cover clause)

- DVLA Vehicle Registration Document plus, if not your own vehicle, the owner's written authority to drive.

- A full valid Driving Licence (not provisional). The new photo style licence is now mandatory in most European countries.

Personal Holiday insurance

Even though you are just travelling within Europe you must take out travel insurance. Few EU countries pay the full cost of medical treatment even under reciprocal health service arrangements. The first part of a holiday insurance policy covers people. It will include the cost of doctor, ambulance and hospital treatment if needed. If needed the better companies will even pay for English language speaking doctors and nurses and will bring a sick or injured holidaymaker home by air ambulance.

Personal Holiday insurance (continued)

An important part of the insurance, often ignored, is cancellation (and curtailment) cover. Few things are as heartbreaking as having to cancel a holiday because a member of the family falls ill. Cancellation insurance can't take away the disappointment, but it makes sure you don't suffer financially as well. For this reason you should arrange your holiday insurance at least eight weeks before you set off.

Whichever insurance you choose we would advise reading very carefully the policies sold by the High Street travel trade. Whilst they may be good, they may not cover the specific needs of campers, caravanners and motorcaravanners.

Telephone 01580 214000 for a quote for our Camping Travel Insurance with cover arranged through leading leisure insurance providers.
Alternatively visit our website at: alanrogers.com/insurance

European Health Insurance Card (EHIC)

Make sure you apply for your EHIC before travelling in Europe. Eligible travellers from the UK are entitled to receive free or reduced-cost medical care in many European countries on production of an EHIC. This free card is available by completing a form in the booklet 'Health Advice for Travellers' from local Post Offices. One should be completed for each family member. Alternatively visit www.ehic.org.uk and apply on-line. Please allow time to send your application off and have the EHIC returned to you.

The EHIC is valid in all European Community countries plus Iceland, Liechtenstein, Switzerland and Norway. If you or any of your dependants are suddenly taken ill or have an accident during a visit to any of these countries, free or reduced-cost emergency treatment is available – in most cases on production of a valid EHIC.

Only state-provided emergency treatment is covered, and you will receive treatment on the same terms as nationals of the country you are visiting. Private treatment is generally not covered, and state-provided treatment may not cover all of the things that you would expect to receive free of charge from the NHS.

Remember an EHIC does not cover you for all the medical costs that you can incur or for repatriation - it is not an alternative to travel insurance. You will still need appropriate insurance to ensure you are fully covered for all eventualities.

Travelling with children

Most countries in Europe are enforcing strict guidelines when you are travelling with children who are not your own. A minor (under the age of 18) must be accompanied by a parent or legal guardian or must carry a letter of authorisation from a parent or guardian. The letter should name the adult responsible for the minor during his or her stay. Similarly, a minor travelling with just one of his/her parents, must have a letter of authority to leave their home country from the parent staying behind. Full information is available at www.fco.gov.uk

Travelling with dogs

Many British campers and caravanners prefer to take their pets with them on holiday. However, pet travel rules changed on 1 January 2012 when the UK brought its procedures into line with the European Union. From this date all pets can enter or re-enter the UK from any country in the world without quarantine provided they meet the rules of the scheme, which will be different depending on the country or territory the pet is coming from. Please refer to the following website for full details: www.defra.gov.uk/wildlife-pets/pets/travel

Been to any good campsites lately?
We have

You'll find them here...

The UK's market leading independent
guides to the best campsites

Also available on iPad alanrogers.com/digital

... also here...

101 great campsites, ideal for your specific
hobby, pastime or passion

Also available on iPad **alanrogers.com/digital**

Want independent campsite reviews at your fingertips?

You'll find them here...

Over 3,000 in-depth campsite reviews at
www.alanrogers.com

...and even here...

FREE Alan Rogers bookstore app
- digital editions of all 2013 guides
alanrogers.com/digital

An exciting **FREE** app for
both iPhone and Android
www.alanrogers.com/apps

Open All Year

The following sites are understood to accept caravanners and campers all year round. It is always wise to phone the site to check as the facilities available, for example, may be reduced.

Town & Village Index

Town & Village Index continued

NETHERLANDS

Index by Campsite Region & Name